BABY BOOMERS—

Sandwiched Between Retirement & Caregiving

BABY BOOMERS—
Sandwiched Between Retirement & Caregiving

by Sandra W. Haymon, Ph.D

TATE PUBLISHING & *Enterprises*

Published by Tate Publishing & Enterprises, LLC
127 E. Trade Center Terrace | Mustang, Oklahoma 73064 USA
1.888.361.9473 | www.tatepublishing.com

Tate Publishing is committed to excellence in the publishing industry. The company reflects the philosophy established by the founders, based on Psalm 68:11,
"The Lord gave the word and great was the company of those who published it."

Book design copyright © 2009 by Tate Publishing, LLC. All rights reserved.
Cover concept by Sandra W. Haymon, Ph.D.
Illustrated by Kristen Polson
Interior concept by Sandra W. Haymon, Ph.D.

Published in the United States of America

ISBN: 978-1-60696-861-1
1. Family & Relationships, Eldercare
2. Business & Economics, Personal Finance, Retirement Planning
08.11.13

ADVANCE REVIEWS OF:

Baby Boomers—
Sandwiched Between Retirement and Caregiving

"I laughed a lot, I cried a lot, and I learned a lot as I turned the pages of Dr. Haymon's incredibly brilliant book. *Baby Boomers—Sandwiched Between Retirement and Caregiving* provides readers with a myriad of highly useful information and is truly a gift for the heart, mind, and soul of the Baby Boom Generation—my generation. This book literally changed my life by bringing into focus the humanity of our situation in the midst of the emotional chaos most of us live in. Her practical style of writing gives readers a wealth of information that is easy to read, understand, digest, and put to good use!"

"The fact that Dr. Haymon shares personal and painful experiences establishes immediate credibility and instills compelling trust in her sage advice and sensible suggestions. I truly believe the timeless information provided in *Baby Boomers—Sandwiched Between Retirement and Caregiving* will become the catalyst for restructuring and improving millions of personal situations and relationships. This is a MUST read for everyone, no matter what generation you were born into!"

-Patricia Rubino-Brunetti,
Board Chairman and Secretary/Treasurer,
Valley View Packing Company, San Jose, California

"As an R.N., an author, and the guardian for my late, disabled father, I applaud Dr. Sandra Haymon for the invaluable information in her new release: *Baby Boomers—Sandwiched Between Retirement and Caregiving*. This book will be an incredible help during a heartbreaking time that's sure to come for all of us, at some level, sooner or later, if we live long enough. I predict this resource manual will be on bookshelves for at least thirty years!"

-Nancy Arant Williams,
R.N., Author: And The Heaven's Wept, Stover, Missouri

"The psychological and medical consequences of caregiving, long ignored in the literature, have only recently been recognized and examined as a distinct problem. Dr. Sandra Haymon's important new book, *Baby Boomers—Sandwiched Between Retirement and Caregiving*, brings the emotional, physical, spiritual, and even the bureaucratic pitfalls into clear focus. Comprehensive in scope, thoroughly researched, and exquisitely detailed, *Baby Boomers* anticipates the unforeseen landmines awaiting caregivers and offers concrete strategies to prevent, avoid, and overcome them. The inevitable unexpressed anger and associated shame felt by many caregivers receives a compassionate and understanding discussion. *Baby Boomers* is the most useful and readable exposition of the caregiver problem I have ever encountered. This superb volume belongs in the library of every clinician and counselor."

-Jean Posner M.D.,
Neuro-Psychiatrist, Owings Mills, Maryland

"*Baby Boomers—Sandwiched Between Retirement and Caregiving*" is a masterpiece! Dr. Haymon previously gifted caregivers with *My Turn*. Now, in her exceptional new book, she expands that information and addresses every aspect of caregiving. Dr. Haymon's firsthand knowledge, gained through personal struggles, in addition to her professional experience, offers invaluable information to help guide caregivers and their loved ones through this passage of life. I highly recommend *Baby Boomers—Sandwiched Between Retirement and Caregiving* to every family caregiver and all professionals who work with elderly individuals or caregivers. *Baby Boomers* is an incredible reference to have at your fingertips."

-Ellen McNally,
Sage Eldercare, Summit, New Jersey

"*Baby Boomers—Sandwiched Between Retirement and Caregiving* is a testimony to Dr. Haymon's enduring commitment to enhance the quality of life of those with whom she comes in contact. I have known her for over twenty years as a trustworthy, compassionate, and dedicated professional colleague. Even though I have now progressed beyond the "sandwich," I will undoubtedly continue to refer to the many informative chapters in her book as I face life's ageless and never-ending challenges. Her literary style, her research, and her life's experiences will enable readers to easily learn valuable lessons that will help them plan and prepare for their futures regardless of age, gender, or ethnic background. I believe *Baby Boomers— Sandwiched Between Retirement and Caregiving* is a book that individuals will read, re-read, and then repeatedly consult as an invaluable reference for making important and often emotionally–charged financial and personal decisions."

-Gary W. Peterson, Ph.D.,
Professor Emeritus, Florida State University,
Tallahassee, Florida

"*Baby Boomers—Sandwiched Between Retirement and Caregiving* contains a wealth of information and is a must read for all baby boomers! As a former owner and director of an assisted living and retirement community, I applaud Dr. Haymon for passionately sharing her personal struggles of dealing with her own aging parents. Dr. Haymon's vast research and tireless efforts put into the consolidation of this material can help all of us wisely prepare for our own retirement. This is a well-written, informative, and marvelous research manual for anyone wanting the information necessary to fully experience "retirement living at its finest."

-Debbie Griffiths,
RNC, President, Pinecone Management Company, and
Author: *Little Lady, BIG DREAM,* Thomasville, Georgia

"*Baby Boomers—Sandwiched Between Retirement and Caregiving* is appropriate for all generations. As a daughter of baby boomers, I realize it will soon enough be "my turn." Having read this book, I know I will be much better prepared to deal with the financial, legal, and emotional facets of caregiving when it does become my turn. I truly appreciate Dr. Haymon's honesty in sharing her personal experiences and stories. I highly recommend this book!"

-Amy L. Greenwald,
Attorney At Law, Shreveport, Louisiana

PAST PRAISE FOR:

My Turn: Caring For Aging Parents & Other Elderly Loved Ones—A Daughter's Perspective (Haymon, 1996)

My Turn: Caring for Aging Parents & Other Elderly Loved Ones – A Daughter's Perspective (Haymon, 1996)

"The best 'how-to' manual I've ever read. The question-and-answer approach makes *My Turn* not only very readable but also poignant, truthful, and significantly powerful. I recommend Dr. Haymon's labor of love to every caregiver and to all of us who want to better understand what our own children will be facing in the years ahead."

-Andrea Personette,
Education Coordinator, HealthSouth
Rehabilitation Hospital, Tallahassee, Florida

"Simply superb...Dr. Haymon has written more than an excellent resource book—she has crafted a very readable and moving story about a subject that probably will end up touching most of us...thank you for *My Turn*."

-Kit Bauman,
Editor of Elder Update, State of Florida, Dept.
of Elder Affairs, Tallahassee, Florida

"*My Turn* is not only an informative, compassionate, and useful guide through a difficult passage in one's lifetime, but it is also a work that blends insights acquired from Dr. Haymon's own life's experiences as a caregiver with knowledge gained from her meticulous research as a professional psychologist."
-G.W. Peterson, Ph.D.
Florida State University Professor and Licensed
Psychologist, Tallahassee, Florida

"Dr. Haymon's personal trial is transformed to empower the reader to appropriately and lovingly see more choices to attend not only to their aging loved one but to themselves as they face this most difficult and challenging time of life. *My Turn* is a must read for helping professionals who choose to live and teach pro-activity."
- Brenda Y. Crawford, LPC, CEAP, Coordinator,
Civilian Employee Assistance Program, Marine
Corps Logistics Base, Albany, Georgia

"I want to congratulate you on your wonderful book, *My Turn.* People who turn their experiences into something that can be shared by others are, I believe, both gifted and gracious. Your book nicely exemplifies that. It really fills a void."
-A. Ruggieri, MD, FACP, FACR,
Tallahassee, Florida

"*My Turn* is a timely resource for caregivers. As a professional working directly with persons who face the challenges of caring for a loved one, *My Turn* is refreshing and gratifying. It provides support from a person who has walked in "their shoes." I highly recommend *My Turn.*"
-Annie F. Todd,
Social Worker, Alzheimer's Project of Tallahassee, Florida

"*My Turn* is a must for Employee Assistance libraries and personally for employees who are caring for an ill or aging loved one. Dr. Haymon has addressed all of the issues caregivers face. Just reading the book reduces stress and offers hope. Both the *Red Flag Checklist* and the *Resource List* are invaluable contributions to the world of eldercare. Plus, Dr. Haymon has included the legal documents necessary to ensure medical decisions are carried out. I highly recommend *My Turn!*"
-Cindy Lee, Ph.D.,
Apalachee Employee Assistance
Program, Tallahassee, Florida

"Reading *My Turn* is more than reading a book. It's a visit from a friend, a friend who's been there, a friend who understands. The warmth and compassion shared in Dr. Haymon's personal stories is truly comforting. I highly recommend *My Turn* to everyone caring for an ill or aging parent."
-Grazyna Bergman,
Executive Director, The NeuroScience Center at
Tallahassee Memorial Hospital, Tallahassee, Florida

"Here at the Alzheimer Resource Center, we speak daily with the children of persons with Alzheimer's Disease who have to step into the heartbreaking and demanding role of taking care of their parents. *My Turn* is a great resource to save them time and to educate them about the many ways they can help their loved ones. I recommend it highly for both the factual information and the way you tackled the difficult emotional issues. Your book is an excellent addition to a much needed resource base."
-Tom McGough, MS,
Executive Director, Alzheimer Resource
Center, Tallahassee, Florida

"*My Turn* truly touches the hearts of all who deal with the care of an aging loved one. Dr. Haymon covers emotional issues in an informative and uplifting manner."
-Kay Hind,
Executive Director, SOWEGA
Council on Aging, Albany, Georgia

This book is dedicated to my husband, *Marvin*,
the kindest and most gentle man I have ever known.
It is also dedicated to
my best friend and spiritual sister, *Patty*,
the most unselfish and generous person I've ever known,
and
to my dear friend *Pat*
whose friendship and influence transcend and
continue beyond the grave.
The three of you are truly the greatest blessings of my life.

Thank you for loving me just as I am.

Sandra

ACKNOWLEDGMENTS

Part of this publication is based on my personal experience of caring for my mother and stepfather when they could no longer care for themselves. Part of it is based on my present and ongoing experiences of planning for my own retirement, while part of it is current research on general issues and concerns associated with retirement, as well as concerns related to caring for elderly loved ones.

I had a lot of emotional support from friends and family while I took care of my folks. There are too many to name, but I know who you are and thank you from the bottom of my heart. Thank you for listening to me, allowing me to vent and to cry, and for helping me to see the humor and for encouraging me. The journey would have been a lot tougher without you.

I am eternally indebted to my husband and my best friend, Patty Rubino-Brunetti, who were there for me during some very trying times over the past decade. They were especially supportive while I wrote this book. I'm not sure I would have made it without them.

I will be forever grateful to Gary W. Peterson, Ph.D., for his time, his friendship, his wise counsel, and for his editorial comments, once again. I am blessed to have had him as my friend and mentor for the past two decades.

My cousin Louie was my number one supporter as we peddled *My Turn* across the state of Florida. I lack the vocabulary to thank him for his labor of love and pray for him as he continues to take his *turn*.

I also want to thank my dear friend Debbie Griffiths, who encouraged me to submit this work for publication and generously offered editorial comments. My friend and financial advisor, Davey Owens, provided invaluable editorial reviews, and Karen Nevels did an outstanding job updating the list of resources. I truly appreciate you all.

My dear friend Pat Russell remains in my heart and mind and continues to influence my choices and decisions. Thank you and I miss you.

Cresyl, Amy, and Hippie were my loyal feline companions when I wrote *My Turn*. Unfortunately, they are no longer here. I miss them, too.

I am blessed to have many friends who have graciously given their time and energy because they believed this to be a worthwhile project with the potential of helping millions of others as they face the challenges of retirement and caring for elderly loved ones. Thank you all for helping to make this possible.

I had and continue to have lots of help from guardian angels. Thank you for protecting me and continually lighting my path down unfamiliar roads.

Most of all, I thank my Father in heaven for my life and for being able to live in a free country where I can share my thoughts in print!

Sandra W. Haymon, Ph.D.

TABLE OF CONTENTS

Experience is what you get when
you don't get what you want.
(Dan Stanford)

SECTION ONE: Caregiving – 33

If all difficulties were known at the outset of a long
journey, most of us would never start out at all.
(Dan Rather with Peter Wyden in *"I Remember")*

Oh No! Not Alphabet Soup Again! – 35

Dr. Haymon gets a second helping of alphabet soup. This
time it is served by financial planners rather than healthcare providers. The alphabet fragments/acronyms in this
bowl (AT/TX, PT/TD, IRAs, ROTHs, MUNIs, SEPs,)
remind her of similar fragments in the alphabet soup
served to her by medical and legal professionals when she
was the caregiver for her elderly parents.

Caring For Elderly Loved Ones – 38

Learn how caring for elderly loved ones was handled in
the past, how this is presently being handled, and specula-
tions about how this may be handled in the future. Don't
be caught off guard when it's your turn to care for an ill or
elderly loved one.

Our Turn – 45

Many baby boomers may be required to take several turns
at caregiving, and these turns could occur simultaneously.
Learn from the experiences of others how to be better prepared when it becomes *your turn*.

Overview of My Turn – 52

Dr. Haymon offers an abridgement of her personal encounters while taking care of her mother and stepfather. In a very honest and forthright manner, she openly discusses *her turn* in hopes others will learn and benefit from her experiences.

SECTION TWO: Becoming Aware Before You Get a Wake-Up Call – 61

> To think too long about doing a thing
> often becomes its undoing.
> (*Eva Young*)

Red Flag Checklist – 64

Are your elderly loved ones home alone? Should they be? Assess the situation before you and they are in crisis. Use the enclosed *Red Flag Checklist* to evaluate your loved ones' cognitive, physical, general, and social level of functioning, as well as their ability to handle money matters. There is also a critical checklist that screens for potential endangerment to self or others and an alcohol specific checklist, which uncovers alcohol related problems. Don't ignore indicators suggesting your elderly loved ones are no longer safe living alone.

Denial – 71

Learn to recognize and confront common myths and denial mechanisms you may possess about your elderly loved ones' ability to care for themselves. Don't ignore early warning signs that could cost your loved ones or others their lives.

family members. Learn to make decisions that are in the best interest of your family, not just what's best for your elderly loved ones. Explore ways to include your siblings, spouse, adult children, and grandchildren in the caregiving process. Discover ways to encourage family members to talk about their feelings and how to handle emotions appropriately.

Emotional Issues of the Elderly – 153

Individuals may grieve many losses during the final stage of life—their sense of personhood and identity, physical and mental health, lifelong relationships, and often their very homes. Many also experience end-of-life concerns, worries, and fears. Learn how to engage in empathic presence and how to help elderly loved ones find value and meaning in their lives. Empower them to resolve past issues, to forgive, to accept forgiveness, and to set goals for this final stage of life.

Closure—Saying Good-bye – 170

Discover ways to say good-bye before and after the death of loved ones. Learn how to resolve unresolved issues appropriately before it's too late. Find strength through forgiveness and comfort in loving and being loved. Give loved ones permission to die. Consider the notion that relationships don't end with death.

SECTION FOUR: Making Choices and Decisions – 201

When you have to make a choice and don't
make it, that is in itself a choice.
(*William Young*)

Medical Choices and Advance Directives – 203

Consider healthcare choices and make informed decisions in

advance. A medical crisis in an E.R. is not the time or place to make end-of-life decisions or determine whether you can legally make decisions for elderly loved ones. Examine the pros and cons of CPR, feeding tubes, and artificial respiration. Advance directives such as Do Not Resuscitate Orders (DNRs), Do Not Hospitalize Orders (DNHs), Living Wills, Durable Power of Attorney (DPOA), and others are explained in clear, easy-to-understand language. Decide which ones are appropriate for you and your loved ones.

Living Arrangements – 232

Consider various care options and living arrangements: in-home assistance, adult day care, assisted living facilities, nursing homes, and Alzheimer's units. Review important considerations prior to moving an elderly loved one into your home. Understand your loved one's needs and level of functioning. Gain confidence in your choice of care options and living arrangements.

Assistance Programs – 254

Explore numerous assistance programs. Gain a better understanding of Medicare Parts A (Hospital Insurance), B (Medical Insurance), C (Advantage Plans), and D (Drug Benefit Program); HMOs, PPOs, and POSs; Medicaid; Optional Supplemental Income (OSI); Supplemental Security Income (SSI); Veteran's (VA) benefits, and others.

SECTION FIVE: Preparing for Retirement – 281

Retirement should be based on
the tread, not the mileage.
(Allen Ludden)

Baby Boomers Retire – 283

Review the history and present status of Social Security. Gain a clearer understanding regarding the mishandling of Social Security funds. Examine probing questions and consider possible solutions to problems associated with our present Social Security system.

Silver Tsunami Expected to Hit with a Vengeance – 307

Understand the domino effect that will be created as 78 million baby boomers, America's Silver Tsunami, turn 62 over the next two decades (ten thousand every day) and vacate their positions in the US workforce. The annual trillion dollar question is: How will the mega costs, associated with Social Security, Medicare, and healthcare for baby boomers be funded? Explore possible answers.

Are There Enough Eggs in Your Basket? – 311

Answer probing questions to determine if you are financially ready for retirement and learn ways you might become even better prepared. Discover ways to avoid unnecessary income taxes, estate taxes, and probate. Compare retirement investments—IRAs, SEPs, ROTHs, 401ks, and others, as well as variable, fixed, and indexed annuities. Clarify the differences between *qualified* and *non-qualified* plans. Learn more about trusts, wills, and other valuable documents that could help you manage and preserve your estate. Review important considerations regarding long-term care insurance.

A Dress Rehearsal Before You Retire – 339

Plan a *dress rehearsal* before you retire. Learn how to get your finances in order as well as how to anticipate and project retirement expenditures. Answer retirement questions that could help you prepare for the type of retirement you've dreamed of.

Where will Boomers Choose to Live? – 345

Explore traditional and non-traditional retirement lifestyles. Consider adult retirement communities, R.V. parks, retirement learning centers, and other possibilities for your ideal nirvana.

SECTION SIX: Conclusion – 349

> Yes, there is a nirvana; it is in leading your sheep
> to a green pasture, and putting your child to
> sleep, and writing the last line of your poem.
> *(Kahil Gibran)*

Conclusion – 351

Dr. Haymon shares personal insights gained while writing this book. She also invites readers to consider the eternal aspect of relationships and the importance of listening to our own internal voice. She outlines her ongoing process of planning for her own retirement and suggests that solutions to problems are perhaps contained within the problems themselves. Always remember the password is *love!*

SECTION SEVEN: Additional Information – 359

> Change starts when someone else sees the next step.
> *(William Drayton in Esquire)*

Resources – 361

Review a complete, up-to-date referral resource list with more than 250 references, including Web sites, addresses, and phone numbers. Find information on virtually every aspect of caregiving and retirement.

Glossary – 415

Reference a most extensive list of medical and legal terminology, including acronyms used by medical and legal professionals. More than 150 terms with accompanying definitions.

Sample Letter Regarding Social Security – 446

Dr. Haymon encourages readers to write to their senators, representatives, AARP, and others regarding the problems associated with Social Security. She also includes a *sample letter* to help make it easier for others to voice their opinions and urge their representatives in Congress to open this dilemma to political process, which allows all citizens to vote on possible solutions.

FOREWORD

It is a rare privilege when one has an opportunity to influence people of all ages, even those she does not know. Dr. Sandra Haymon is now in this position, and we would be wise to take advantage of her research and personal experiences. *Baby Boomers—Sandwiched Between Retirement and Caregiving* is a fantastic glimpse into one woman's experience and how she's been able to turn it into something that can help all of us on some level. Her conversational style, matter-of-fact language, and her ability to touch and encourage others will motivate readers to begin planning for the future. She explores the dilemma facing most baby boomers: "How do we cope with caring for our parents during our retirement years?"—a most difficult and challenging question.

In her groundbreaking book, Dr. Haymon openly explores emotions that accompany this life-altering task. Most of us would rather not think about our parents aging and becoming ill; however, Dr. Haymon makes a convincing case for early planning and preparation. Most of us need to start forming and perhaps executing a care plan not only for our aging parents but also for ourselves in regard to both retirement and aging issues.

As I reflect on Dr. Haymon's experiences, Vicktor Frankl's words resonate in my mind—"The last freedom is the freedom to choose our attitude." The caregiving scenario is often heart wrenching; however, the author reminds us that attitudes make a tremendous difference in the perception of the experience.

With this information, readers will be better prepared to discuss their wishes regarding end-of-life issues with their doctors. Dr. Haymon does an excellent job of explaining documents necessary to ensure that one's choices are honored. It is imperative that everyone sign advance directives to specify their wishes *before* a crisis occurs.

In addition to guiding the reader through the entire process of caregiving and explaining the "alphabet soup" of health-care providers, she also explores financial options for our own retirement. As a physician, a husband, a father, and a son, I so appreciate Dr. Haymon legitimizing and validating concerns about money issues. For many health care providers, including myself, the subject of money has typically been considered taboo. Dr. Haymon uses terms that demystify the vocabulary of financial and investment gurus. She offers a platform that allows us (even physicians) to discuss health-care and our financial future in the same sentence. This is extremely important as boomers move toward retirement because no care is free, even when it's provided by those who care.

After reading *Baby Boomers—Sandwiched Between Retirement and Caregiving,* I feel inspired, renewed, and motivated. Dr. Haymon tackles tough subjects. Yet, her style inspires hope, and her words empower readers to confront denial and take action. This book is destined to become the definitive work on caregiving as we take our turn.

Dr. Haymon reminds us that things do not just *happen* to us—we are only *victims* if we choose to be. We can always choose our attitudes, plan for our futures, and understand beforehand how death, illness, caregiving, and finances affect all of us. Enjoy this book; share it with your friends, family members, and those you love. It will make those last few years with your loved ones sweeter—for you and for them!

Jose Rodriguez, M.D., Author, Professor, The College of Medicine, Florida State University, Tallahassee, Florida.

PREFACE

One infamous Valentine's Day in 1994, a single phone call changed my life. I had pretended for years that my elderly mother and stepfather would always be able to live on their own. That was a myth I desperately wanted—needed—to be true. It wasn't, yet my entire family danced the dance of denial until we were in crisis. My folks were not safe living alone. The phone call to my mother was clear evidence of that. My stepfather was only semi-conscious, and my mother was oblivious to the seriousness of the situation. I spent the next two years overwhelmed much of the time, while I tried to navigate the turbulent waters of Social Security, Medicare, Medicaid, medical choices, advance directives, and living arrangements.

I never set out to write a book about my frustrating experiences of dealing with what seemed to be an insane bureaucratic system. However, my friends and colleagues knew that I had inherited the responsibility of caring for my folks and started coming to me for advice. Then one day, a friend who worked for a community agency called and said her office was bombarded daily with calls about problems and concerns associated with caring for elderly relatives. She asked if I would be kind enough to give a seminar addressing these issues. I quickly begged to be let off, explaining that I did not have the answers. She replied with, "Sandra, you know more about this topic than anyone—you're living it!" I reluctantly agreed, and we decided on a title for the one-hour seminar: *"Are Your Parents Home Alone? Should They Be? This is Your Wake-up Call."* I was soon giving lectures all over the country with demands from participants that I put my experiences in writing. I guess the rest is history, as they say.

My Turn: Caring for Aging Parents & Other Elderly Loved Ones—A Daughter's Perspective was released in early November 1996. By Thanksgiving, I had been invited to be on ABC's *Good Morning America—Sunday,* and CBS' *Late, Late Night with Tom Snyder.* Mr. Snyder's own mother was blind and in a nursing home at that time, and he was taking *his turn.*

Sandra at the studio of ABC's Good Morning America, New York City, November, 1996

Sandra at CBS studios, Los Angeles, CA, November, 1996.

Sandra & her best friend of nearly forty years (Patty Rubino-Brunetti) the night Sandra was interviewed by Tom Snyder, CBS studios, Los Angeles, CA, November, 1996.

When I wrote *My Turn*, I was primarily concerned about how and where my folks would live out their retirement years and for how we would pay for their care. Although there were hundreds of thousands in that boat with me, I was about ten years ahead of the curve because my parents were "older" when I was born. Millions of fellow baby boomers have caught up with me, and it is now "their turn" to take care of ill and aging parents or other elderly loved ones. Ironically, the information in *My Turn* is more relevant now than it was when I wrote it twelve years ago.

In *Baby Boomers—Sandwiched Between Retirement and Caregiving,* I have updated and included most of the original information from *My Turn.* I've also written about my personal experiences during the last years of my parents' lives and the emotional toll that process took on us. They have now passed away, so I've written about how I said good-bye and brought closure to that passage in my life. I believe relationships continue whether loved ones remain physically present or not. I also believe the concerns discussed in the chapters on *Emotional Issues* are perhaps the most important part of the caregiving process.

Since I will turn sixty-two in 2011, I'm not only looking at ongoing concerns associated with caring for elderly relatives, I'm looking at my own future. I'm now concerned about many issues related to my retirement. I'm concerned about how and where I will live, as well the *quality* of my life while I live out my retirement years.

Just as I had to figure out how to pay for my parents' care, I now have to figure out how I will pay for my own care when that time comes, and if I live long enough, that time will surely come. Since most of my friends and colleagues belong to the baby boom generation, we are all in the same boat—sandwiched between retirement and caregiving. However, instead of hundreds of thousands, this time, there are over 78 million in this boat with me!

As I approach retirement, I have many questions about the economic and social context in which millions of us will be retiring. I have tried to look into my future—our future—and address as many concerns as possible. I have looked within myself and researched many sources for information I believe to be vital as we move through this passage of our lives.

In *Baby Boomers—Sandwiched Between Retirement and Caregiving,* I have included everything I could think of to help make this voyage easier. As boomers, we have faced many challenges and have wrought positive change in our nation. We are once again faced with great challenges—challenges associated with our own retirement as well as caring for our elderly loved ones. Boomers shaped the past, and we will also shape the future.

Because this book is intended to be a smorgasbord—written in a way that allows each chapter to stand alone, it does not have to be read in any particular order. Although you may read it straight through, you might also choose to skip chapters and go to one that seems particularly pertinent to your situation at any given time. It is a resource book that you will perhaps refer to again and again over the next twenty years and then pass on to your children as they take their *turn* taking care of you!

My heart truly goes out to each of you. It is my hope that you will have an informative, insightful, engrossing, and enlightening journey through *Baby Boomers—Sandwiched Between Retirement and Caregiving.*

Sandra W. Haymon, Ph.D.
Baby Boomer, Caregiver, Psychologist,
Author, and soon to be Retiree.

Sandra's mother and stepfather (Carl and Mildred Williamson) on the cover of the original brochure for My Turn: Caring for Aging Parents & Other Elderly Loved Ones—A Daughter's Perspective, *1996.*

SECTION ONE:
CAREGIVING

OH NO! NOT
ALPHABET SOUP AGAIN!

CAREGIVING CAREGIVING

The most important thing in
communication is to hear
what isn't being said.
(Peter F. Drucker)

My husband and I were among thirty to forty other baby boomers at a dinner meeting. We'd all come to learn about investments and how to best protect our "nest egg" intended for our retirement. However, I was unaware of the others as I sat staring at the speaker, his words swirling around my head. I thought my eyeballs must have been spinning as I watched him writing on his flip chart and explaining the differences between AT/TX, PT/TD, AT/TD, and AT/TF.

Starting with AT/TX (after-tax/taxable) investments. He cautioned us not to invest in these type investments: CDs, stock portfolios, mutual funds, and savings accounts. Next, he addressed the PT/TD (pre-tax/tax deferred)—IRAs, 401ks, 403Bs, and 457s. That's when I became almost comatose. I was barely coherent enough to hear something about ROTHs, MUNIs, and SEPs. Yet, it seemed like déjà vu.

I knew I had felt this same feeling before, overwhelmed with so many acronyms, a language I didn't speak or understand, but where? My mind raced between paying attention to the present and scanning past memory files. Had I attended such a meeting in the past? No. No, I would not have forgotten such an experience. Perhaps I'd heard all of this in another life. No. I didn't believe in that. Yet, I was sure of this feeling. I was sure I had experienced this before, but where? I was startled back into the present when the waiter asked, "Soup or salad?"

"Soup! Alphabet soup!"

"Excuse me?" he said quietly.

"I mean salad. I'll have salad."

I knew he was staring at me, but I didn't care. I was remembering—it was all coming back to me. It was another helping of "alphabet soup!" My mind raced through the files I had tucked away over a decade ago when it was "my turn" to figure out where and how my elderly parents would live, given they were no longer safe living alone. I had also written a book titled *My Turn: Caring for Aging Parents & Other Elderly Loved Ones—A Daughter's Perspective (1996),* and in the book, I had shared my initial taste of what I called "alphabet soup."

My first helping of *alphabet soup* came when I took my mother to an assisted living facility, and the administrator said, "You do understand this is an ACLF. I see your mother has SS. Does she have SSI? How about OSS? Does she have A and B?" I remembered feeling overwhelmed and paralyzed, not knowing what she was talking about. I now felt those same feelings. I also felt sad, sad that my folks were no longer alive and sad as I realized it was now *my turn* to plan my own retirement. Once again I sat staring into space, blinking back tears as I relived that day when my mother sat looking at me with such trust, the day I could no longer deny our roles had reversed, the day I realized it was *my turn* to take care of her.

As I stated then, I found no comfort knowing there were millions in the same boat with me trying to figure out how to best care for aging parents or other elderly loved ones. Once again, I find no comfort in knowing there are nearly eighty million others in the present boat with me. Nearly all of us are now trying to figure out how to plan for our own retirement in addition to caring for elderly loved ones, helping adult children out financially, and perhaps still raising kids who have not yet left the nest, or raising grandchildren or great-grandchildren. In fact, it feels like we're all sinking!

I've looked back at some things that helped and some that didn't as I treaded the stormy waters of caring for my aging parents. During that time, beacons from lighthouses were few and far between, and there were no life rafts in sight. I was carried mostly by the currents of desperation and determination, which sometimes dragged me under and often slammed me against the rocks and reefs. Thankfully, I survived and have hopefully charted the waters so others will have a less difficult time finding their way when it's *their turn*. In addition to updating the information I included in *My Turn*, I also offer new and improved directional finders intended to help us navigate the turbulent and confusing waters of Social Security, Medicare, retirement options, and our present healthcare system, in hopes we might successfully negotiate our transition from work into retirement still in one piece and safely on the shores of our ideal nirvana.

Sandra with husband (Marvin Minton)
on their wedding day, 11/21/1998.

CARING FOR ELDERLY
LOVED ONES

We are called to honor our parents
and respect those who are aging
(Leviticus 19:32).

The reason most of the information I shared in *My Turn* is more relevant today than it was when I lived and wrote it over a decade ago is because the majority of baby boomers are now moving into retirement age, and subsequently, their parents are moving into old age. According to the American Association of Retired Persons (AARP), the number of people over 65 years of age has more than tripled since 1900. This "older population" in the United States is expected to double again—from 36 million in 2003 (12% of the population) to 72 million by the year 2030. This will comprise more than 20% of our population. And most elderly people will require their adult children, grandchildren, or others to take care of them at some point before they die. Consequently, millions of baby boomers now find themselves in situations similar to the one I was in a few years ago—one of caring for elderly loved ones.

The following section, as well as several other sections, are written in an interview style so that a lot of information might be offered straightforward and to the point. Many of the questions asked in My Turn are included in these sections with updated responses.

Interviewer: Most of us realize it won't be long before it's "our turn." In fact, many of us are dealing with this, even as we speak. It's an age-old problem. How did we get here, and where do we go from here? Have things really changed that much?

Haymon: As we approach midlife, many of us find we no longer have to crusade for every cause that comes along, nor do we have to try to right every wrong that's occurred throughout the millennia. Most of us have spent the past few decades educating ourselves, raising children, and establishing ourselves in careers. Now, just when we thought we could relax and coast for a while, we're asked to walk an unfamiliar road. We're given no maps, no landmarks, and no directions. We're asked to accept responsibility for caring for our aging parents or other elderly loved ones.

How can this be? It seems only yesterday we argued with them for our independence. Many of us rebelled against the power our parents held over us. We rallied against everything they stood for and blamed them for the state of the world. We despised their self-discipline and hated their rules. I don't know about your parents, but mine thought they knew the *right* things for me to do and the *right* way for me to live and to be. Yet when I so desperately needed their answers, they had none.

I find that most of us want to care for our loved ones in the *right* way. We just don't know what the *right* way is. It is quite ironic that as many of us (boomers) marched and protested together, we felt empowered by numbers. It didn't matter what the issue was; we felt we were in it together. Now we are not comforted knowing there are millions in the same boat with us. Our anxiety actually increases as we talk to friends and relatives who are in similar situations and just as lost as we are.

I: Dr. Haymon, who normally ends up being the one to take care of aging parents?

H: Traditionally, the primary responsibility of caring for elderly people fell to women who did not work outside the home. Now, even women with jobs are still expected to assume this responsibility. More than 90% of caregivers for elderly people are women who may or may not work outside the home and who may or may not have children still at home. Here is something else that may surprise you—it is customarily the youngest daughter. Even when this responsibility falls by lot to a son—

I: Let me guess, it becomes his wife's job.
H: You got it. He delegates that responsibility to his wife. The stark reality is that the decision of who will assume the primary caregiving for aging relatives historically has been, and continues to be, one of default. That default is to women.

I: Dr. Haymon, you stated in your previous book that the number of people over 65 has more than tripled since 1900, yet the number of people to take care of them has dropped from fourteen to four. How can that be?
H: Well, let's think back to 1900 and what our culture was like at that time. We were primarily an agrarian society. The majority of the people farmed, and they had large families. It was not uncommon to have eight, ten, or even twelve children in one family. Kids were needed to work the farm. During that time, it was not only understood, but it was expected that families would take care of Grandma and Grandpa, like the Waltons. During that period in time, it was not uncommon for two, three, maybe even four generations to live on the same farmland—sometimes even in the same house. So there were lots of individuals of various ages to help take care of Grandma and Grandpa when they got old. During that period in time, growing old and dying were accepted as a natural part of the process of living.

Then we moved from an agrarian society into an industrial society. Since many people did not have automobiles, they left the farms and moved into town so they could be closer to the factories and stores. However, many elderly people refused to leave their farm homes. Physical distance created emotional distance. Then World War II came along, and men went off to war while many women went to work in the factories. This was the first time in our history that a large number of women entered the paid work force. When their husbands came back from the war, not all women went home. Many stayed on the assembly lines, and others went into service industries. The focus in our country during that time was on productivity and consumer goods. The government saw the need for women, as well as men, to stay in the work force. So "Uncle Sam" assumed responsibility of providing places where our aging relatives could live. For the first time in our history, we delegated the responsibility of taking care of aging loved ones to total strangers.

In some families, there was the proverbial "old maid" daughter. Today, we would probably refer to her as the "independent woman who chose not to marry." It was understood that if she would take care of Grandma and Grandpa, she would be given the old home place, the china, or some other tangible perk when they died. That was true in my own family. My Aunt Katie, my mother's sister, remained faithful in taking care of Grandma and Grandpa until they both died. Even though my grandmother lived about ten years longer than my grandfather, Aunt Katie never married while either of her parents remained alive.

Those families who didn't have an *Aunt Katie* had little choice except to put Grandma in a nursing home. During that time in history, there was extreme stigma attached to that choice. Neighbors would whisper about how awful it was to "put her in a home," but what else could they do? There were house payments, car payments, and TV payments to be made, as well as children to be sent to college. By this time, many families had become dependent on two incomes, so they had little choice but to put Grandma in a nursing home. I say Grandma because women normally outlive their husbands, and people commonly refer to their own parents as Grandma and Grandpa or Grandmother and Grandfather because that's what they teach their own children to call them.

I: Was there also an Aunt Katie on your father's side of the family?
H: Unfortunately not, and even if there had been, she would not have been able to manage the demands of caring for my paternal grandmother. I actually remember the very day we placed Grandma in a nursing home. It was 1954, and I was not quite five years old. Even though I didn't understand why, I knew placing Grandma in a nursing home was an embarrassment to our family. My mother and I would go to visit her almost every Sunday after church. And although it was his mother, my dad rarely visited. I looked forward to visiting her. She had lived in our home since before I was born, and once she was in a nursing home, I missed her. I really looked forward to taking flowers from my mother's yard and things I had drawn and colored for her. Yet I knew my mother would cry every time we left. I saw that was true for many families. Many would come to visit, and their Grandmas would beg to go home with them. So some of them stopped visiting, except for birthdays and holidays. I now think it broke their hearts to have to leave their loved ones there, and they just couldn't handle the guilt they felt.

At the time, although I was very young, I absolutely understood why Grandma couldn't come back home to live with us. My grandmother had broken her hip. Of course, the technology to replace hips was not available in the early 1950s—at least not to us. Thus, a broken hip was truly the kiss of death. My grandmother was also a large woman, and when she became bedridden, we couldn't physically manage her very well. Since I hadn't yet started to school, I was available to do lots of chores, which included emptying and washing out Grandma's bedpan. I also had to help my mom change Grandma's bed sheets, and that was an extremely difficult task, especially for a four year old.

My mother would stand on one side of her hospital bed, and I would stand on the other. I had to stand on a wooden box because the hospital bed was higher off the floor than normal beds, and I was short and small. Mother would pull Grandma onto her side while I pushed the soiled bed sheet underneath Grandma as far as I could reach. Then we would change sides. I would carry my box to the other side as fast as I could. Mother would then turn Grandma onto her other side while I pulled the soiled sheet from underneath her. Then I would spread the new sheet on the bed and push the other half underneath Grandma. I would grab the box, and Mother and I would change sides again. Mother would roll Grandma over, and I would pull the clean sheet from underneath Grandma and spread it as best I could. Being rolled from one side to the other was painful for Grandma, and she would sometimes yell out and tell us to hurry. This procedure occurred sometimes three or four times a day because Grandma had lots of "accidents." I would become anxious because I didn't want her to hurt. The wooden box was heavy for me to carry, and no matter how fast I hurried from side to side, Grandma still cried out and hollered for us to hurry.

Grandma also dipped snuff, so another chore assigned to me was to empty her "spit jar" and wash it out. I was actually proud to be able to do so many things to help out. Plus, I got praise from other relatives and neighbors. They would comment on how they could hardly believe such a little girl could do so much. I still remember comments like, "Mildred, you would never be able to handle all this if Sandra were in school and not here to help you." I now think my early exposure to such weighted responsibilities contributed to my belief that I could "fix" my own parents' problems, which would enable them to continue living alone. So when the time came to move Grandma to a nursing home, I knew why. My mother had grown tired and weary. My paternal grandfather, as well as my grandmother, had also lived with my folks for years but had died before I was born. My mother had already taken one *turn* as caregiver for him. Although I really missed having Grandma in our home, I knew even at that young age how much work it was just trying to keep her clean and dry.

Sandra's paternal grandmother (Drucilla Gilder), about 1950.

During that same period, sometime in the early 1950s, our society entered into what would become known as the *information age.* Now, with computers, the Internet, cyberspace, e-mail, and the World Wide Web, many of us are able to work from our homes. It seems we've now come full circle. We used to work at home. Then we left our homes to go to work each day. It may be we're returning to our homes to work just in the nick of time. For many of us, it truly is the eleventh hour; "Uncle Sam" is broke and "Aunt Katie" is now a successful CEO living with a significant other. Neither one of them is going to take on the responsibility of taking care of our elderly. My guess is that if you're reading or hearing this, it's your turn.

OUR TURN

CAREGIVING CAREGIVING

The important thing is this: To be able
at any moment to sacrifice what we
are for what we could become.
(Charles DuBois)

Many of us may be required to take several *turns* sorting out
elder care issues for parents, in-laws, siblings, friends, or a
spouse, as well as for ourselves. In addition, these *turns* might
occur simultaneously, even while we have minor children still
at home. Since I was the youngest in a family of five daughters
and one son, it was always understood, on an unspoken level,
that I would be the caregiver for my mother. I inherited this
responsibility about ten years before most boomers face these
challenges, primarily due to the fact that my folks were older
when I was born. My mother was 37 and my father was 44.
Nearly 60 years ago, that was considered "old to still be having
children." I actually have a sister (Nita) who was married and
had a son of her own before I was born. She is now 76 years old
and in extremely poor health with heart problems, COPD, and
dialysis three times a week due to kidney failure. I am listed as
her *Durable Power of Attorney* and may yet take another *turn*
at caregiving. My husband, Marvin, also the youngest in his
family, currently has a brother in a skilled nursing facility and
one recently released from a rehabilitation center secondary to

a fall that resulted in a broken knee and a subsequent stroke. Chances are Marvin will sooner than later be given the opportunity to take a *turn* at caregiving.

Most of my own friends and acquaintances and many of my clients are now taking *their turn*. One couple, I'll call them Mary and Glen, spent the last twelve years taking care of her mother, who had Alzheimer's Disease. The month after Mary's mother died, Glen's mother was also given a diagnosis of Alzheimer's. In addition to caring for her mother, Mary has been fighting a rare form of blood cancer for the past six years. Glen, a financial planner, recently told me that nearly every one of his clients, as well as his friends, are presently dealing with issues related to caring for elderly parents. He said this topic comes up at almost every business or social function and usually ends with them shaking their heads and throwing up their hands in bewilderment as to what to do. He went on to say that over the past year, he's watched his mother change from being the most loving and sweet personality into a person neither he nor any of his family members recognize. His parents have been married for over sixty years. Glen says he's never known either of them to raise their voice, nor had he ever heard a swear word uttered from either of their mouths. However, his mother has recently become aggressive, and she attacks his father. Plus, she screams and "swears like a sailor."

His parents have had two kitchen fires due to his mother forgetting she left food cooking on the stove. Once, his father's hands were severely burned as he tried to throw a skillet of burning oil out their back door. In an attempt to keep them safe, Glen moved them from their home of more than fifty years to an assisted living facility. Unfortunately, his mother has started to wander outside the building. She is now considered high risk and in need of supervision. Consequently, she will have to move to a facility that offers a greater level of care. This is breaking all their hearts, especially his father's.

Glen said there have been only two times his parents have ever spent a night away from one another in their sixty years together, both when his mother was hospitalized giving birth to him and his sister. Unfortunately, this will probably be the beginning of several moves that will require his parents to live apart in separate care facilities.

Another example is the current situation of my dearest friend, Patty, who was the only child of "older parents." Patty is now caring for her 99 year-old mother, who has difficulty walking and hearing. Patty's mother, Ms. Rubino, is one of the strongest women I have ever known and insists on living alone in her own home. Patty would love for her mother to move in with her and her family, but her mother refuses. Her refusal is not given because she is stubborn or selfish but out of love for Patty. Ms. Rubino says she remembers when her own mother lived with her, her husband, and Patty for nearly twenty years—Patty's entire childhood. And although Ms. Rubino loved having her own mother live with them, she understands certain stressors associated with taking care of an elderly parent while caring for your own child and husband. Ms. Rubino says she realizes Patty has the additional stress of running a business, in addition to caring for her own two children and a husband, and she does not want to add to Patty's stress load.

After a recent fall that left her with extreme hip and back pain, she finally agreed to allow Patty to install a PERS (Personal Emergency Response System) to use in the event she should fall again or have some other emergency. This relieves some of Patty's anxiety about her mother living alone.

Patty was one of many boomers who postponed marriage until she was 38, had her first child at 40, and had a second one when she was nearly 44. Consequently, at 60, she still has a daughter in high school. Her life more resembles a "Dagwood Special" than a simple boomer sandwich. She could be the poster child for the *sandwich generation*. She's sandwiched between caring for her mother, a daughter in high school, and a son in college, as well as running a business and overseeing rental properties, all while needing to plan for her own retirement. The stress of this multi-layered sandwich has taken an enormous toll on her physically, mentally, emotionally, and spiritually.

She is unable to make plans for herself because every waking moment is consumed with her daughter's endless school activities, her mother's doctor appointments, and the demands of her business. Her phone rings constantly with never-ending calls from attorneys, realtors, therapists, doctors, teachers, estate planners, her office staff, the gardener, the plumber, her daughter and son, and so on.

Her father's unexpected death and his failure to plan ahead left a huge financial mess, which resulted in mega losses to taxes and years in probate. In addition to addressing the problems left by her father's unplanned estate, she's spent several years trying to ensure that her mother's estate is planned and as protected as possible. Consequently, she's not had much time to handle her own affairs, which would include planning for her own future.

She's angry that her father's lack of financial planning left her tied up in legal battles for more than twenty years. She's angry that his lack of planning has cost her huge amounts of time, energy, and resources that could have been avoided. She's angry that she and her mother had to pay hundreds of thousands of dollars in taxes, which could have also been avoided if her father had planned ahead. She has said that one of her greatest fears is that she will die before she gets her own affairs in order, thus leaving her two kids in a financial mess similar to the one she inherited.

She also fears she will never have time to do the personal things she wants to do. She is very happy her mother is still living. She feels blessed her kids have had the opportunity to know their grandmother and that she has had the honor and privilege of caring for her mother. What she regrets is not having her own children earlier so she would not have such weighty responsibilities on both sides of the coin now.

She states that she never truly enjoys anything because when she's with her kids or her husband, she feels guilty because she's not spending that time with her mother, and when she's with her mother, she feels guilty because she's not spending the time with her husband and kids. She's constantly torn between two realities: her kids will not always be kids, and her mother will not live forever.

Most recently, she's come to the realization that she will not live forever. The next ten years—those between ages 60 and 70—are perhaps the best years she has left, and she grieves. She grieves the losses of her father to death, of her mother to poor health and old age, of her children's childhoods, of her own life script (hopes and dreams that will never be realized), of plans that will never come to fruition, and of the loss of personal freedom. She describes herself as being "trapped in the undertow," carried along only by the currents of life and often feeling helpless and hopeless.

Patty Rubino-Brunetti with her family: Husband (Michael); Son (Mike); Daughter (Tricia); Mother (Mrs. Grace Rubino), 2006. Mrs. Rubino was ninety-seven years old and still very beautiful!

We are the boomers. We demanded to have *it* all, and now that we've got *it*, we don't know what to do with *it*. *It* has become the Frankenstein that may destroy us, or at least take away our sense of peace and well-being, to say nothing of our physical health. How ironic. Many of us were the *flower children*—males as well as females wearing flowers in our long, flowing hair. Some draped symbols of peace around their necks and painted peace signs on their vans, book covers, and vests. A common greeting was the universal symbol of peace—index and middle fingers spread apart while our thumbs held down our ring and little fingers. Many of us rebelled against the establishment, protested inequality, rallied for change, and vowed to live our lives differently than our parents had lived theirs.

It seems such a paradox that we were all about peace, and now many seem to be drowning in a cesspool of anxiety, frustration, depression, and anger—everything but peace. It is also ironic that this same cluster of symptoms is now referred to as the "caregiver syndrome." Our overt expressions of protest have given way to internalizing our feelings of dissatisfaction. In the 1960s, protests included recruiting thousands for marches, staging sit-ins to represent the masses, and chaining ourselves to fences, lest anyone should misunderstand our position on the controversial issue of the day. These media attention displays have now been replaced with unseen, individual, internal protests. However, it is also ironic that once again, millions of us are simultaneously protesting in hopes of affecting *change*. But now, our voices of protest are heard loudest in the quiet recesses of our very soul. Thus, the *change* we affect is now negative and detrimental to us—to our very physical, mental, emotional, and spiritual health.

We often yell at those with foreign accents on the other end of the phone nearly half a world away as we desperately attempt to get information. We ask our questions over and over, only to be put on hold or even worse, to be disconnected and have to start all over again. We shake our heads in disbelief at the constant barrage of mistakes and misinformation offered by sales clerks, receptionists, doctors, lawyers, bankers, accountants, and financial advisors. God forbid we try to obtain *accurate* information from anyone connected with Medicare, Medicaid, or Social Security. Most of those folks are more confused and know less than we do. Our blood boils when we realize they are just telling us *something,* anything, to get us off the phone. To add insult to injury, most of what they say doesn't even make sense. Thus, our blood pressure goes up, gastric juices pour into our stomachs, and negative neuro-chemicals flood our brains, causing a chain reaction throughout our entire bodies.

The damage done by our internal protests is revealed when we seek medical attention for high blood pressure, angina, gastro-esophageal reflux disease (GERD), chronic fatigue, insomnia, erectile dysfunction, depression, anxiety, obesity, memory loss, joint pain, diabetes, and a host of other ailments secondary to stress overload. They quietly rob us, like a thief in the night, of our sense of peace and well-being. We're often left feeling overwhelmed, exhausted, irritated, alone, and afraid.

OVERVIEW OF MY TURN

I have found that among its other benefits, giving
liberates the soul of the giver.
(Maya Angelou)

I: Dr. Haymon, could we start with an overview of "your turn"
then perhaps explore some of your experiences in greater detail
later?

H: Sure. For about a year prior to convincing my folks to move
to Tallahassee, we had regular arguments about whether they
were safe living alone, particularly since they lived quite a distance from neighbors. My mother would often tell me if that
was all I'd come to talk about I could just go home. Finally,
out of desperation, I put a huge guilt trip on my stepfather,
telling him that if anything happened to Mother as a result
of them continuing to stay there alone, I would not only hold
him personally responsible for it, I would also never forgive
him for allowing it to happen. I recruited him to help me convince Mother that they must move closer to me so I could
help take care of them or accept the inevitable consequences.
Since Carl had no children of his own, I was the daughter he
always wanted. I knew he loved me and valued my opinion. He
also knew I loved him. I hated to have to resort to that sort
of emotional blackmail, but I'd tried every other persuasion

to no avail. We decided he'd tell Mother they needed to move closer to me because of *his* health, and they would keep their house so they could go back on weekends. I found the perfect townhouse for them, and the move took place around the first of September in 1993.

That was only about five months before the infamous Valentine's Day incident in 1994. At that time, I was 44 years old and had accomplished many of my life's goals. In addition to surviving an abusive childhood while living with my mother and biological father, I had put myself through college. I'd gotten a private pilot's license. I'd run a marathon. I had earned a Ph.D. I thought there was nothing I couldn't handle. Yet on that day, I was presented with the greatest challenge of my life and the one for which I was least prepared. Within a twenty-four-hour period, I had to decide what to do with my 80-year-old parents who could no longer remain in their home and take care of themselves.

I: I can't imagine that you would have been willing to take care of them, considering how difficult your childhood had been.

H: Growing up with alcoholic parents is horrible; there's no doubt about it. The last thing I wanted to do was to have to take care of them, but nobody else was willing to accept that responsibility. So I had to let go of my anger and my emotional pain. I realized I was taking care of them not because of who they were but because of who I was. My definition of my role as a daughter had nothing to do with their definition of their role as my parents.

Whether you had a horrible childhood with abusive parents, and many of us did, or whether you had a great childhood with loving parents, the issues remain the same. Overnight I had to make major medical decisions for my stepfather, find a place where my mother could be cared for, move her from her home, and figure out how to pay for everything. I was confronted with some of the most difficult questions I had ever been asked, and I didn't have the answers.

I: What were some of those questions?

H: Whether you're in an emergency room or admitting your parents to a care facility, you will be asked about end-of-life medical decisions. For example, you will be asked whether they have a living will. I want to take a minute here to mention something about these, because living wills tend to lull people into a false sense of security. Most address only one issue, and that is whether the individual would want to be placed on artificial life support, such as feeding tubes or artificial respirators. And while it is important to make this decision, you also need to know there are many other decisions that need to be made.

For example, another decision is whether to administer CPR in the event of cardiac arrest or respiratory failure. I didn't know my folks had a choice, nor had I ever thought about why they might not want CPR.

You might also be asked whether they have a *Do Not Hospitalize Order* (DNH). Again, I didn't know we had a choice. I had never considered the notion that we might not want to hospitalize them—we might rather treat them at home or in the care facility. Actually, we have many choices regarding medical decisions. The point I want to make here is that we do have lots of choices, as long as we make those choices *in advance.* However, *we give up our choices* when we don't plan ahead.

I: How can we plan ahead?

H: By discussing end-of-life choices with our elderly loved ones and insisting they make these decisions for themselves. We also need to ensure they complete the necessary forms so their wishes may be carried out. I was also asked whether my folks had *advance directives.* At that time, I had no idea what an advance directive was.

I now know advance directives are legal documents that allow you to make your own medical decisions while you're competent to make them. There are many advance directives—*Living Wills, Do Not Hospitalize, Do Not Resuscitate, Surrogate Caregiver, Durable Power of Attorney, Guardianship,* and others, which allow personal choices to be carried out.

At this time, I only want to make you aware of these documents and to remind you that if your parents don't make decisions for themselves, chances are you will have to make these heart-wrenching decisions for them.

I: Were there other ways you could have been prepared for that day when it became your turn?
H: Yes. If I had known then what I know now, not only would I have talked to my folks and insisted they make their own end-of-life medical decisions, I would have made sure they had regular physical and mental evaluations and insisted my stepfather receive treatment for his alcoholism. I would have also been more knowledgeable regarding their finances and insurance policies, but sometimes that's easier said than done.

In my mother's case, she had a unique filing system. My mother was a Southern lady who had lived through the Depression and grasped the concept of recycling before we even had a name for it. She never threw anything away and had saved every one of her old purses for the last fifty years. She used those old purses as her filing cabinets. She had red purses and brown purses, black purses and blue purses. She had big purses and little purses, fat purses and flat purses. In no particular order, my mother kept their insurance policies, burial policies, bank statements, and other important and unimportant documents in those old purses.

She also kept every greeting card ever sent to her and hid money in the envelopes of those cards. Then she hid the cards in those old purses and hid those old purses in the tops of closets, under the beds, and between the mattresses on the beds. I believe my mother kept every piece of mail addressed to "Occupant" in those purses. So when it became my turn and I had to come up with their birth certificates, marriage certificates, insurance policies, and other important documents, I had to go through every envelope in every purse. It took me a solid week, working nonstop. That was the bad news.

The good news was that I found nearly $2,000 hidden in those old purses and in the toes of old shoes. So you know what? I bought them some new furniture and a filing cabinet to take to the care facility.

I would also have been more knowledgeable about Medicare, Medicaid, and other government assistance. Consequently, in hopes of helping others not to be as overwhelmed as I was, I have provided phone numbers and Web sites of helpful references in the *Resource* section near the end of this book.

I: Many people are worried about how they will pay for long-term care. Could you give us some idea of how much these facilities cost?

H: Elder care in our country is extremely expensive. In 2007, the average private-pay nursing home cost for a semi-private room, in which persons share a room with another resident with only a curtain between their beds for privacy, was $183 per day ($5,566 a month/$66,795 per year). A private (single occupancy) room was $206 per day ($6,266 a month/$75,190 per year), and these costs steadily increase about 5% per year. As you can see, a lifetime of savings could easily evaporate within a few short months.

I: So how in the world do people pay for this?

H: Some folks first spend their life savings, and when that's gone, they depend on government assistance. Others who have no savings depend primarily on government programs or other public or private sources. Some have investments such as annuities, which provide a steady income stream in addition to their Social Security, or perhaps they have long-term care insurance. Others depend solely on their adult children to pay.

I: Could you have seen this day coming?

H: You know, at some level, I had known for years that I would be the one to inherit the responsibility of taking care of my mother and stepfather. However, I pretended that day would never come. Although there were lots of red flags indicating the day had already arrived, I just ignored them.

I: Don't you think most people ignore the flags?

H: Absolutely. Here are some examples of red flags I ignored. Both my mother and stepfather fell on several occasions, and even though some of their falls resulted in broken bones, we attributed those falls to loose rugs, the lights not being on, or any number of external reasons. They also had difficulty remembering things. My mother would leave pots burning on the stove. On more than one occasion, they got lost within blocks of their own house. Yet, I just shook my head and kept going about my normal routine.

I: So why didn't you put your parents in a care facility earlier?

H: I've explored that question, both within myself and with others who waited until they were forced to do something. Many of us don't admit that our folks need to be moved into care facilities earlier because we're either in denial or we don't want to see them lose their independence. Or maybe we don't want our own lives to change. It could be that all of these reasons are at play. It could also be that we don't want to face our own mortality.

I: Can you tell me briefly what you mean by the term "denial"?

H: Denial happens when we stick our heads in the sand and pretend nothing has changed. We actually hide from reality. While this might protect us from some emotional pain, it may also allow life-threatening situations to occur, not only for our elderly loved ones but for other people as well. For example, there were many warning signs that indicated my stepfather was not competent to drive, but I just looked the other way. I didn't want to take away his independence by taking away his truck keys. Then one day he mistook the accelerator for the brake and caused a three-car accident in a shopping center parking lot. It was a miracle nobody was killed.

I: So, Dr. Haymon, how do we avoid staying in denial in a situation like that?

H: It's very important that we pay attention to signs that tell us something is not quite right. If it looks like something's wrong with the picture, then there's probably something wrong with the picture. Check out your suspicions. Ask other family members, friends, and neighbors how they see your elderly loved ones. Keep a journal. When abnormal events happen, jot those down and date it. Then, when you take your loved ones for their medical or mental evaluation, take that information with you. Review it with their doctor. Get the doctor to help you decide if there's reason to be concerned. By all means, don't ignore red flags that might indicate you need to get your loved ones evaluated by a geriatric psychiatrist or psychologist, as well as a medical doctor. I've also created a *Red Flag Checklist,* which I hope will enable other caregivers to assess their loved ones current level of functioning and help them determine if she/he is safe living alone.

I: When we realize our parents are no longer safe living alone and are unable to take care of themselves, what are our choices? To borrow your phrase, where do they go when they can't go home?

H: There are actually many choices. You may decide to hire someone to come live with them in their own home. It's important that elderly people be allowed to stay in their homes as long as they can *safely* do so. *Safely* is the operative word here. You may decide to move them into your home, or you may opt for an adult personal care home. Other choices include adult day care, assisted living facilities, nursing homes, Alzheimer's units, and state hospitals. There are many options, but in order to make a good decision, you have to know your loved one's true level of functioning. There are different facilities for different levels of care. Placing them in an inappropriate facility may result in a number of unnecessary moves. My situation is a good example. In just eighteen months, I moved my stepfather ten times and my mother eight times. This primarily occurred because I had not placed them in an appropriate facility at the outset.

I: I had no idea there were so many options. How do you feel when you look back on this time in your life?
H: Honestly, when I look back at all of that, it looks absolutely crazy! Even now, it is hard for me to believe I was in such heavy denial and stayed there so long. Another part of me is thankful they were not seriously injured and that no one else was hurt or killed because of my inability to see things as they were and act accordingly.

However, once I finally got my folks placed in a facility appropriate for their needs—a wonderful Alzheimer's unit that was about a ninety-minute drive from my home—I felt a great sense of relief and resolution. They were together and seemed happy. They also appeared to feel safe and secure, as evidenced by their decreased levels of anxiety and agitation.

As I stated in *My Turn,* those several years were "the worst of times and the best of times." The old saying that one person's garbage is another person's treasure suggests the notion that we have a choice about how we experience life events. So it is with taking care of aging relatives. It's not inherently joyful, nor is it inherently burdensome. We are wonderfully free to choose how we experience it. I truly hope that what I share with you about *my turn* will help you and others have a much less difficult time when it becomes *your turn.*

SECTION TWO:
BECOMING AWARE BEFORE
YOU GET A WAKE-UP CALL

CAREGIVING   CAREGIVING

RED FLAG CHECKLIST

DENIAL

ONE PHONE CALL CHANGED

EVERYTHING

The following checklist is intended to help determine whether individuals are safe living alone. You may find it helpful to ask friends or relatives who are not emotionally involved with the person being evaluated to use this checklist to help you assess your elderly loved one's current level of functioning. Certainly the more "red flags," the greater the likelihood the individual is not safe living on her/his own. However, if even one flag on the Critical list is checked, immediate intervention is indicated. Once completed, take this checklist along with your loved one for further screening by her/his medical doctor, psychiatrist, psychologist, and/or other health-care providers.

RED FLAG CHECKLIST

Early Warning Signs:
Any one of these may indicate a decreased ability on the part of your loved one to safely function alone.

Decreased Cognitive Functioning

❑ General confusion
❑ Gets lost in own neighborhood
❑ Can't remember names of family members
❑ Short-term memory loss
❑ Forgets and leaves the engine of her/his vehicle running
❑ Confuses the heat thermostat with the air conditioning controls
❑ Wears more than one outfit at the same time (several shirts/blouses; pants/dresses)
❑ Forgets to feed pets or clean cat litter pans
❑ Forgets to retrieve mail from mailbox for several days
❑ Does not remember eating meals
❑ Forgets appointments frequently
❑ Leaves keys hanging on the outside of doors
❑ Calls police frequently for unapparent reasons or because she/he hears imagined noises

❏ Doesn't know the identity of the U. S. President
❏ Inability to count backwards from 20
❏ Cannot remember/recite the alphabet
❏ Hears voices not heard by others
❏ Sees things not seen by others
❏ Accuses spouse of having affairs even when spouse can barely stand or walk

Decreased Physical Functioning

❏ Lacks coordination
❏ Bladder/bowel incontinent (soils underclothes)
❏ No longer able to shave
❏ Inability to hear phone/doorbell
❏ Stays in bed even when not sick
❏ Requires help getting out of bed/chairs
❏ Unusual shakiness of hands and/or legs
❏ Unexplained bruises/injuries (check out possibilities of physical abuse, especially if bruises/injuries occur on upper body or face)
❏ Night sweats
❏ Frequent diarrhea
❏ Seeing several physicians for the same or similar complaints
❏ Difficulty using a telephone
❏ Difficulty operating a television set
❏ No longer able to operate washing machine/dryer properly

Decreased General Functioning

❏ Overly suspicious (inappropriately questions the motives of others)

- ❑ Paranoid behaviors (bars doors/windows; looks under beds and in closets without reason)
- ❑ Appears unusually anxious
- ❑ Misplaces things and accuses others of stealing them
- ❑ Becomes upset easily (cries/laughs inappropriately)
- ❑ Appears more depressed than usual
- ❑ Appears depressed more frequently
- ❑ Becomes extremely afraid of animals
- ❑ Becomes obsessed with a pet or treats pet as having human qualities
- ❑ Accidental hypo- or hyperthermia (exposure to extreme temperatures—hot or cold)
- ❑ Outbursts of
- ❑ anger/aggression
- ❑ Extremely restless/fidgety
- ❑ Frequently goes to bed two to three hours earlier than usual at night
- ❑ Nighttime sleep is accompanied with several brief awakenings
- ❑ Nightmares
- ❑ Insomnia
- ❑ Frequent use of sleep aids
- ❑ Night prowls (cat naps during the day then wanders around the house during the night)

Decreased Social Functioning

- ❑ Conflicts with neighbors
- ❑ Social withdrawal
- ❑ Isolation/estrangement
- ❑ Becomes hostile for unapparent reasons
- ❑ Diminished social skills

❑ Inability to carry on two-way communication

Decreased Eating Habits

❑ Eats food that is not fresh
❑ Eats unbalanced meals (consuming lots of sweets)
❑ Hoards food
❑ Cooks food and forgets to eat it
❑ Refuses to eat

Decreased Personal Hygiene/Cleanliness of Environment

❑ Does not take regular baths or shampoo hair
❑ Does not brush teeth or keep dentures clean
❑ Does not keep fingernails and toenails clean and groomed
❑ Wears soiled clothes
❑ Mixes clean and soiled clothes together
❑ Does not wash clothes regularly
❑ Does not change bed linens regularly
❑ Does not keep shoes clean and in good repair
❑ Does not keep bathrooms clean and fresh
❑ Fails to maintain a clean home environment
❑ Allows garbage to collect inside house
❑ Does not keep dishes washed and put away
❑ Does not discard old food from refrigerator and clean it
❑ Does not keep litter boxes clean

Disorientation

❑ Doesn't know the time of day, day of the week, month of the year, seasons, or what year it is
❑ Doesn't know where she/he is physically
❑ Doesn't know what city or state she/he is in

Decreased Ability to Handle Money Matters

❏ Hides/loses money and cannot remember where it is—accuses others of theft

❏ Careless in bill paying (paying bills more than once or not at all)

❏ Unintentional shoplifting (takes goods without realizing they're not paid for)

❏ Uncontrollable spending sprees—may order things from phone solicitors and not remember

❏ Orders excessively from shopping networks and/or catalogues

❏ Pays money to strangers for work that is not performed

❏ Gives money to strangers

❏ Careless with checks (signs blank check and gives to others)

❏ Puts new acquaintances on checking/savings accounts

❏ Withdraws money from the bank for strangers

❏ Easily manipulated by unscrupulous vendors

❏ Makes drastic changes in wills or trusts to include mere acquaintances or charitable organizations and/or excludes family members

Critical Red Flags:

If even one flag on this list is checked, immediate intervention is indicated.

Signs of potential physical harm to self or others

❏ Chokes on food

❏ Leaves gas stove on with no flame

❏ Forgets pots are cooking on the stove

❏ Burns food frequently

❑ Inability to take medications properly

❑ Inability to safely drive automobile yet continues to drive

❑ Cigarette burns on clothing/furniture

❑ Often loses balance/stumbles/falls frequently

❑ Carelessness with firearms

Alcohol-Specific Indicators:

Due to a change in physiology in elderly persons, consumption of alcohol could lead to problems even when the amount consumed is minimal. One daily cocktail combined with some over-the-counter as well as many prescribed medications may be dangerous.

❑ Continues to drink in a social context while taking medications

❑ Obvious intoxication

❑ Previous history of alcohol abuse

❑ Diagnosis of cirrhosis of the liver

❑ Previous arrests/tickets for DUI

❑ Alcohol-related accidents

❑ Previous hospitalizations for alcohol-related problems

❑ Hides alcohol

❑ The presence of empty alcohol containers

❑ Frequent trips to neighborhood stores for the purpose of buying beer/wine/liquor

❑ Previous history of behavioral problems

❑ Previous history of psychiatric problems

❑ Impairments in the ability to process verbal information/ drinking oneself into oblivion

❑ Passes out from alcohol

❑ Vomits in bed (This is extremely dangerous due to the possibility of choking on vomit.)

❑ Delirium tremens (DTs)

Many of these red flags also apply to individuals with a history of addiction to pain medications, muscle relaxers, anti-anxiety medications (benzodiazepines), amphetamines, and/or other prescription, over-the-counter, or street drugs. Suddenly stopping alcohol, nicotine, or other drugs could result in serious withdrawal symptoms, including seizures, and the result could be fatal. Therefore, do not abruptly stop alcohol, nicotine, or other drugs/medications without medical supervision.

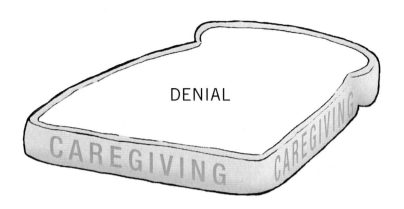

DENIAL

CAREGIVING CAREGIVING

Eyes have they, but they see not.
(Psalm 135:16)

I: Let's talk more in detail about denial. You say you stayed in denial for over a year and a half. There must be many people who, if they weren't in denial, would recognize right now that it is their turn to take charge of things that need to be done for their parents. Would you share some of your personal experiences?

H: I'd be happy to. Once, when I just happened to visit my folks, I pulled into their drive and noticed smoke coming from their kitchen. My parents were nowhere to be seen. I went into their house just in time to turn the stove off before it caught fire. It wasn't that Mother had forgotten she had left the pot cooking; she didn't even remember she had put the pot on the stove. The pot had actually melted into the burner. As crazy as this may seem, similar events happened on several other occasions; plus, they each fell several times before I was willing to admit they could no longer safely live alone.

As I mentioned, in September 1993, I finally got my folks to agree to move to a neighborhood near me—one that had lots of close neighbors. I thought that by moving them closer to me, I could check on them frequently and provide the additional assistance they needed so they could continue living fairly independently. Had I not been in denial, I would have immediately recognized their need not only for assistance but for greater care, including supervision.

I: So, there were obvious red flags all along the way.
H: Oh, there were lots of red flags that screamed, "These people are no longer able to take care of themselves." However, I just disregarded all of them. I ignored all indicators that something was wrong with the picture.

I: I loved the story you shared in My Turn about the pets. Would you tell it again?
H: The story about the pets is funny now—from a safe distance. However, at the time, it was anything but funny. It is another example of how denial plays out at an individual level.

I knew the value of elderly people having pets, so I wanted my folks be able to move some of their pets with them. *Some* is the operative word here. My folks had lived in a rural environment for a number of years, and they had many animals they lovingly referred to as their pets. They had dogs, cats, ducks, chickens, turkeys, goats, pigs, and an occasional raccoon, opossum, or snake. I also knew we couldn't move all those animals into a city neighborhood. So I talked with my folks, and we agreed to move two dogs and five cats with them. We found good homes for the rest of their animals. Also, since our city had a leash law intended to prohibit animals from running loose on the streets, I paid to have the yard of their new townhouse fenced to accommodate these pets.

I: Even the snakes and the opossum?
H: No, I hoped those poor souls would return to their natural habitats. However, and most unfortunately, a snake had taken up residence in one of the flowerpots and was moved into their new townhouse. I am terribly afraid of snakes, so just getting it out of their living room was a traumatic experience for me. Actually, the guy putting up the fence was there working, and I got him to get it out of their house.

Another event I was unprepared for was the fact that one of their dogs was pregnant. In short order, we went from having two dogs and five cats to eleven dogs and five cats. For several weeks, I was called at my office on a daily basis to handle some pet crisis. I was called by my mother, who informed me some of the puppies had crawled underneath the fence. They were stuck in drains and ditches, and she wanted me to come free them. I was called by neighbors who reported some of the puppies were in their carports, crying, and others were under cars and wouldn't come out. Still others were running up and down the streets. Cars had to drive on the edges of yards to keep from hitting them.

I: I'm sorry, how many puppies were there?
H: Nine.

I: You are a saint.
H: Two adult dogs, five cats, and nine little puppies. Well, I was also called by officials of the city, who informed me we were in violation of the leash law. Other neighbors called to complain that the cats were climbing onto their cars and leaving scratches.

Then one day, a neighbor, who sounded hysterical, called and told me that when she tried to put two of the puppies back over the fence into my mother's yard, my mother thought she was taking the puppies away. So, my mother went after the lady with a pair of scissors. Of course, I immediately left my office and went to my mother's house. Mother confirmed the story that she had tried to attack the neighbor with a pair of scissors then threatened the woman again. I was extremely embarrassed. The woman my mother had tried to attack was the wife of one of the professors at our state university. He was a man I liked and respected, and he and his wife had been very kind and helpful to my folks.

But you know, besides being embarrassed, I was frightened by my mother's behavior. I knew if my mother continued to

SANDRA W. HAYMON, Ph.D.

have such outbursts, she would be committed to a psychiatric hospital. At the very least, she might be admitted to an Alzheimer's unit. Realizing that, I worked very hard to get all those pets taken care of. I put an ad in the paper and soon found homes for all the puppies. We were back to two dogs and five cats, and I was relieved to no longer be dealing with them. However, I was still in denial. I was unwilling to admit that my parents could not take care of themselves, much less care for their pets.

I: I can't imagine you having to deal with all that, but you tell it now with great humor, as a funny story.

H: Carol Burnett once said that comedy is tragedy, plus time. There has been enough time now, since some of my tragedies, to turn them into comedy. Some of the funniest stories I now remember are the very ones that seemed horrific when they happened. But I'll tell you what's not funny, and that's when I look back and realize my denial could have cost my parents and others their lives.

I: We all talk about denial and you gave us a brief explanation earlier, but what is it really? Put on your psychologist hat for a moment.

H: Actually, denial is a way of coping. Sometimes, when things are emotionally painful, we hide behind the proverbial wall of denial in order to take care of ourselves. It is very common for caregivers to be in denial of their loved one's true level of functioning.

I: What's so bad about being in denial?

H: I'm not saying denial is bad. Denial may be beneficial in protecting us from emotional pain. However, it may also be debilitating. It may keep us from taking any action at all. At the very least, denial influences our judgment, which may cause a multitude of other problems. It certainly did for my folks and me.

I: I'm still not sure I understand. Would you go a step further?

H: Let's talk about families in terms of a systems approach. Families are actually systems made up of organized patterns of beliefs, attitudes, and behaviors. Those basic beliefs serve as a structure for relationships within a family. Those beliefs are also formed around rules, rules either spoken or unspoken, rules by which members of the family agree to operate. However, sometimes the foundation of those beliefs changes, yet family members continue to hold the same beliefs, attitudes, and behaviors they held prior to the fundamental change. Although one or maybe all family members realize something is different, they pretend nothing has changed. This unwillingness to adapt to the change is referred to as denial. Denial usually has several layers that serve to protect those basic beliefs although they are no longer true.

If we use an artichoke as a metaphor, we might envision the heart of the artichoke as the false belief held to be true by family members. Just as with the heart of the artichoke, there are several layers of protection, leaves that have to be peeled away in order to get down to the heart—the basic belief.

I: What was the situation in your family?

H: My mother, stepfather, and I had an image of them as strong, healthy, and independent. This could be likened to the heart of the artichoke. This mindset held true until they were about seventy-five years old. However, by Valentine's Day of 1994, it was no longer an accurate image. In reality, they couldn't take care of themselves. This fundamental change had occurred at the very heart of our family system. Yet even in the face of much evidence to the contrary, we continued to interact in the same ways we had for years. None of us wanted to be the first to admit things had changed. If we admitted the truth, then our attitudes and the way we interacted with each other would have to change. We were operating in a superficial comfort zone none of us wanted to leave.

I: It also seems if you had admitted what bad shape your parents were in, they would have lost their independence, and you would have lost yours. Isn't that true?

H: Sure, that was true. I can see that as I look back now. However, none of us were conscious of that at the time. I didn't want them to be dependent on me. I didn't want to be the caregiver.

I: Besides protecting us from emotional pain, are there other reasons denial might occur within families?

H: Yes. One reason denial may exist is to maintain the status quo within the family system. When things are at the status quo, nothing has to change. As long as family members agree to deny anything has changed, they can continue to behave and interact as though things are just as they've always been. Therefore, the family system remains intact, although it may not be working very well. In many ways, denial seems to be a passive way out. People, in general, do not like change and are likely to take the path of least resistance. Denial may also exist because people fear the unknown. Even though things are not as individuals might want them to be, at least everyone in the family knows the spoken or unspoken rules. Therefore, with some degree of accuracy, they may predict what might happen. Often that seems preferable to the unknown.

I: Could you give us an example of how denial protects us from emotional pain?

H: Sure. The losses associated with growing old are many and may be extremely painful. Denying certain signs of aging may enable individuals to buffer themselves from the realization that things are not as they were in the past. Denial may protect them from the pain of looking at their lives and realizing things will probably never be as they once were or perhaps as they had hoped for.

I: You say denial influences our judgment. How so?

H: The most obvious problem with denial is that denial is a

distortion of information. In order to make informed decisions, we need accurate information, not distorted information. Decisions based on inaccurate information are rarely good decisions. Sometimes denial keeps people from taking any action at all. As long as we look the other way or stick our heads in the sand, we don't have to do anything. For example, if I refused to look at my parents' situation, I wouldn't have to take away Carl's truck keys because the danger wouldn't exist in my schema. Carried to its extreme, denial helps to create situations that are dangerous and sometimes even cost people their lives.

I: So did you just ignore everything?
H: Not only did we ignore the truth, we came up with reasons to justify why the accidents were not their fault. We created a whole tapestry of reasons to explain why they fell and why Mother kept forgetting the stove was on. If any of us had admitted they could no longer see, hear, walk, or remember as well as they used to, then our roles—our family relationships—would have to change. My relationship with them as a daughter would then change, and I would become the caregiver. Their perception of being independent would change to one of dependence if we came out of denial.

I: So, you or your sisters might have to take charge, huh?
H: Ironically, many folks either stop or significantly reduce the frequency of their visits to their elderly loved ones as the time nears when roles need to be reversed. They don't want to see it. The red flags keep getting bigger and redder, screaming something has changed. If they visit their elderly loved ones, they run the risk of seeing those flags. The paradox is that the closer we move toward it, the further away we want to get. In our case, we just did nothing.

The next disaster, for us, occurred on a Sunday. My stepfather still had, but should not have had, his driver's license. Consequently, he drove Mother to their old neighborhood to see one of the neighbors to whom she had given her chickens, and the woman gave three chickens back to Mother. Well, Mother brought those chickens home with her, then killed and cleaned them—on her front porch! My mother thought nothing of wringing chickens' necks, dipping them in a pot of boiling water, and plucking the feathers off of them. She was merely cleaning them so she could cook them.

I: *This was at their house in Tallahassee?*
H: Yes, in their townhouse in the middle of a neighborhood with many close neighbors. Not only were chickens not allowed due to city ordinance, but several of the neighborhood children gathered to see what this old woman was doing to these chickens. They had never seen a chicken killed before, much less on someone's front porch. The first news I got of it was when one of the mothers called and asked if my mother was performing some sort of Satanic ritual. I asked her not to call the police and assured her I would take care of it immediately.

I: *You seem to have maintained a wonderful sense of humor about all of this.*
H: It makes the journey a lot easier if you keep a sense of humor. From the safe distance afforded me by time, I can now enjoy these stories. However, I also realize the serious implications my denial could have had. While I was solving problems associated with pets and chickens, there were other problems occurring that were much more serious.

Mother certainly could no longer safely prepare meals. It wasn't even safe for her to be around a stove. So I enlisted a community service to transport my folks to a senior citizens' center, where they could go every day to eat lunch and engage in other social activities. This did not work very well, nor did it last very long. Mother was hardly ever ready when the van arrived to pick them up. Of course, the driver could not wait long for them as he had other people to pick up. Thus, Mother would get upset because she thought he didn't want them to go. On the days she was ready and went to the center, as soon as she and Carl finished their lunch, she wanted to go home.

However, the van was not intended to function as a private limousine for my folks but was scheduled to leave at a certain time with all the passengers on board. Once again, this upset Mother, who said, "They won't let us leave." By the time I got all that worked out, their health had declined so that traveling to the center was no longer an option. At that point, I enlisted the services of Meals-On-Wheels, a wonderful organization that delivers meals to elderly people who are housebound.

I: Do most cities have that?
H: Yes, they do. Meals-On-Wheels and congregate meals are usually listed in the white pages of phone directories. You could also call a local Elder Care office or the Eldercare Nationwide Locator, and they would be happy to refer you to those services. You could also go online and locate one nearby.

Every day this wonderful service brought more food to Mother and Carl than any four people could eat. Having lived through the Great Depression, my mother understood the importance of not wasting food, or anything else for that matter. Her motto was "waste not and want not." As I mentioned earlier, she practiced recycling long before we even had a name for it. Not only did she save every Styrofoam container the food came in, she also saved every salt and pepper packet and every bit of food. What's more, she refused to eat the fresh food until all the old food was gone. I'm all for conservation, and this may not seem such a big problem. It may even solicit commendation from some, but there was another problem.

We lived in Florida, and my mother would often mistakenly turn on the heat, thinking it was the air conditioning. It was not uncommon for the temperature in their house to be over 100° Fahrenheit with the doors and windows closed. Well, you can imagine what happened. I had to go over twice a day in attempts to discard all the old food and try to prevent them from getting food poisoning because she'd forget to put the food in the refrigerator.

Mother became upset if she saw me throwing anything out. I would often have to call my sister Wanda to come and help me. One of us would entertain our folks while the other went to the kitchen and threw all the stuff away. We thought we had solved the problem.

I: Why did you think you had solved the problem?
H: Because we were going over there and dumping all of this stuff—old food, Styrofoam boxes, plastic spoons and forks—not just in the garbage can in her kitchen, but we were taking all this stuff out to the street to a big dumpster. We were getting rid of all the old food so they would only have fresh food. Within a few days, Mother caught on to what we were doing. She then started going outside to the dumpster, getting the old food out, taking it back inside, and carrying on with her plan to consume the old food first.

I: Let me guess—you and your sister were both still in denial about your mother?
H: That's probably the understatement of the year.

I: So then what did you do? What's the rest of the story here?
H: My sister and I continued in our fight against the food and Styrofoam boxes. We won some of the battles, but we were losing the war. There was no way we could keep up with all of it. So I hired a cleaning service to come twice a week to discard the old food. That didn't work very well either. Do you know what I finally had to do? I had to go to my mother's house every day, throw out the old food, and take her garbage home with me to keep her from going outside and retrieving the discarded food. However, I was still not willing to reconsider my belief that they could live alone.

I: Dr. Haymon, you've been remarkably honest about your personal denial regarding your own parents' situation with leaving pots on the stove, pets, old food, and whatever. Was giving up driving a big issue with your stepfather?

H: It was a huge issue because he loved to drive. For most of his life, Carl drove a taxi for a living. After he retired from that job, he went to work for the government, where he drove a truck for the forestry department. Driving was who he was; that's how he identified himself, and he was very proud of that. Plus, he had a wonderful driving record.

However, Carl could not see or hear well, and his circulation was very poor. He often had leg cramps so severe that he could hardly use the brakes on his truck. Plus, he had gout in his feet, which was extremely painful. Many times I asked him not to drive. I assured him I would take him and Mother to the grocery store or wherever they wanted to go. Yet he persisted in driving. He not only drove on neighborhood streets, but he continued to drive on the

Interstate. Then one night, I came home from a business meeting to retrieve several phone messages.

One of the messages was from a deputy sheriff, who stated my folks had been in an accident but were not injured. He checked their address and saw that they were only about five blocks from their house. Now remember, we live in Florida, and about 30% of our population is over 65. This deputy sheriff was quite accustomed to seeing elderly people driving, so when he saw that they were only a few blocks from their house, he released Carl to drive himself and Mother home.

The next message I got that night was from a state trooper, who said my parents were driving on the wrong side of the road when he stopped them. They were northbound in the southbound lane of a two-lane street. He called the number on my business card. The telephone rang into an answering service for the mental health agency where I was doing an internship. Since I couldn't be reached, my boss was contacted, and the third message was from him.

He said that he and his wife had rescued my folks and had driven them home. Although my boss knew what street they lived on, he didn't know their house number. It was very sad. He told me that he drove up and down the street several times because my folks couldn't remember which house was theirs. The street they lived on was only two blocks long, yet neither my mother nor stepfather could identify their home. They were obviously upset about the accident, the sheriff, and the state trooper. They were anxious and scared and couldn't remember.

I: Did this finally crack your wall of denial?
H: Not even a hairline. I still tried to explain why they couldn't remember and that it was not their fault. They had an aluminum boat, and according to my boss, Mother finally said, "Oh. That's our boat. That's where we live." My boss made sure that they got into their house safely. In his message, he further stated he had left their truck at a gas station and gave me the address. I got a friend to take me to pick their truck up so I could take it to their house. My stepfather had been cited for a moving vehicle violation and was extremely upset. I talked with him and tried to comfort him.

The incident had occurred when they went grocery shopping at a store near their house. This store was located in a strip mall with many other shops and lots of pedestrian traffic. While he was backing out of his parking space, he mistook the accelerator for the brake. Another car was moving behind him. Poor Carl, he thought his foot was on the brake, and he just floored it, knocking the moving car into a parked car and that car into a tree.

When I read the accident report the following day, I cried, realizing that if someone, some child, had been walking behind Carl's truck, she/he would have been killed. I had no choice. I took his truck keys and cried some more. I did not want to take away this grown man's independence, but I had no choice.

The wall of denial had finally been cracked. I was finally able to admit he was no longer safe to drive.

I: Was that the first tough decision you had to make?
H: The first tough decision was the one requiring them to move from their home. It's hard to make decisions that take away another adult's independence. However, even after all of this, we continued to maintain our family relationships just the way we always had. The decisions I had to make in the next layer of denial were associated with even greater health risks for my folks.

Since my stepfather was mentally more alert than my mother, he had assumed responsibility for their medications. Unfortunately, he kept confusing them. He'd take hers and give her his, or they'd both take too much one day and wouldn't take any the next. I thought that if I could just explain it more clearly to him, he would understand and be able to handle it. Stuck in the next level of denial, I again relied on my own creativity.

I: You were going to save the day again; I can see it coming.
H: Absolutely. I knew I could fix this one. So guess what I did? Once a week, I would sit down with them and explain their medications. I put appropriate doses in separate envelopes, one envelope for each day of the week for each of them—fourteen total envelopes. Plus, I wrote their names and the dates on each envelope. That seemed simple enough to me for him to follow. Compliance with using the envelopes lasted only a few days. I went over there one afternoon and discovered they had taken the medication intended for an entire week in just two days. I was frustrated and bewildered. I didn't know what to do.

I had solved a lot of problems in my life, but I didn't know how to fix this one. Then one day, I was at the pharmacy we commonly used. I was just standing there, waiting for their prescriptions, when I saw what I thought must have been the most ingenious invention in the whole world. There it was—a plastic box with seven columns and four compartments in each column. This would work! There was a column for each day of the week and a compartment for morning, noon, afternoon, and evening. All they would have to do was lift the lids of each little compartment and take the pills out. I bought two of them and went racing over to their house. I was so excited! I'm not kidding you. I was thrilled.

I: Solve the problems, and they can stay at home.
H: I was so excited to show them the boxes. I explained how it worked, especially to Carl. I went over it in detail. I wrote Mother's name on the top of one box and Carl's name on the other. About three days later, I realized this wasn't working any better than the envelopes had. In fact, it was worse. As Carl would try to open the little compartments, the plastic lids of other compartments would open, and pills would go flying everywhere.

I found pills scattered all over their kitchen—on the tops of counters, under the edge of cabinets, under the door of the refrigerator, on the floor, and in the sink. I knew they could not continue taking prescribed medication in this haphazard manner. It was dangerous for them. They weren't supposed to be taking each other's medications. They weren't supposed to be taking a whole week's worth in two days and taking none for three or four days. Yet I knew I couldn't go over there four times a day. I was exasperated.

I: Did it ever come to mind that maybe you should put them in a nursing home?
H: No. That thought never occurred to me. I just thought the problem was me. I kept thinking that somehow I could get this right. If I tried hard enough, I could take care of everything, which would allow them to live independently. So, I kept trying really hard.

ONE PHONE CALL
CHANGED EVERYTHING!

CAREGIVING CAREGIVING

Anyone can hold the helm when the sea is calm.
(Publilius Syrus)

I: You were so good at maintaining their situation through your denial. What finally jump-started you into doing something about it?

H: What finally shocked me out of denial happened that infamous Valentine's Day in 1994. Although it had only been five months, it seemed more like five years, since I had moved my folks near me. I'm not exaggerating; if you multiplied all the things I've talked about by ten, you would still have only the tip of the iceberg of problems I dealt with. As I shared earlier, I went to their house every day and sometimes several times a day trying to take care of things so they could continue to live in their home.

Sometimes I would find their house keys hanging in the front door, where they had forgotten them. One evening, before I had to take Carl's truck keys, I found his truck engine running. He and Mother were inside watching television, totally unaware the truck engine was running with the doors locked and the keys in the ignition. I often stopped by on my way to work to make sure my folks had made it through the night okay. If I had early morning meetings, I would go to their place on my lunch hour.

Here's what finally happened. As I mentioned, at that time I was completing a residency in psychology and was putting in long hours each day. Since I had gone to work early that morning, I did not stop by their house. On that particular day, I had seen clients back-to-back all day and had not even taken a lunch break. Consequently, I had not seen or talked to my folks since the previous afternoon, so I called my mother to find out how they were doing. I also wanted to let her know I would come by after work but that I would probably be working until about eight o'clock that night. I had Valentine candy and cards for them, and it was important for me to take them their gifts. When I asked Mother how they were, she said she was fine, but Carl had gone to bed shortly after I had left them the previous afternoon and had not gotten up since. I quickly calculated that Carl had been in bed nearly twenty-four hours. I asked her if he had talked to her, and she said, "Well, I talked to him several times, but he didn't answer. He didn't say anything." I asked her if he was breathing. She replied, "I don't know." I was stunned! I took a deep breath and said, "Mother, please go see if you can get him to talk to you and stay right there with him."

Well, my sister Wanda is a registered nurse, and she worked at a hospital near their house. I called her and explained the situation because I knew she could get there quicker than I could. I asked her to go over and see what was going on. She did, and within a matter of minutes, she called back and told me Carl was breathing but not verbally responding. She said she had already called for paramedics, and as soon as they came and took Carl to the hospital, she would take Mother home with her. I told her I would meet the paramedics at the hospital.

It was during those next few hours that I was asked all

86

those questions about CPR, hospitalization, and advance directives. I was overwhelmed. The reality of their condition hit me squarely in the face. I so wished I had done something sooner. I wished I had somehow seen they were in such pitiful shape. The emergency room was hardly the time or place for me to be trying to figure all this out.

Sometime around midnight, the questions had been answered, I had filled out all the forms, and Carl was resting in a private room. It seems he'd had an adverse reaction after mixing his prescription medications with several cans of beer. I remember walking out to my car and another shock hit me. I thought, *oh my goodness, what am I going to do with Mother?*

I: Oh, boy. Where was your mother?
H: Wanda had taken Mother home with her. So I called my sister, and she said it was okay for Mother to spend the night with her. However, I would need to come and get her first thing the following morning because she had to be at work by 6:30 a.m. She lived alone, and there would be no one at her house to stay with Mother.

I also lived alone and worked fifteen-hour days, trying to finish my residency. Even if I moved my mother home with me, I would not be there the majority of time to see about her. Knowing her history of turning on stoves and the unfamiliarity of my house, I knew she couldn't be left alone. I felt guilty because I thought she *should* come home with me, but that certainly was not a viable option. I felt so overwhelmed. First thing the next morning, I called my boss to let him know the situation. I picked Mother up from Wanda's and promptly started calling care facilities. Not only did I find out they didn't have any rooms or even any bed space, I also learned they had waiting lists that were months long.

I: When you say care facilities, would most people know that to be nursing homes?

H: Actually, I didn't call any nursing homes. I still couldn't admit my mother needed nursing home care, even though she did. I was in the next level of denial—remember the artichoke? She and Carl both actually needed skilled nursing care months prior to that event. However, I still couldn't see it.

So instead, I called several adult congregate living facilities (ACLFs). These accommodations are like small apartments. Individuals have their own large bedroom and bathroom, but they don't have kitchens because they aren't allowed to have stoves. There is a large dining room where residents eat prepared meals together. I called these types of facilities because I was still in denial about my mother's true level of functioning. I was only willing to admit Mother couldn't live alone, and I had to find a place for her to live.

I: And did you finally find one?
H: Yes. I found a facility that had a room, and I told them immediately that we'd take it. Then the next eye-opener came for me. The lady said, "We'll have to interview and evaluate your mother. Then we will decide whether your mother meets the criteria for this room or not." That was a real shock for me. I had so many choices about other things, yet I didn't really have a choice about that. Nor did I have any idea what "to evaluate" meant. I only knew I wanted my mother to pass whatever evaluation she needed to so she would have a place to live.

Mother and I arrived early for her evaluation at this care facility. The admissions director who met with us was a tall young woman in her late twenties, with blond hair and blue eyes. She wore glasses and was either plump or pregnant. I couldn't tell which because she wore an oversized top. She was pleasant, and after a short introduction, she opened a folder and served me my first helping of alphabet soup. Without even looking up or taking a breath, she said, "You do understand this is an ACLF. I see that your mother has SS. Does she have A and B? Does she have SSI? How about OSS?" I was stunned—completely stunned! I had never heard so many acronyms in my entire life. I felt as though I had been dropped off on another planet and didn't speak the language. I had no idea what she was talking about. I guess she could feel me staring at her because she looked up over her glasses, just for a second, and then she continued. "Is she eligible for the Medicaid Medically Needy Program?"

I felt paralyzed. I was caught somewhere between not having a clue to what she was talking about and wanting desperately to respond appropriately so she would accept my mother. I'm not sure how long I sat there, staring into space. I was hoping that somewhere in all of my life's experiences I had recorded some information in long-term memory that would at least help me fake this one. The next thing I heard was, "You will need proof of your mother's eligibility for these programs; otherwise, private pay is $1,935 a month."

I: Oh my, how much?

H: Nineteen hundred and thirty-five dollars a month. This was in 1994, and I was completing a residency program. At that time, I didn't even make $1,900 a month.

I was so overwhelmed. I could feel the tears in my eyes. Yet I knew I didn't have the luxury of crying. Even if I did, who was going to comfort me? My mother sat there with a childlike smile on her face. She didn't know what day it was, where she was, or what was going on. I remember she looked at me with such a look of trust. I could no longer deny our roles had reversed. It was then, indeed, my turn to take care of her. So I took a deep breath and swallowed the lump in my throat.

I then admitted to this admissions director, "This is my first experience in taking care of my parents, and I don't know what to do. I want to do a good job. I just don't know where to start." I continued, "Quite frankly, I don't even know what you're talking about." She was kind enough to write down all the acronyms—those fragments of the alphabet and the words they represented.

She also agreed to evaluate my mother since we were already there. "I need to know about her ADLs." Again, I sat staring at her, unsure of what I was feeling but quite sure I had never heard of "ADLs." She stared back at me for a few seconds. Finally, her ability to read body language must have kicked in because she said, "Oh, I'm sorry. ADLs are activities of daily living." That didn't help a lot, so I waited for her to continue.

She first asked me if my mother could dress herself. Flashes of recent times when my mother had put on several layers of clothing passed through my mind—dresses over pants, shirts over dresses. There were even times when Mother would have on her underwear and a shirt but no long pants, totally oblivious to her appearance. Bless her heart. It seemed as though her cognitive functioning either got interrupted or ceased completely in the middle of dressing, as well as when doing other things.

I'm not sure how long I sat watching those reruns in my mind before I heard the question repeated. "Can your mother dress herself?"

"Yes, of course she can dress herself," I replied. Somehow I knew not to add the additional information regarding Mother's ability to dress herself.

"Is she continent?" Continent was not a word I ever remembered using. I had written my dissertation on "Work Addiction," and I was used to working with white-collared CEOs. The question of whether an individual was continent had never come up. In my overwhelmed emotional state, I was not efficiently processing information.

I became acutely aware this young woman was directing every question to me, as though my mother was invisible. I wondered if at some level Mother was aware she was being ignored. I felt a bit embarrassed talking about her with her sitting right there. "Your mother is continent—right?"

"Yes. Yes, she is."

I was startled back from my mini-mental vacation, and although I was still not exactly sure what she was talking about, I knew that by the way she phrased the question the correct response was yes. "How about toileting—can your mother toilet herself?" By then I assumed the correct default response was yes, so I responded accordingly. I did not volunteer the fact that Mother would often not make it to the toilet on time and thus went through several clothing outfits a day.

"Does your Mother need help bathing?"

"Well, I've been running her bath water and helping her into the tub. I ensure her ears, underarms, and other areas are washed. I also wash her hair, help her out of the tub, and dry her off." I felt I needed to expand my answer because I did not want Mother to slip and fall or burn herself with hot water. So I answered her honestly. From the look on the director's face, I knew immediately that I had said too much.

"We normally require that residents need no assistance with bathing. However, we can assist her but it will cost extra. She *is* able to feed herself, isn't she?"

Maybe I was getting paranoid, but I thought the director was losing patience with me. I did not want to do anything to annoy her, so I quickly replied, "Yes, she eats very well."

She did not hesitate. "Does your mother have difficulty ambulating?"

Again, I responded quickly. "No. She can also walk very well." I wanted to get this evaluation over as soon as possible. I felt mentally drained, emotionally exhausted, and was still on the verge of tears.

"Good, because our license requires residents to be able to get themselves out of the building in the event there should be a fire," she explained. She then gave me several forms to fill out and said she would need a copy of Mother's Medicare and Social Security cards, as well as her driver's license or another photo ID.

"She hasn't driven for years, so she doesn't have a photo ID," I replied. I was then informed I would need to take her to the DMV (I actually knew this meant the Department of Motor Vehicles) and get a photo ID for her.

We were then told they would hold the room for her until the next day. At that time, either we had to produce approved eligibility forms for government assistance, or we had to agree to private pay before she could move in. Next, this very kind woman directed me to the appropriate state agencies. Please recall this was the day after Carl was admitted to the hospital, and I had been up until after midnight in the emergency room with him. I was not only tired but needed to be at work. Anyway, during the next few hours, I felt as though I was in a time warp with all these aliens speaking a strange language.

I met with representatives from a number of state agencies and explained my situation. I explained it over and over to different people in different departments. I filled out forms until my eyes crossed, plus I had to make several trips to get birth certificates, bank statements, and Medicare and Social Security cards.

I even had to produce an itemized statement of all their personal belongings. The one good thing about continuing to run back and forth to Mother's house was that I could personally check on her every couple of hours in addition to calling her in between my trips. By late that afternoon, I was told everything looked to be in order, but they needed to interview my mother personally prior to approving her for assistance.

I: So you did find assistance? You had a place for her to go, and you were able to get financial assistance for her, right?
H: Yes, if she passed this last interview.

I: Another test to go through? Goodness sakes.

H: I looked at the clock, and I had about forty-five minutes to drive across town, get my mother, and then drive back to this state office before they closed. I was so frustrated. None of the people to whom I had been providing information, and there were many, not one of them ever indicated they would need to talk to my mother. If I had known that, I could have brought Mother back with me during one of the trips when I was running back and forth for all those documents. Instead, they waited until just before closing to tell me they had to interview her. Remember, the care facility was only going to hold the bed for her until the following morning, so I didn't have the luxury of waiting until the next day to do this.

Once again, I had to stuff my feelings. I couldn't afford to vent my frustrations. These people had power; they held the magic pen that could just as easily check the "denied" box as the "approved" box. I asked how long the interview would take, and I was told only a few minutes. If I could get Mother back there before five o'clock, someone would interview her that afternoon. I thanked them profusely and promised I would be back with my mother before they closed.

Then I hurried out of the state building, ran to my car, and drove as fast as I could. I picked up my mother and flew back across town. We got into the state building with five minutes to spare. They interviewed Mother, and thank goodness, she was approved. We had the needed assistance, and we had a room.

I silently offered prayers of thanksgiving. With the approved forms in my hand, I called the care facility and announced that my mother and I were en route to the furniture store to purchase the furniture they had specified, and we would be there within a couple of hours. This particular facility required specific furniture—single beds, nightstands, and chests-of-drawers but not dressers. My sister Wanda met us at the furniture store. We quickly chose appropriate furniture and hurried to the facility. I had to pay the delivery men extra money to get them to deliver the furniture, since it was after hours, but I was happy to do so.

I: Luckily you had the $2,000 from the purses to buy the furniture.

H: And a filing cabinet. Well, as I moved my mother in, I had to face another painful belief that I had held. I believed nursing homes represented the last place prior to death. I guess that belief originated in my childhood, when we placed my grandmother in a nursing home and she died a couple of years later.

I supposed that I could postpone my parents' deaths by postponing a nursing home. Even though this first placement was not a nursing home but rather an assisted living facility, I still had to face the fact that my parents would never live alone again.

Now you're probably wondering, how I could have continued to ignore such blatantly obvious signs, signs that clearly indicated my mother and stepfather were incapable of living on their own. The answer is quite simple: I was in denial and therefore, I could not see the signs. I couldn't take in any new information that contradicted my basic belief that my folks were strong, healthy, in control, and able to live alone.

That's what denial does. It blocks any information that contradicts our basic belief, whether the belief is true or not. There is another level of my denial I feel I need to talk about because it's so prevalent in many families, and that is the level of denial created by alcoholism.

Alcoholism among the elderly is a huge, hidden problem. While accurate figures are difficult to determine, current estimates suggest more than three million people over 60 years of age are problem drinkers. About twenty percent of all persons treated for alcoholism are older than 55 years of age. A particular growing problem is late-onset alcoholism, which appears to be a response to stressful life events, including multiple losses.

Unfortunately, alcoholism among the elderly often goes undiagnosed primarily because elderly people are not screened for it. Sometimes they are diagnosed with depression or Alzheimer's disease, when in fact many of their symptoms, such as frequent falls, shaky hands, and forgetfulness, are alcohol-related. Consequently, treatment addresses the symptoms rather than the problem.

I: Were both of your parents alcoholic?
H: Yes, both my mother and stepfather were severely alcoholic. Also, my biological father had been alcoholic most of his adult life. Consequently, having grown up with alcoholic parents, I had learned from a very early age to deny any reality I didn't want to be true. It's like an example in the book *An Elephant in the Living Room.* The elephant is actually the drinking—the alcoholism, and everybody pretends the elephant isn't there. There is a child in the story who sees the elephant and wonders why nobody else does. The child tries to talk about it, but no one in the family is willing to validate this child's reality.

It's as though no one else sees it. At least they're not willing to admit they do, and they certainly are not willing to talk about it. So the child learns to pretend there's no elephant. She too begins to deny that it's real. The unspoken rule is to not admit there is an elephant in the living room and to not talk about it. So the child learns not to trust herself.

Since no one else validates her reality, she learns to first ignore the elephant and then to not even see it. Individuals who grow up in families with addictions learn numerous ways to avoid seeing things they don't want to see. In addition to pretending certain things don't exist, they stick their heads in the sand or put on rose-colored glasses. They look the other way and call black white and white black. They do whatever it takes to avoid situations they've been taught to ignore and perhaps have even been punished for seeing.

I: Dr. Haymon, I can see how you would have been more likely to be in denial, given the fact that you were an adult child of alcoholic parents.

H: My mother continued drinking until her mid-seventies, and my stepfather drank until the time he was actually moved to a nursing home. Remember when I told you my folks fell several times, and some of those falls resulted in broken bones? Not once did I attribute their falls to alcohol. Instead I pretended it was caused by a loose rug or not enough light.

Alcohol was often responsible for much of their confusion and forgetfulness, yet my folks and I continued in our denial. Not once did we talk about the elephant in our living room.

I: I can see how denial keeps people from placing their parents in a care facility, but why would you ask your 70 or 80-year-old parent to stop drinking so late in life?

H: That's a good question, which many people ask. Some people say, "They're probably only going to live a couple more years anyway, so why even bother trying to get them to quit?" I think my story paints a very clear picture why. You might have no other choice than to place them in a care facility, forcing them to stop drinking, smoking, or using smokeless tobacco, because most facilities don't allow residents to indulge in those.

My parents were in an adult living facility, and the residents who lived there were expected to be somewhat independent and responsible. For the most part, this facility didn't mind if residents had a beer or a glass of wine, but Carl was clearly alcoholic. He couldn't stop with "a" beer or even two beers. Carl grew up on a farm. He was "country" and wore bib overalls. He would go to the convenience store next door to the assisted living facility and buy a six-pack, sticking cans of beer in every pocket. He would come waddling back to the facility thinking nobody noticed, even though he looked like he had gained forty pounds in the interim.

I: That was clever.

H: Alcoholics always are. That's a good way to put it. When individuals are addicted to any substance, they become very clever, very creative in figuring out ways to meet that need. Well, his beer drinking didn't seem to be causing any problems. I think the staff at the facility just sort of looked the other way. Perhaps they thought, *here's this old man, who just wants to have his beer. He's not rowdy. He's not hurting anybody.* So they let him get away with it. for several months. Then one day he paid somebody to bring him a bottle of whiskey.

I: I'm not sure I understand. Who brought him the whiskey?

H: Oh, I don't know exactly whom he paid to bring it. When I asked him, he didn't even know the person's name. He said it was just somebody who worked there. I quickly learned that getting someone to bring whiskey (or other substances) to a care facility, or even to a hospital, is not that difficult. For a few dollars, workers or family members of other residents or patients are more than happy to accommodate. Individuals can also call and pay taxi drivers to purchase and bring alcohol to them. Even some contracted workers, such as those who do the lawns or plumbing, etc., are more than willing to make a few extra bucks.

Well, that particular day, they were outside, and Carl was pushing Mother in her wheelchair, which they both enjoyed. He would often push her up and down the driveway in front of the facility.

Then, when he was going up the driveway toward the street, he just decided to keep going. My mother had the bottle of whiskey between her legs in the wheelchair. Carl had taken several drinks and given my mother several drinks. Not only was he intoxicated, but Mother was too. Since Mother was mentally out of it, she obviously didn't understand what was happening. According to the report, the head nurse first learned they were missing when the police called to say an old man was pushing an old woman in a wheelchair a few blocks from the facility. Mother and Carl had been spotted at the intersection of a four-lane highway. Naturally, the police assumed they had wandered away from the nearby facility.

I was very frightened when I heard about the incident. I later learned that Carl had pushed Mother along a four-lane highway that was on a thirty-degree incline. If he had slipped or stumbled, my mother would have gone flying into four lanes of traffic. Not only could she have been killed, but she might have been injured severely enough to suffer for days, weeks, or months in a hospital. Naturally, I was not surprised when I was asked to move my folks as soon as possible. I was not even given the normal thirty-day notice. Care facilities cannot be subject to that kind of liability.

I: So then what happened?
H: I had to find another place for them to live. However, this time I knew they needed to move into a nursing home. I was finally able to admit they needed more supervision than assisted living facilities could offer. I knew that even if I could get them into another assisted living facility it would only be a matter of time before I would be dealing with similar problems. They needed twenty-four-hour supervision.

Once again, I was very fortunate because I was able to find a nursing home that I could move them both into at the same time. The good news, I thought, was that the nursing home did not allow alcohol. Sadly, although Carl's physician knew he was alcohol dependent, he did not prescribe treatment for alcohol withdrawal. So within a short period of time, Carl became so agitated and combative that he had to be admitted to the psychiatric unit of a local hospital.

He stayed there a couple of weeks and received treatment.

Then he was dismissed and returned to the nursing home. Less than two weeks later, he was sent back to the psychiatric unit, where he stayed for two more weeks. During that time, I was notified that I had to move him to an Alzheimer's facility. His acting-out behavior was attributed to irreversible dementia. The closest we ever came to addressing his alcoholism was when the attending physician said it was okay for Carl to have non-alcoholic beer.

Now, placebos work in many situations, but placebos are not appropriate for alcohol withdrawal. Because I couldn't find local placement, I had to move him to another part of the state. Not only did this mean he and my mother had to be separated, but it also meant I would have to drive several hours round-trip to check on him. Also, placing him in an Alzheimer's unit created yet another problem. He was not allowed to continue using snuff there. Consequently, he had to withdraw from nicotine as well as alcohol.

I: So he wasn't treated for tobacco withdrawal either?
H: No, and I want to cry every time I think about what this man went through. He was asked to withdraw from a seventy-year habit of using smokeless tobacco—snuff. It was horrible. The poor man was not only suffering from physical withdrawal from alcohol, but he had to withdraw from nicotine without patches or any treatment for withdrawal symptoms. You know, it truly is a miracle he lived through it. Some individuals don't.

In my denial, I made many mistakes. There is no doubt about that. I cannot go back and correct those mistakes, but I certainly learned a lot. Now I've become an advocate for elderly people. I truly want others to benefit from my mistakes, in hopes this will not happen to them or to their loved ones. I would never want another elderly person to be asked to give up a lifetime habit of drinking or smoking without being properly treated for withdrawal.

I've included specific *red flags* for individuals who may

have a history of alcohol, nicotine, prescription, or over-the-counter drug dependency in the *Red Flag Checklist,* which is included at the beginning of this section. Hopefully this will help others better access their loved ones level of functioning.

SECTION THREE:
FACING EMOTIONAL CHALLENGES

CAREGIVING CAREGIVING

FEELINGS CHECKLIST

EMOTIONAL ISSUES OF THE CAREGIVER

EMOTIONAL ISSUES OF OTHER FAMILY MEMBERS

EMOTIONAL ISSUES OF THE ELDERLY

CLOSURE—SAYING GOOD-BYE

The following is a list of over one hundred emotions reported as common among caregivers. This list is intended to help you appreciate the breadth and complexity of emotions you may experience while caring for your loved ones. Please take a moment to check every feeling you have felt or are presently feeling regarding caring for elderly loved ones. If you check more negative than positive feelings, you may need to explore your endorsements with a counselor, psychologist, family physician, or clergyman. A noticeable negative slant may indicate you are experiencing depression, anxiety, and/ or grief issues.

FEELINGS CHECKLIST

- ❏ Abused
- ❏ Afraid
- ❏ Agitated
- ❏ Agonized
- ❏ Alienated
- ❏ Alone
- ❏ Angry
- ❏ Annoyed
- ❏ Anxious
- ❏ Apathetic
- ❏ Apologetic
- ❏ Appreciated
- ❏ Appreciative
- ❏ Ashamed
- ❏ Assertive
- ❏ Burdened
- ❏ Centered
- ❏ Comfortable
- ❏ Compassionate
- ❏ Confident
- ❏ Confused

- ❏ Contented
- ❏ Curious
- ❏ Defeated
- ❏ Delighted
- ❏ Demoralized
- ❏ Depressed
- ❏ Determined
- ❏ Devoted
- ❏ Disappointed
- ❏ Discouraged
- ❏ Disgusted
- ❏ Dissatisfied
- ❏ Embarrassed
- ❏ Empowered
- ❏ Energized
- ❏ Enraged
- ❏ Enthusiastic
- ❏ Envious
- ❏ Exasperated
- ❏ Excited
- ❏ Exhausted

- ❏ Fatigued
- ❏ Fearful
- ❏ Flattered
- ❏ Forgiving
- ❏ Forgiven
- ❏ Frustrated
- ❏ Glad
- ❏ Good
- ❏ Grateful
- ❏ Gratified
- ❏ Guilty
- ❏ Happy
- ❏ Helpful
- ❏ Helpless
- ❏ Honored
- ❏ Hopeless
- ❏ Horrified
- ❏ Hostile
- ❏ Humiliated
- ❏ Hurt
- ❏ Hysterical

- ❏ Immobilized
- ❏ Indebted
- ❏ Indifferent
- ❏ Indecisive
- ❏ Intolerant
- ❏ Isolated
- ❏ Jealous
- ❏ Joyful
- ❏ Limited
- ❏ Lonely
- ❏ Loved
- ❏ Loving
- ❏ Lucky
- ❏ Miserable
- ❏ Misunderstood
- ❏ Negative
- ❏ Optimistic
- ❏ Out of control
- ❏ Overjoyed
- ❏ Overwhelmed
- ❏ Paralyzed
- ❏ Paranoid

- ❏ Passionate
- ❏ Peaceful
- ❏ Perplexed
- ❏ Pleased
- ❏ Positive
- ❏ Powerful
- ❏ Powerless
- ❏ Privileged
- ❏ Provoked
- ❏ Reassured
- ❏ Regretful
- ❏ Relieved
- ❏ Remorseful
- ❏ Resentful
- ❏ Respected
- ❏ Rewarded
- ❏ Sad
- ❏ Sarcastic
- ❏ Satisfied
- ❏ Shocked
- ❏ Stressed
- ❏ Strong

- ❏ Stubborn
- ❏ Stupid
- ❏ Successful
- ❏ Supported
- ❏ Surprised
- ❏ Suspicious
- ❏ Sustained
- ❏ Sympathetic
- ❏ Thankful
- ❏ Thrilled
- ❏ Tired
- ❏ Tolerant
- ❏ Unappreciated
- ❏ Understood
- ❏ Unhappy
- ❏ Unprepared
- ❏ Unsuccessful
- ❏ Used
- ❏ Useful
- ❏ Valued
- ❏ Weak

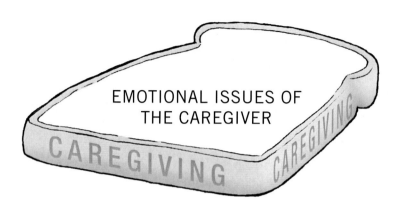

EMOTIONAL ISSUES OF
THE CAREGIVER

To every man (and woman) is given the key to the
gates of heaven. The same key opens the gates of hell.
*(Richard Feynman, Nobel Prize, Physics,
1965, quoting a Buddhist Monk)*

*I: Dr. Haymon, could you talk with us about emotions common to
caregivers?*
H: There are two primal emotions—love and fear. As I see
it, all other emotions stem from one of these two emotional
origins. Love is a positive, uplifting, and energizing emotion.
Most of us know what love is. Love is kind. Love is patient. Love
is tolerant. Love is long-suffering. Some of the emotional fruits
of love are feelings of joy, happiness, peace, and gratitude.

Fear is the opposite of love. Fear is a subtractive and counter-productive emotion that is draining and defeating. Some
of the emotional fruits of fear are anxiety, impatience, frustration, anger, sadness, discouragement, and depression. These
emotions often manifest as physical and emotional pain. One
of the primary problems with fear is that it is negative. Therefore, decisions that are made from fear based emotions never
serve us well. It's the *Law of the Harvest*. We cannot gain
something positive from something negative any more than
we can get corn when we plant potatoes.

Backing up yet another step, emotions and subsequent

behaviors are the products of our thoughts. Cognitive Behavioral Theory lends itself to the notion our emotions have nothing to do with anything outside our own skin. This concept dates back thousands of years in recorded history and was taught in the Old Testament of Christian scriptures. Two examples of this are: "As you think it in your heart so it is" (Proverbs 23:7) and "Know my heart and know my thoughts" (Psalms 139:23).

Our feelings are not secondary to what has happened or what someone did or said but rather what we tell ourselves about what happened or what was done or said. We are not emotional victims of our environment. If we don't like what we are feeling about something or someone, we can change our feelings by simply changing our thoughts, what we tell ourselves, what we believe—all or some of which may or may not be true.

For example, a friend (we'll call her Mary) might say something critical to us. That's what actually happened. We might tell ourselves: "Mary has no right to say something so hurtful. She should not judge and criticize me. I don't deserve to be talked to that way." Our emotional response would probably then be one of hurt and disappointment and perhaps anger. Our behavioral response might be to verbally blame Mary for our feelings by saying, "Mary hurt my feelings and made me really angry. I'm so disappointed in her."

Those thoughts project us into Mary's emotional equation, which is a bit egocentric. Such thoughts also reflect a Stimulus-Response (SR) model and clearly indicate we have given up our personal power—our ability to think before we respond. These thoughts could lead to emotional distancing from Mary. We also might retaliate with unkind words of our own.

Or we could tell ourselves: "Mary must be under a lot of stress. I know she cares about me and would never intentionally say anything unkind. I'm sure she doesn't even realize how critical she sounded. I wonder what I could do to help lighten her load." Those thoughts reflect a Stimulus-Organism-Response (SOR) model that allows us to evaluate what happened and then choose how we will respond.

Such thoughts would also keep us out of Mary's emotional equation and enable us to maintain our personal power, which frees us to act rather than react. Based on these thoughts, our emotional response might be one of compassion, and our behavioral response might be to offer help and words of encouragement. As you can see, what actually happened did not change, but our thoughts did. What a huge difference changing our thoughts can make in the way we feel and the way we behave!

Nothing and no one can *make* us feel. We are all born with the wonderful ability to choose our feelings by choosing what we tell ourselves. Understanding and embracing that concept not only empowers us but also frees us. The idea that others have the omnipotent power to *make* us angry, mad, sad, or happy is irrational thinking. I'm personally glad others do not possess the power to *make* me feel. Just imagine what an insane world it would be if humans could control the emotional responses of others. We would all be mere puppets, waiting for someone to pull our strings in order to get a response. Our feelings and emotional responses would always be at the mercy of everyone and everything in our environment. Thank goodness no one can plant in our emotional garden but us.

Now, if someone held a loaded gun on us, most of us would do pretty much anything that person told us to do. However, the gun holder would never know what we thought or felt unless we chose to share it.

Feelings, whether positive or negative, always influence a person's judgment and subsequently the decisions she or he makes. Decision-making is actually a behavior based on what we've told ourselves about the information we have. Decisions influence outcomes.

Negative feelings negatively influence our judgment and yield negative outcomes. Not only do our emotions influence the decisions we make, but negative emotions may be so overwhelming that we become immobilized and unable to make any decision at all.

Human emotions vary from person to person and are often complex. A common assumption is that no one could possibly understand what we are feeling. This is perhaps due in part to language, which is used to express the nuances of emotions. It may well be that we can never truly understand what another is feeling. However, there are common emotions that accompany the responsibility of caring for elderly loved ones, which might include anger, guilt, grief, helplessness, and general feelings of being overwhelmed. These negative, counter-productive emotions originate from a fear base and are often painful. I have personally felt many of these emotions and learned the consequences of denying some of them.

In addition to the emotions of anger, guilt, grief and feeling overwhelmed, caregivers often experience feelings of sadness, resentment, and of being depressed. These feelings originate from fear. However, one might feel honored and privileged to have the opportunity to serve other human beings when they cannot do for themselves. This perception might be accompanied with feelings of peace, joy, excitement, and a sense of pleasure and personal satisfaction, all which originate from love.

Mixed Feelings

> The way I see it, if you want the rainbow, you gotta
> put up with the rain.
> (Dolly Parton)

It is also common for individuals to have mixed feelings or to bounce from one feeling to another. Caregivers who enter their caregiver role with mixed feelings about their loved ones may experience extreme discomfort created by internal struggles.

I: What do you mean by that?

H: Individuals might be torn between loving their parents yet disliking them at the same time. They might also harbor unresolved childhood feelings of anger and resentment toward their parents. It might be that a loved one was abusive or emotionally unavailable. Some people are torn between wanting their loved one(s) to come to live with them and at the same time knowing this would not be the best decision for their family.

Others might be torn between what they think is best and a different opinion from a spouse or some other family member. Some vacillate between what they would prefer to do and what they think society expects them to do. One might also have made previous promises or commitments to a loved one, but now, due to a change in circumstances, it is no longer possible to fulfill those promises or commitments.

Feelings certainly do not have to be acted on. However, the intensity of our feelings might signal a need to identify and acknowledge them in order to make decisions and solve problems. It might be helpful to remember that feelings are usually identified with just one word.

Feelings Are One Word

> Words can sometimes, in moments of grace, attain
> the quality of deeds.
> *(Elie Wiesel)*

I: What do you mean by one word?

H: If you tell me you feel like running down the hall screaming, I won't have a clue how you feel because you have just described a behavior, not a feeling. I won't know if you are running down the hall screaming because you are angry or afraid, or because you are happy. Here is a technique I use when I am trying to determine exactly what I am feeling. I close my eyes and locate where I'm experiencing the feeling in my body.

Negative emotions are typically felt in specific areas of our bodies and often manifest as stress and tension. Some report feeling negative energy in their necks, lower backs, and/or legs, while others feel stress and tension in their stomachs, chest, and/or head. Sometimes folks say the areas where this negative energy localizes feels tight, and some say that their heart feels hard.

Positive emotions are often first felt in one's heart and face. Some report feeling a warm or burning sensation in their bosoms that spreads throughout their bodies when they feel love, joy, happiness, and other positive emotions. Others say their hearts feel big and full, as though it fills up their entire chest.

After I've located where the feeling has localized in my body, I close my eyes and allow myself to get in touch with the sensation in order to determine whether it's positive or negative energy. With my mind's eye I try to visualize what that area inside my body looks like.

Then, with my eyes still closed, I try to see the color of the feeling. Research suggests certain feelings are associated with specific colors. For example, anger is associated with red, blue with sadness, and green with jealousy and envy. My grandmother knew this intuitively. She'd say, "He's so angry he can see red," or "He must be really mad. Look how red his face is." When someone was sad or depressed, Grandma would say, "She's got the blues. She needs to get outside in the sunshine," or "It's the green-eyed monster of jealousy."

Using Karelian photography, research now shows what Grandma knew intuitively. In one study, individuals who were diagnosed with clinical depression were photographed, and surely enough, there was a blue hue in their auras (the energy field that surrounds all living things). Individuals who scored high on anger scales had a red hue to their auras, just like Grandma saw.   Grandma's belief that getting outside in the sunlight would help depressed folks feel better is also now validated scientifically. Through research, we now know that sunlight triggers the release of serotonin (our natural anti-depressant). Depressed folks who live in areas with little sunlight are encouraged to sit in front of a bright light for a few minutes each day. This has been shown to help relieve symptoms of depression as well as Seasonal Affective Disorder (SADs).

When I've isolated the feeling, determined whether it's positive or negative, and visualized the color, I try to accurately name it. I complete the sentence, "I feel _____." I insert only one word. "I feel *sad*." "I feel *happy*." "I feel *guilty*." "I feel *thankful*." "I feel *depressed*." "I feel *angry*."

Anger

> Anger is a symptom, a way of cloaking and expressing
> feelings too awful to experience directly—hurt,
> bitterness, grief, and most of all, fear.
> *(Joan Rivers, Still Talking)*

I: What would folks be angry about?
H: Some folks report being angry that they have fallen lot to the role of caregiver, angry at the situation, angry that others do not help, angry that there are not other choices, angry that healthcare is so expensive, angry that they don't have more money, or angry that they are left to make decisions that their loved ones could have made for themselves years ago. Others report feeling angry because there are so many decisions to make or angry with their loved ones for their irritating behaviors and lack of gratitude.

Others are angry because it seems that no matter how much they do, it is never enough and never good enough. Sometimes caregivers are angry with their spouse or other family members because they add to their level of stress. Some report getting angry with their superiors and co-workers because they don't seem to understand when they have to be away from their jobs to tend their loved ones. It is not uncommon to be angry with doctors and other professionals. Some people are angry with God.

Sometimes people are angry with themselves because they didn't anticipate and plan for the need to take care of their loved ones. Sometimes people are angry with themselves for being angry. More often we are angry and don't take the time to identify the thoughts we are telling ourselves that result in angry feelings.

Anger is a negative emotion that stems from fear. Therefore, the products of anger will be negative and destructive. Anger often manifests in physical symptoms and blocks creative energy. It can also be destructive to other people as a result of hurtful words and harmful behaviors. Anger could also distance us from people who might be able to help us.

When we look beneath our anger to see what is driving it, we often come face-to-face with our fears. We may fear that we will make wrong decisions, that we will not do something "right," or that others will criticize us. Our anger might be driven by the fear that our loved one(s) will die or fear regarding our own mortality.

When our parents die, our generation is next. That's a very frightening thought for some people. Rather than deal with their fear, many people find it easier to express anger. Our society accepts anger more readily than it accepts fear.

Many of us were taught not to be afraid or at least not to let anyone know we were afraid. When we acknowledge our anger and look at the fear that's feeding it, we will be better able to challenge and replace it with more realistic and positive thoughts that will result in positive feelings. When we clear out negative emotions, positive ones will surface.

What really helped me identify my emotions was for me to talk with a close friend about my feelings, as well as what I was thinking and telling myself. Although I wasn't necessarily looking for advice, it was helpful to have someone to just talk with. There is great therapeutic value in talking about our emotions. I strongly recommend that individuals talk about their feelings with a close friend, relative, counselor, member of the clergy, or perhaps another caregiver, but talk with someone.

I: What are some other ways people might deal with their anger or other negative emotions?
H: Individuals might try whatever they've used in the past that helps them to cope, whether it's cleaning out a closet, exercising, or journaling. For some, it is deep breathing or meditating, going for a walk, chopping wood, gardening, or taking a relaxing bath. For others, praying about their concerns offers a sense of peace and calmness.

Feeling Helpless

Some people strengthen the society just by being the
kind of people they are.
(John W. Gardner)

I: Dr. Haymon, you mentioned helplessness as one of the feelings commonly experienced by caregivers. Help us understand how the caregiver is the one feeling helpless.
H: Helplessness is another feeling that stems from fear, yet many individuals report feeling helpless while taking care of an elderly loved one. It may be they fear not being able to help their loved one or being ineffective as a caregiver. Other feel-

ings that stem from fear, but common to caregivers, include feelings of incompetence, powerlessness, and feeling overwhelmed and out of control. These feelings can be demoralizing. Negative feelings are often exaggerated when we are tired, have multiple life stressors, and/or are in the midst of a pile of bureaucratic forms related to Medicare and other health related agencies.

Other aspects of our lives continue even though we might have inherited responsibility for our elderly loved ones. Feelings of helplessness and powerlessness are also intensified when we're unable to find doctors or other professionals who understand our problems. Often, feelings of being overwhelmed result from attempting to handle too many things at the same time.

Feeling Overwhelmed—Relaxation Exercise

> Every problem contains within itself the seeds of its
> own solution.
> *(Edward Somers in National Enquirer)*

I: How can we deal with feeling overwhelmed?
H: Here's a relaxation exercise you might try when you're feeling overwhelmed. Take three deep breaths—one for your body, one for your mind, and one for your spirit. Try to bring all three parts of you together as you do this exercise. If you're where you can, close your eyes, but if not, do the breathing exercise anyway. Inhale slowly through your nose until your lungs are filled with oxygen. Then slowly exhale through your mouth, blowing out as much carbon dioxide as you possibly can, relaxing into the exhale. Pause in between breaths, drop your shoulders down, and find your place of centeredness, which is normally around your navel. Repeat this for at least three deep breaths, more if possible. This exercise takes less than two minutes but offers

amazing benefits. The calming effect of oxygen is more powerful than Valium or other anti-anxiety medications. Plus, oxygen improves our alertness, as well as our memories.

Next, make two lists. On the first list, write down the three most important tasks you feel you need to accomplish. Put them in order of importance, but only put three on this first list. On the second list, write down the smaller things you need to do that might be handled relatively easily or within a short period of time. Next, decide to whom you could delegate the tasks from either or both lists. Then do exactly that. Delegate everything you possibly can.

A typical day for any caregiver might include taking one or both parents to one or more doctors, completing medical and insurance forms, doing their laundry, shopping for their groceries, preparing their meals, helping them with their baths, going to the pharmacy, cleaning their house, feeding their pets, or making minor home repairs. Of course, this would be in addition to an already full schedule of things in her/his personal life, which might include a fifty to sixty hour work week, as well as other family, community, and church responsibilities.

Caregivers might be surprised to learn a friend or relative would be glad to pick up grocery items while doing their own shopping. Perhaps a neighbor wouldn't mind feeding the pets. This might save you an unnecessary trip to their house. Perhaps there's a transportation service that could safely transport your loved ones to their appointments, and you could meet them there if necessary. Many of us are not accustomed to asking other people to help, when in fact there are many people who would be more than willing to lend a hand. Caregivers need to remember to take care of themselves. The journey of caring for elderly loved ones could go on for a decade or more. This task might be nearly impossible to complete should you burn yourself out. Consider the example of being on a plane and the flight attendant giving instructions that should cabin pressure drop you need to put your own oxygen mask on first and then help children or others. The realization is that you are of no use to others unless you take care of yourself.

I: How about those of us who can't delegate, who say, "Nobody can do it as well as I can?"

H: It may very well be true that you could handle all the tasks associated with your caregiving role better than anyone else could. However, as long as things get taken care of, consider them done. This will allow you to narrow your focus and therefore channel your energy. We might think about this in terms of a floodlight. Floodlights illuminate a large area, but the light gets dimmer the further away from the bulb it gets. Next, let's think about narrowing the focus of that same amount of light and channeling that energy into a laser beam. Consider how much more powerful and far reaching the light is when it is narrowly focused. It is the same way with our own energy. When we focus and channel our energy in one direction, we are a lot more powerful than when we spread ourselves so thin.

I: That certainly makes sense. But what if you can't find anyone to delegate to?

H: If you don't have anyone to delegate to or if anything is left on either list after you've delegated everything you can, then decide which ones you will do and in what order you will do them. Prioritize both lists. Should you find yourself getting anxious because something has not been done, stop and ask yourself two questions. Remember, there are two lists, and here are two questions: "What is the worst thing that could happen if I don't get this done today?" "What is the worst thing that could happen if I never get it done?" You might be relieved to learn that perhaps nothing awful will happen either way.

The truth is most things are only important because we have assigned importance to them. In my opinion, few things are important enough to be allowed to rob us of our peace and sense of well-being. We cannot yet live tomorrow nor can we change the past. Remind yourself that you are only one person, and you will do what you can. Then let go of any regrets you have about yesterday or worries you might have about tomorrow.

Regret and worry are negative, subtractive emotions. Negative, subtractive behaviors resulting from these emotions might include immobilization, procrastination, or unproductive random acts. These emotions and behaviors stem from fear and rob us of our peace, energy, and a sense of well-being. When you are feeling regretful and are spending time and energy worrying, listen to your thoughts. Hear what you are telling yourself, and uncover your fears. Challenge and dismiss all negative thoughts, and replace those with more positive, validating thoughts and beliefs. Then pause for reflection and applaud yourself for all that you have already tolerated and taken care of.

Guilt

> The most important story we will ever write in life is
> our own—not with ink, but with our daily choices.
> *(Richard Paul Evans, The Gift)*

I: What about guilt? That seems to be a very common emotion.
H: Unfortunately, you are right. It is quite common for caregivers to feel guilty. Guilt is yet another emotion that stems from fear and thus creates conflict for many individuals. Some caregivers feel guilty for past behaviors toward their loved ones. Some feel guilty about their negative thoughts and for feeling angry and resentful. Others feel guilty about allowing the elderly person to come live with them and interrupting the lives of other family members.

Still others feel guilty about placing their loved ones in a care facility rather than allowing them to move in with them. Others feel guilty because they have to work and can't stay home to take care of their loved ones. As I mentioned earlier, many caregivers feel guilty for spending time with their family and friends instead of spending time with their loved ones because "they might not have much time left." Then they feel guilty for spending time with their elderly loved one(s) and taking time away from their spouse and children.

Other guilt trips include feeling guilty for making promises that can no longer be kept or for resenting the caregiving role. Members of scattered families often feel guilty because they are not close enough to visit their loved ones more often and to help care for them.

Some people report feeling guilty about their loved one's illnesses, even though they know it's not their fault and that there is nothing they can do about it. I felt guilty because I thought I was taking away my parents independence, especially when I had to ask my stepfather for his truck keys. What I didn't understand was that my parents' independence was already lost to poor health and dementia, which had nothing to do with me.

I also felt something similar to survivor guilt. I felt guilty that my folks could no longer live alone and I could, guilty that they could no longer drive and I could, guilty that I could continue with my own life and they couldn't, and guilty that I was healthy and they weren't. Sometimes, just as with anger, we feel tremendous guilt, yet we don't take the time to understand why—to uncover the irrational self-talk that leads to guilt.

Should vs. Could

> When one tugs at a single thing in nature, he finds it
> attached to the rest of the world.
> *(John Muir)*

It is also interesting to note that there is often a *should* command that undergirds guilt. *Shoulds* are moral imperatives imposed by culture. If we don't abide by our cultures' *shoulds,* we are somehow immoral by cultural standards. *Should* implies there is a *perfect* way. Consequently, if we don't adhere to this perfect way, we violate this unspoken moral code. The resulting emotion is guilt. People often feel guilty because they are not perfect and their loved ones are not perfect. When we realize there is no such thing as perfect, we may then realize there is no reason to feel guilty. In reality, there is no perfect way to do or to have done anything. As a matter of fact, there are an infinite number of ways to do most things, perhaps as many ways as there are people doing them.

When you feel guilty, identify the *should* statement. When you find yourself thinking or saying, "I should have," or "They should have," replace the "should have" with "could have." By changing the "should" to "could," we are able to transform self-punishment for not having lived up to some cultural imperative or our own internal standard into an opportunity to engage in sound problem-solving and decision-making. Think of the many ways you *could* have handled whatever situation you're feeling guilty over.

I: This has been helpful because I am constantly saying to myself, "I really should have Mother come and live with us," and I leave it at that. Then I feel terribly guilty that I don't. If I say, "She could come and live with us," what's the difference? Walk me through that. How would that help me get out of the guilt mode?
H: When you think you *should* have your mother come to live with you, the *should* part of this thought process implies that is the *perfect* solution. Visualize your mother living with you, and replace the "should" with "could." For example, you might say to yourself, "I *could* have my mother come to live with us, and if I did, what would I need to take into consideration? Would moving her in with us be the best decision for all involved?"

Then go through a decision-making process. Remember, when we change "should" to "could," it changes internal self-punishment into opportunities for problem solving and decision-making. You might say to yourself, "I could have my mother come to live with us. Now let me look around. Would our house be safe for her? Would there be someone home with her to take care of her?" Using the word "could" might allow you to go through a decision-making process that allows for other possibilities, options that probably would not be considered as long as you've limited your choices to what you thought you *should* do.

I: That's great, because I would then ask myself, "Would she have someone to play bridge with? Would she miss her friends? Would she trip on our stairs?" You have really helped me here. I am suddenly giving up some guilt about where she lives and what I think I "should" do.

The Past—A Pillar of Salt

> The future is the past returning through another gate.
> *(Arnold H. Glasow)*

I: Dr. Haymon, what about the old saying, "Hindsight is 20/20?" I think, when most of us look back at situations, we see things much more clearly.

H: Of course I've heard that old saying, but that too implies accuracy. I'm not sure when I look back on events that I see them with any greater accuracy than I did when they occurred. I only know I see them differently, which may or may not be more accurate.

Unfortunately, when we feel guilty, we spend precious time and energy looking at the past. We may be looking for ways to correct the past and make it perfect instead of letting it go and moving on. When we spend time looking backwards, we are immobilized to move forward. This is another concept taught thousands of years ago.

In the Christian scriptures of the Old Testament in Genesis 19:26, we are given the metaphor of Lot's wife turning to a pillar of salt when she looked back. This image clearly demonstrates the inability to move forward while one is looking to the past.

There is no way to relive our childhoods or undo anything that occurred in the past. Maybe we never liked our parents. Some people even hated their parents, especially parents who were abusive. There is only one way to eliminate negative, subtractive, and self-destructive feelings, and that is through forgiveness. Any other way will merely suppress the negative energy, which will manifest as physical, emotional, mental, and spiritual illnesses.

Forgiveness

> The more a man knows, the more he forgives.
> *(Catherine The Great)*

Forgiveness is more for our benefit than it is for the person(s) we're forgiving. Forgiveness doesn't mean we let her/him "off the hook" and pretend the injustice never happened. Forgiveness simply means we give up our need to judge the other person.

In reality, it is impossible to "forgive and forget" unless you develop amnesia or dementia. We may always remember wrongs that have not been made right.

However, once we forgive the person(s) responsible for the offenses, we remember hurtful events differently. Forgiveness neutralizes injustices and allows us to remember those offenses without the zing and sting previously associated with them. Forgiveness filters out hurt and pain. Forgiveness allows us to make choices based on who we are rather than on whether persons are judged worthy of our care and concern. I learned this lesson when it became my turn to take care of my mother, who had been alcoholic and abusive at times. As I said earlier,

I took care of her and my stepfather not because of who they were but because of who I was and am. Taking care of elderly loved ones is not a time to "get even" or try to "settle the score." Decisions and plans need to be based on what seems best for all concerned.

Perhaps you are the one guilty of inflicting an injustice. If there is something you need to apologize and ask forgiveness for, then do so. If they are coherent enough to understand, that's great, but even if they're not, apologize anyway. Apologizing, just as forgiving, is more for our benefit than it is for the one we've offended.

If there are unresolved issues that need to be discussed and your elderly loved ones are still mentally competent, then by all means talk with them. Lovingly clear your conscious, and lift the burdens from your heart. You and they have much to gain from this.

However, don't expect others to have the same need to clear the air that you do. Often, things we hold vividly in our own minds have long since been forgotten by others. To expect others to remember events in the same light that you do is to set yourself up for possible hurt and disappointment. It could also be a relief that they don't.

Grief and the Grieving Process

> Between grief and nothing I will take grief.
> (*William Faulkner, Nobel Prize, Literature, 1949*)

I: You say grief is another common feeling. Are you talking about when our loved ones die?
H: Yes. The loss of a loved one to death is considered one of the most stressful events in a person's life. Dr. Elizabeth Kubler-Ross, noted for her research on death and grief, identified five stages of grief as denial, anger, bargaining, depression,

and acceptance. These stages also seem to apply to losses other than death.

Individuals grieve differently from one another. Some may follow these grief stages in this order. Others may bounce from one stage to another. Some get stuck in one stage, and it may take years before they're able to move on, if ever.

I personally think there is also a stage of "mourning" that Dr. Kubler-Ross did not include. The mourning stage is perhaps the most personal. During this stage, individuals engage in very personal behaviors intended to comfort themselves. This might include religious traditions that honor the deceased or wearing black or other symbols as an outward expression of their mourning. Some individuals mourn alone, while others find comfort in having friends and relatives surrounding them.

A person's reaction to death is influenced by the nature of her/his relationship to the deceased, as well as personal beliefs about what happens after death. Reactions are also impacted by the circumstances of the death and the age of the deceased. Sudden, unexpected, accidental death illicits profound responses, especially when the victim is a young person. The death of a child can be overwhelming. It is difficult for most folks to make sense out of the insensible. Yet I believe deaths due to suicide are absolutely the most devastating for those left behind. Survivors of suicide victims are often left with tremendous burdens of shame, guilt, and anger.

The death of a spouse is particularly traumatic for most people. Elderly folks who have been together for many years may be especially vulnerable as they try to come to terms with losing their lifetime partner and friend. Their sense of loss and grieving is often compounded as they lose longtime friends to death. In addition to the severe emotional trauma, there may also be significant strain due to secondary financial loss. The death of a spouse who has been the primary source of income may necessitate changes in one's lifestyle, requiring the surviving spouse to seek additional employment or other sources of income. When the spouse has been the primary caregiver, the surviving spouse may no longer be able to remain in her/his own home.

Grieving may occur at many levels. On an emotional level, individuals may express their sadness by crying or wailing, or cursing and becoming angry. Others may attempt to separate themselves from their pain by denying and perhaps keeping themselves too busy to feel emotions. That may seem helpful at first, but at some point (and the sooner the better), they need to allow themselves to feel the strong emotions associated with death and resolve these before they manifest as physical and/or emotional symptoms.

On a physical level, individuals may experience a loss of appetite, sleep disturbance, and/or intestinal problems secondary to acute grief. Others may become physically ill, present illnesses may worsen, or new medical problems may develop. On a psychological level, individuals may develop anxiety or panic attacks or experience chronic fatigue. Some may become withdrawn and depressed and wish they too could die. Profound reactions may include thoughts of suicide.

Even when death is expected, many people report feeling an initial shock that leaves them numb when they first learn that death has occurred. In addition to shock, other normal and common emotions associated with death are disbelief, anger, confusion, sadness, humiliation, despair, helplessness, and guilt. The intensity and duration of these and other feelings varies from person to person. Many individuals report being surprised at how quickly they switch from one feeling to another and thus feel out-of-control. Only time enables persons to absorb the impact of the loss of loved ones to death. Although we may never stop missing them and yearning to be with them again, time eases the pain to a tolerable level.

Individuals grieve many losses associated with death. This type of grieving is often referred to as *bereavement*. This term literally means, "to be deprived by death." Sometimes we not only grieve the loss of the person we referred to as our parent or spouse but also the loss of our relationship with her/him as our friend and confidante. Many folks are fortunate to have loving relationships with their parents and thus grieve their loss on many levels. One's entire lifestyle may change as a result of the death of a loved one.

There are many ways to cope with death. Allowing oneself to grieve is most important. Talking with others about how you feel might help to validate your loss. If you do not have friends or other family members whom you feel free to talk with, then seek out a support group. Be patient with yourself. Sometimes the grieving process takes months or years. Do not dwell on the past or obsess about the deceased. Life is for the living. Take care of your health. Eat healthy foods, and get plenty of rest and exercise. Stay away from alcohol and other drugs as a means of coping. Postpone making any major life decisions, like remarrying or moving, for at least one to two years following the death of a significant loved one. If your grief and sense of loss seem more than you can handle, seek professional guidance through the grieving process. There may be old, unresolved issues that are blocking your progress, keeping you from moving on. Listen to others if they suggest you might want to talk with a psychologist, therapist, grief counselor, or your pastor, priest, or other religious leader.

There are ways we might help others during their time of loss while they move through the grieving process. It is most important we not offer the grieving person false comfort. It does not help to offer shallow comments like "He's better off," "She's in a better place," or "I know how you feel." Perhaps the best we can do is be there for them, listen with an open heart, and offer our empathic presence. We might also offer to do chores that will relieve them of practical burdens. Perhaps we could make phone calls or run errands. We might also offer to sit with an elderly relative or with young children while they take care of other tasks or have a few minutes alone. Give them psychological permission to seek professional help.

Death can be difficult for children, especially when it is a parent who dies. Children may become confused by well-meaning adults who try to protect them. It is best to take time to talk with children at a level they can understand and be honest with them. Since children look to adults as models, it is extremely important that adults are approachable and willing to talk about death. Allow children to ask questions and express their feelings. It is common for children to revert to behaviors that are not age appropriate, such as bed-wetting, thumb sucking, or refusing to be left alone. Offer them security and reassurance, and do not make a big deal about behaviors that are not age appropriate. Drawing attention to such behaviors will only increase the child's anxiety and delay her/his recovery. However, if these behaviors persist more than a few days, or there are other signs the child is not moving through the grieving process, she/he may need to be evaluated by a professional.

It is often difficult for parents to grieve appropriately while they are trying to help a child or children move through the grieving process. Consequently, the adult's bereavement may be delayed.

A lot of people believe the only time we feel grief is when someone passes away. However, as our loved ones age, their health declines, and they lose their faculties, there are many losses to grieve. Sometimes we grieve for the way our loved one(s) used to be and for the qualities that identified their uniqueness. You may grieve the lost opportunity to have the parent(s) you always wanted but never had and now realize you never will have. Sometimes, our grief is over what might have been rather than what really was, because what really was wasn't that great. Whatever our sense of loss, grief is a natural response to loss, and it is normal to grieve losses.

I: Isn't it harder for us to identify grief? It usually seems clear when we are angry. Now I can listen for the "should" statements when I feel guilty, but I'm not sure I know when I am actually grieving.

H: Yes. Grief manifests in many ways. You might find that little things make you sad, or you feel like crying for no apparent reason. Those feelings of sadness are often intensified by fatigue, and sometimes that leads to depression.

Grief is a very complex emotion. When it follows death, it may be overwhelming in the beginning then decrease over time. However, grief associated with irreversible conditions, such as Alzheimer's disease or other dementias, Parkinson's disease, terminal cancer, or kidney failure, seems to go on and on. It shifts back and forth among hopefulness, helplessness, anger, sadness, and loneliness. It bounces back and forth. Just when the condition stabilizes and you think you have adjusted and are coping, the person's condition may change, and you go through the grieving process all over again.

For example, when I had to place my parents in an assisted living facility, I had a long list of losses I was grieving. Slowly, I adapted to our new roles. Just when I thought I had adjusted and was coping, they got worse, and I had to go through the grieving process all over again as I grieved additional losses.

Grief that follows death seems to be understood and accepted by society, yet grief associated with chronic illness is often not understood by people who are not emotionally attached to the ill person. Many caregivers report that feelings of sadness and helplessness worsen as they watch their loved ones suffer while the illness progresses. It is not uncommon for caregivers to think their loved ones might actually be better off if they died so they wouldn't have to suffer anymore.

Nevertheless, in spite of the frustration, anger, and sadness, this final, often difficult, stage potentially offers both the caregiver and the elderly an opportunity for growth at a level not found elsewhere. Often our greatest truths are found in our greatest trials.

Long-term Caregiving—a Marathon

Only a life lived for others is a life worthwhile.
(Albert Einstein, Nobel Prize, Physics, 1921*)*

Caring for aging loved ones could last for years or decades. Therefore, it is important for individuals to give themselves psychological permission to have a meaningful life in addition to their caregiving role. Although caring for an ill or elderly loved one becomes part of your life, and certainly needs to be given appropriate attention, it does not need to consume your entire life.

Taking care of elderly loved ones is similar to running a marathon, which I have also done. Marathon runners have to pace themselves, or they will never make it to the finish line. I cannot tell you how many women I've talked to, all of whom have spent over ten years taking care of one or both parents, who literally burned themselves out in the process. One was hospitalized for exhaustion. Another had spent so much time and energy on caring for her parents that her husband left her. When it was over and she looked around, she was totally alone. Yet another was grieving the fact she had missed so much of her own children's lives because she had been so focused on her mother. The point is that when you put on the caregiver hat, you may be wearing it for a long time. You still have other hats, so be sure to wear those too.

I: What are some things we can do to prevent our caregiving role from consuming our lives?
H: It is vitally important that caregivers schedule downtime for themselves. Most of us already had more on our plates than we could say grace over before we inherited the responsibility of caregiving. Accept the fact that certain responsibilities you used to handle will, perhaps, now have to go unattended unless you delegate those to someone else or hire them done.

By all means, don't try to handle everything you were taking care of prior to becoming a caregiver *and* squeeze in the added responsibilities of caregiving. To do so might be at the risk of losing your own health and sense of well-being.

When you are feeling frustrated because you can no longer keep your house as clean as you once did or think you *should*, or your yard no longer gets "Yard of the Month," and you are feeling guilty that your family is once again eating fast food, stop and ask yourself, "What's important here?" It very well may be that your family would rather have a rested, happy person than a home-cooked meal or the "Yard of the Month" sign on the front lawn. Long-term caregiving requires enormous amounts of physical and emotional energy. Since the human body, mind, and spirit are so interconnected, individuals need to ensure that they take care of themselves on all levels.

Depression

> If you keep saying things are going to be bad, you
> have a good chance of being a prophet.
> *(Isaac Bashevis Singer, Nobel Prize, Literature, 1978)*

I: I'll bet a lot of people become depressed while caring for elderly loved ones.

H: Depression is commonly associated with long-term caregiving. In fact, caregivers are three times more likely to report symptoms of depression and four times more likely to report anger than the elderly person(s) they take care of.

I: Is depression different from being sad?

H: Depression goes beyond appropriate feelings of sadness. When people become depressed, they often feel discouraged, hopeless, and helpless. Many depressed individuals report feelings of despair, and in severe cases, depressed individuals report feeling worthless and suicidal.

Depression often comes on the heels of guilt, secondary

to not being able to keep up with their many *shoulds*. I have also had clients who reported feeling so hopeless, helpless, and such a sense of failure in their role of caregiver that they had thoughts not only of taking their own lives but also taking the life of the person they cared for. They didn't want to leave their loved one with no one to take care of her/him after they took their own life. Tragically enough, there have been a number of suicide-homicides in recent years, where caregivers shot and killed their loved one(s) then turned the gun on themselves. I caution caregivers to be aware of the emotional and physical symptoms of depression.

I: What are some of those symptoms?
H: It is common for people who are depressed to feel tired all or much of the time. Many experience extreme fatigue, beyond normal tiredness, secondary to lack of sleep and rest. Depressed individuals often report feeling restless, anxious, or nervous much of the time. They may spend unusual amounts of time worrying and obsessing.

Depressed individuals often behave in ways that are abnormal for them. They may have temper outbursts over minor incidents or be given to mood swings from euphoria to melancholy. They may become overly sensitive not only to verbal interactions with other people but overly sensitive to light, noise, and temperature. Depressed persons may have difficulty concentrating or staying focused. They often experience forgetfulness, including loss of short-term memory. Sometimes people who are depressed say they fear they are losing their minds. In addition to any or all of these symptoms, depressed individuals may overeat or have no appetite at all. They may oversleep or have bouts of insomnia.

What's more, people who are depressed often begin to experience illnesses. Even people who have almost never been sick in the past develop physical symptoms, such as headaches, allergies, backaches, gastrointestinal problems, shortness of breath, chest pain, dizziness, ulcers, stomachaches, frequent colds, and nervous tics, just to name a few. It is also common for people who are depressed to lose their desire for sex and intimacy.

Symptoms of depression are often manifestations of self-punishment, which is typically tied into moral imperatives defined by *shoulds*. When individuals are unable to fulfill internal or cultural *shoulds*, they sometimes convince themselves they need excuses for not being able to live up to these moral dictates. Physical and emotional symptoms, as well as full-blown illnesses, provide acceptable excuses.

I: So what should—I'm sorry—could we do if we think we're depressed?

H: Because depression is so painful, many individuals attempt to self-medicate. In attempts to reduce the anguish of depression, it is common for depressed people to drink more coffee or other caffeinated beverages than they normally drink, start smoking again after having quit perhaps years earlier, or increase the number of cigarettes they smoke each day.

It is also common for depressed individuals to attempt to self-medicate by using alcohol, sleeping pills, tranquilizers, or other drugs that increase fatigue by depleting what precious little energy they have left. Many of these substances are themselves depressants. Consequently, they contribute to the depression and actually make it worse.

Sometimes, hidden problems, such as anemia, high or low blood pressure, or chronic, low-grade infections, can contribute to their level of fatigue and rob them of much-needed energy. I encourage people to see their medical doctors and schedule regular checkups. I also encourage people to see a counselor if they think they're depressed. Although counseling cannot remove the reasons individuals are depressed, talk therapy might help to sort their problems to a manageable level. Doing so might allow them to handle their problems one at a time rather than remaining overwhelmed. Professional counselors may also help individuals identify and challenge their irrational, counter-productive thoughts, as well as replace them with more rational and productive ways of thinking. Sometimes reframing a problem enables individuals to take the blinders off and view their situation from a broader perspective. Reframing might also allow folks to view their situation as an *opportunity* rather than a *burden*. Depressed individuals tend to obsess about their situation. Therapists might teach them how to use "thought stoppage" to interrupt their obsessions. This could free up creative energy, which might allow them to consider various options.

Whether you seek professional help or talk with a friend, relative, or maybe a member of the clergy, it is helpful to talk with someone about your situation. These individuals might not be able to do anything except to listen to you, but that may be all that is needed. In fact, you might tell them up front that you do not expect them to have answers or to solve your problems and that you only need to vent. However, sometimes we can't see the forest for the trees, so sharing our problems with others may give us a chance to see our problems from a whole different perspective. Sometimes others may offer alternatives we had not considered.

Caregiver Support Groups

> In the West there is loneliness, which I call the leprosy of the West. In many ways it is worse than our poor in Calcutta.
> *(Mother Teresa, Nobel Prize, Peace, 1979)*

Caregiver support groups are especially helpful in offering a plethora of options, possibilities, and alternatives. It may be that you are not the type to talk in groups, particularly not to strangers. Many of us do not want to, as my grandmother used to say, "air our dirty laundry in front of strangers." That's okay; join a group anyway. Some find it comforting just to be with others who can relate to what they're going through. Even if you don't want to talk, it may be helpful to listen. If there's not a local group or you can't leave your loved one long enough to attend, you might go online and participate in an online group. There are many online caregiver support groups.

Oftentimes, other people in the group may have already gone through a very similar situation to yours and are happy to share what has worked and what has not worked for them. These suggestions may save you enormous amounts of time, energy, and money. So while you may think you are not the type to join a group or that you can't afford the time to attend a group, it may very well be that you cannot afford not to.

There is tremendous benefit from just talking about one's situation. Talking truly seems to be the oil that soothes the soul. Right now, call up that special friend and set a date to get together and just talk. Make it a weekly date, and no matter what comes up, keep that date every week. If possible, maybe you could get in some exercise by walking while you are talking and visiting.

My friend Darby and I scheduled dinner together every Monday night. She allowed me to vent about my situation with Mother and Carl for half the evening, then I listened to her frustrations for the second half. Even caregivers need a caregiver!

When the need to provide care continues for years and there is not enough of you to go around, stop and think of ways you have been neglecting yourself. One of the first things to go, besides sleep, is proper nutrition. It is vital that individuals eat well-balanced meals regularly. There are lots of other things you can do to take care of yourself.

Quiet Time—A Personal Story

> We do not remember days; we remember moments.
> (*Cesare Pavese, The Burning Brand*)

If you are unable to have quiet time at home, then go to a

movie, even if you have to take children or parents with you. Chances are they will be preoccupied for that couple of hours, and you can either escape into the movie, sleep, or just sit there and rest. Allow me to share another true story.

About two years after I inherited the responsibility of care-giving for my mother and stepfather, I decided to take them to a movie. I also wanted to spend some time with my little five-year-old friend, Chelsea, who lived next door to me. So I took them all to see *The Lion King*. I planned an additional half hour of travel time because my parents walked very slowly, and it took extra time to get them in and out of the car. I was very glad I had allotted time for that. I was so proud of all of us. We made it into the movie on time without a single incident. About halfway through the movie, Carl fell asleep and started snoring loudly. Chelsea started giggling, so I gently shook Carl to wake him up and to stop the noise that was now disturbing other people. He awoke and let out a loud yawn that seemed to go on for a full minute. I was terribly embarrassed. Then to my relief, the people sitting around us also started laughing. Their laughter prompted my laughter and my little friend was still giggling, so we missed two or three minutes of *The Lion King*. Carl, who remained blissfully unaware of what had happened, just sat there and began to watch the movie.

Exercise and Rest

> I think God's going to come down and pull
> civilization over for speeding.
> *(Steven Wright)*

I: Well, it's comforting to know things like that even happen to the experts. Dr. Haymon, I hear so much about the importance of exercise.

H: Exercise is vitally important. When we think we don't have enough time to exercise, that's the very time we need it the most. Many caregivers say they feel guilty when they take time to exercise and think they "should" be doing other things. I remind folks of one clear and simple fact: exercise increases your energy level. Consequently, you will be able to perform other tasks more efficiently and will actually save time in the long run.

It is also extremely important for caregivers to get plenty of rest. Enlist relatives or friends to give you a respite, hire a professional sitter, or take your loved one(s) to a care facility for a few days several times a year to give you time away from your caregiving responsibilities. Remember, you will not be able to care for anyone else if you don't take care of yourself. It is not uncommon for long-term caregivers to develop diabetes (even when there is no family history of diabetes) and/or die before the person they are caring for does. In addition to not getting sufficient rest, caregivers often fail to get their annual physicals and/or neglect to take their own prescribed medications. Self-neglect is another symptom of depression.

Summary of Emotional Issues of the Caregiver

> Happiness is a conscious choice, not an automatic response.
> *(Mildred Barthel in Ensign)*

Caring for elderly loved ones is often like being on an emotional roller coaster. The downside of that roller coaster might include frustration, anger, guilt, resentment, sadness, and depression, as well as feelings of helplessness and of being overwhelmed.

The upside might include feelings of honor, privilege, acceptance, joy, and peace. It is important to identify our feelings in a single word, as well as the thoughts behind them. Counter-productive and subtractive feelings are fear driven.

Feelings do not have to be acted on. The process of caregiving could go on for ten or twenty years, so caregivers need to take care of themselves. Schedule downtime, eat properly, exercise, get plenty of rest, have regular physical checkups, and talk about your feelings. Find sources of help and assistance for your loved ones and for you.

The end stage of life can be an emotional time for you, for other family members, and for your elderly loved ones. Tensions and resistance can often be held to a minimum when individuals are patient with themselves, with those they're taking care of, and with other family members. Let go of past hurts and focus on the moment.

Perhaps you have been chosen to care for this other human being for a reason. It would be counterproductive to exchange your time, energy, and emotions for anything less than a wonderful opportunity to grow and learn and to connect not only with the other person but also with yourself at a level of intimacy possible only through the unselfish deeds of serving others.

EMOTIONAL ISSUES OF
OTHER FAMILY MEMBERS

CAREGIVING   CAREGIVING

For the Husbands, Wives, and Children of Caregivers

> What lies behind us and what lies before us are tiny
> matters compared to what lies within us.
> *(Ralph Waldo Emerson)*

I: Dr. Haymon, thank you so much for helping us understand more about the caregiver's feelings as they go through the process of taking care of elderly loved ones. I am curious to know how this could affect the caregiver's husband or wife.

H: It's not uncommon for the spouse of the caregiver to report confusion as to what his or her role actually is in the caregiving process. Perhaps one of the reasons for this confusion is that there are perhaps as many different roles as there are caregiving situations. I'll give you some examples at both ends of this spectrum and one in the middle, with an understanding that there are an infinite number of combinations in between.

The Case of Betty and John

> When I cease to be indignant, I will have begun
> my old age.
> *(Andre Gide, Nobel Prize, Literature, 1947)*

The first story was told to me by a friend of mine. I will call him John, but of course, that is not his real name. John said his wife, whom I will call Betty, moved her father into their home. Although Betty's father was alcoholic and had been abusive to Betty, her mother, her brother, and her sisters while they were growing up, Betty felt it was her duty to take care of him during his last years. Betty's father had emphysema. He was also on dialysis, which required special meals and trips to a dialysis clinic three times a week.

John said he didn't mind Betty's father moving in with them. Their house was certainly large enough to accommodate another person. Plus, Betty was not employed, so there would be no problem with her taking her father to dialysis. He said what he did mind was Betty's attitude during the process of taking care of her father.

John said Betty grew angrier by the day, and she vented her anger toward him and their two daughters. Betty was not only angry with her father but also angry with her mother for divorcing him and felt her mother should be the one taking care of him.

She was also angry that neither her three sisters nor her brother were willing to assume even partial responsibility for their father. Her siblings attributed his poor health to his own choices in life, which included smoking heavily and drinking excessively. They did not agree with her decision to move their father in with her but felt she ought to do whatever she thought she needed to. They just didn't want any part of it.

Betty could not control her siblings, and it enraged her that she could not make them accept part of her perceived burden of their father. She complained to her husband and daughters every day and became more and more unpleasant to be around. She started showing signs of depression and became hypercritical of John, their daughters, and practically everything and everyone around her.

SANDRA W. HAYMON, Ph.D.

John said he and their daughters did everything they could to relieve Betty of her burden. He would take her father to the dialysis clinic, and their oldest daughter would bring him home as she returned from school. Soon he and their daughters were doing all the house cleaning and washing dishes after every meal. Plus, they assumed the responsibility for all the laundry in addition to the yard work and keeping their cars clean, which he was already doing. This left Betty free to cook and prepare her father's special meals, dispense his medicines to him, and take him to his medical appointments.

But no matter how much John and their daughters did, it was never enough and never good enough for Betty. She rarely gave them credit for helping at all. She continued to complain about how bad she had it and how unfair it was that she had all this responsibility.

Then an interesting thing happened. One sister changed her mind and invited their father to live with her and her family for a while. During that time she prepared his meals, dispensed his medicines, and took him to dialysis, in addition to taking care of her own household chores, which included cooking and cleaning up after a husband and two young children. She wasn't as interested in taking care of their father as she was in giving Betty a break. She took care of him for several months before returning him to Betty.

In addition, when their father was hospitalized, which he frequently was, while he was living with Betty, another sister either personally took her turn sitting with their father or hired an off-duty nurse to sit in her place. On more than one occasion, the sister who lived out of town would fly home and spend a week or so staying with their father while he was in the hospital.

No matter how many people helped Betty take care of her father nor how much any of them did, Betty continued to cling to her anger and play the role of victim, criticizing everything and everybody around her. It's now been over twenty years since Betty's father died, yet Betty continues to describe the experience of caring for her father as one she endured totally alone, without any help from John, their daughters, her sisters, or anyone else. Betty is still angry, and she still holds much resentment toward her family.

John told me that the process of caring for Betty's father could have been very different, and perhaps could have even been a pleasant experience, were it not for Betty's attitude. John was quick to say that after Betty's father stopped drinking, he was actually a pleasant man to be around. John described him as being intelligent and well read and said he contributed much to their conversations. John was sad the experience had been so negative for Betty, yet he realized that it was only negative because Betty chose for it to be. It wasn't inherently so.

The Case of Pat and Karen

> I used to think getting old was about vanity—but actually it's about losing people you love. Getting wrinkles is trivial.
> *(Eugene O'Neill, Nobel Prize, Literature, 1936)*

This story is probably somewhere in the middle of the spectrum. I will refer to these people as Pat and Karen.

At the point when Pat's mother could no longer safely live alone, Pat moved his mother in with him and his wife, Karen. Karen did not want Pat's mother to move in. She had never enjoyed a relationship with her mother-in-law, and she surely did not want to be involved in taking care of her.

Pat's mother had too many assets to qualify for Medicaid, yet she didn't have enough money to pay the private rate for skilled care. So Pat felt he had no choice but to move his mother into his home. He assured Karen he would take care of his mother. He would do her laundry, take her to her medical appointments, and take care of everything for her. He realized this was his responsibility, and he didn't expect Karen to help.

This went okay for a few months until Karen became jealous that Pat was doing so much for his mother. Karen's perception was that Pat was "always" involved with things associated with his mother, and he no longer had time for her. She resented this and started picking fights with him. Soon, Karen began setting up situations so Pat would have to choose between her and his mother.

The tension and stress became almost too great for Pat to handle, and he frequently became sick. He told me he reached a point when he no longer enjoyed anything and felt depressed much of the time. He dreaded going home, and he began drinking heavily, which only added to his conflict with Karen. This situation lasted for about five years until Karen filed for divorce.

That was several years ago. When I last talked with Pat, he said his mother had passed away about two years after Karen divorced him. Karen remarried and has two children and a stepchild. Pat said that he lives alone and still has many mixed emotions about his decision, all those years ago, to move his mother into their home.

He told me he now takes things one day at a time; he learned a lot about himself and his relationships. But most important of all, he quit drinking the day his mother passed away. He said he's concerned about his own future, since he has no children of his own. He wonders who will take care of him when the time comes that he can no longer live alone.

The Case of Carol and Tom

The average man does not know what to do with his life, yet wants another one which will last forever.
(*Anatole France, Nobel Prize, Literature, 1921*)

The last story I want to tell you is at the other end of the spectrum from the case of Betty and John. This particular story involved two close friends of mine.

I will call them Carol and Tom. Tom's mother, Ann, had an irreversible lung disease, and his stepfather was diabetic. His stepfather, Ben, had no living relatives willing to assume the responsibility of taking care of him, so Tom's mother and stepfather came as a package.

Even though Carol and Tom were both professionals and although it was Tom's relatives, Carol accepted the role of primary caregiver. It wasn't that Tom was unwilling to take care of his mother and Ben, he simply felt inadequate for the task. Carol had maintained a loving relationship with Tom's folks for many years. Consequently, they trusted her to make decisions for them. They knew she would make decisions in their best interest. Carol told me she felt overwhelmed. She described her experience to me this way:

Tom's mother and stepfather lived in Connecticut. As a result of diabetes, Ben's left leg had to be amputated. Carol took time off from her job and flew to be with Tom's mother and stepfather during that period of time. She arranged for home healthcare workers to come and assist Ben as soon as he was released from the hospital. These care assistants were supposed to be there the very day he came home.

However, help did not arrive for several days. Since Ann was not physically able to take care of her husband, Carol had to postpone her trip home so she could stay and help toilet, bathe, and dress Ben. Carol said this was embarrassing for all of them. She told me about one particular time when she had just finished helping Ben bathe and he told her, with tears in his eyes, how much he appreciated her taking care of him.

Carol said she realized, at that moment, how pretentious modesty and ego really are. She said something else I will never forget; she said she had never felt as good about herself as a person. She realized she had no apparent obligation to this man, yet she knew there was an obligation that exceeded legal, marital, or family ties. That obligation was human-to-human. She said she understood, for the first time in her life, what it meant for her to be her "brother's keeper."

Within a few months after Ben's leg was amputated, it became obvious that he and Ann were in need of greater assistance than home healthcare visits. So, Carol flew to Connecticut and moved them to Tallahassee, Florida, where she and Tom lived. She and Tom hoped they could provide enough assistance so his folks could remain in their own home. Moving them was complicated by the fact that Ben had been a successful attorney and had acquired many material possessions. This included not just one home but three homes located in different parts of the country. In addition to their primary residence in Connecticut, they had a winter home in Coral Gables, Florida, and a summer home in the mountains of North Carolina, so it fell to Carol to handle the disposition of all these properties, as well as their furnishings.

Unfortunately, Ann and Ben were unable to remain in their new home for even a year before they needed to move to assisted living. Carol found a beautiful facility and once again handled everything.

Only a few weeks after moving to the assisted living facility, Ben needed to go for a medical checkup. Since it was his left leg that had been amputated, Ben could still drive. Consequently, he and Ann felt confident they could manage on their own, so they did not ask Tom or Carol to go with them.

After the appointment, Ann helped push her husband in his wheelchair to their car. Since she had problems with her lungs, this was extremely taxing for her. On the way home, she began having trouble breathing and had a stroke in the car that required hospitalization. She became comatose and was placed on life-support. Carol said the decision to turn off the life-support machines was the most difficult decision they had ever had to make.

Furthermore, she and Tom had never thought his mother would die before his stepfather. Carol was honest to tell me that she and Tom had, at some level, blamed Tom's stepfather for the death of Tom's mother. On another level, they knew he certainly was not responsible, but in their minds, if Ann had not been pushing him in the wheelchair, she wouldn't have exerted her lungs to that extent and might still be alive.

Carol was quick to say that she and Tom also blamed themselves, and they both felt very guilty. Now I want you to hear the "*should*" statement that was underneath their guilt.

Carol said she and Tom believed they *should* have known about the medical appointment and *should* have gone with them, even though Tom's mother and Ben had chosen not to tell them. Of course, this was irrational thinking, which led to their feelings of guilt. Shortly after his wife's death, Tom's stepfather declined to the level that he needed to be moved to a nursing home. So, once again, Carol found a skilled-nursing facility and moved him.

Several months later, Tom's stepfather died. Carol says that when she looks back on her caregiving role, she views it as the greatest learning experience of her life. She said she developed a capacity for tolerance and compassion she had never before experienced.

Out of curiosity, I asked Carol how she became the primary caregiver for Tom's mother and stepfather. She said Tom was so overwhelmed that he was virtually paralyzed.

Since there was no one else to take care of them, she felt she had no choice but to take control of the situation. Decisions had to be made, and someone had to take action. Carol became another statistic in the research that indicates the decision regarding who will assume responsibility for elderly parents is often one of default, to women, even when it is the husband's parents.

I also asked Carol what she would have done differently if she'd had the choice to do so. She told me she would have spent more time with Ann and Ben. She said the experience brought her and Tom closer together. She said Tom was so appreciative and grateful for all she had done for his folks, and he compensated her in a thousand ways. She ended by saying she was thankful for the opportunity to be the caregiver for Tom's mother and stepfather because she truly believed that experience prepared her for her upcoming role as caregiver for her own mother and father.

I: What strikes me is that we truly do have choices as to how we frame our experiences, as well as how we respond to difficult situations. Would you now help us better understand how caring for elderly loved ones affects grandchildren and great-grandchildren?
H: Some caregivers may still have children at home, especially if it's a granddaughter or grandson who has inherited the responsibility of caring for their elderly loved one(s). So the children I talk about might actually be the great-grandchildren of our parents. For the sake of example, I will simply refer to them as "your children."

Whether the elderly person is coming to live in your own home or your children will just be visiting them, it is important for you to take time to talk with them about the elderly person's condition. You might need to help the child understand differences between problems associated with aging and problems associated with particular illnesses and impending death. However, you only need to go into as much detail as the child can understand based on her/his age. Remember to keep it simple.

When children understand elderly people cannot help being the way they are, it is easier for them to tolerate certain behaviors and not take things personally. Children are often much more accepting and forgiving than adults.

I: Could you give us some examples?
H: If the grandparents are frail and unable to walk as far or as

fast as they once could, you might only need to tell the child that as we grow older, our bones and muscles are not as strong as they once were. That is the reason Grandma or Grandpa moves so slowly.

I: What if the elderly persons have dementia?
H: Then simply explain that for whatever reason, the brain has become diseased, and parts of the brain have been destroyed by the disease. Help the child to understand that sometimes information is destroyed or erased. That is why their grandparents cannot remember names or places or what they had for lunch. It is helpful to use analogies the child can understand.

With younger children, you might liken this to an Etch-A-Sketch toy. Perhaps even allow them to draw something on it. Then erase it so they can see that the drawing that was once there is now gone. No matter how hard they shake the box, the drawing will not reappear.

With older children, you might liken it to a computer. Allow the child to input some numbers or type something. Then, without saving the information, turn the machine off and back on again. Help them understand that the machine did not forget the information just to be mean. Once the information is gone, the machine, like the diseased brain, cannot get it back.

It is also useful to help the child understand that elderly people do not pick up objects and misplace them to be mean or to aggravate them. They simply cannot help it. Explain to them that many elderly people may pick up something, and by the time they turn around, they have forgotten what they were going to do with it or where they got it from.

You might encourage children to put personal items that they don't want others touching in a special place that is not obvious to the elderly person. Try to anticipate what behaviors your children will view as strange, and talk with them about those. It may be that their grandparents can no longer toilet themselves and need to wear diapers. Perhaps they have had a stroke, and they have difficulty talking or moving an arm or a leg. No matter what the disability, talk to your children and allow them to talk to you about it.

We also need to give our children psychological permission to say whatever they need to say and feel whatever they feel. Don't add guilt by telling them they *should* or *should not* feel a certain way.

It is common for children to feel frightened of their grandparents, especially if the grandparent no longer talks, walks, or looks the way she/he used to. Sometimes children are even afraid to touch them. They don't want to hug them because they are afraid they will "catch" whatever the grandparent has. It is important here to allow children to set their own boundaries. You may also need to reassure them that old age is not contagious.

I: That's interesting. I've never thought of that.

H: Children also need to know they cannot make their grandparents worse. Explain to them that sometimes things they do might upset their grandparents temporarily. However, their grandparents will probably forget the incident very quickly. At any rate, they will not make their grandparents sicker.

Children are often afraid their grandparents will die. Since that is a real probability, don't be afraid to talk with them about death. Allow them to ask questions and talk about what death means to them. Explore how they feel rather than telling them how they *should* feel. Don't just assume that children are not bothered by their grandparents' condition. Observe them as they interact with their grandparents, then find some quiet time and let them talk about their feelings. By all means, do not try to force children to participate in activities they are uncomfortable with. This is a difficult time for all of you, and every person copes with stress differently.

I: What are some of the most frequent issues that come up for children?

H: When talking about their grandparents, they say such things as, "They smell funny. They have no teeth. The way they eat is sickening. They act crazy. I'm afraid of them. They're always touching me and messing with my hair, and I hate that. I have no privacy with them around. They're always coming into my room and bothering my stuff. They are hard of hearing, so we have to scream at them. We have to play the TV so loud it hurts my ears. We can never go anywhere because of Grandmother or Grandfather."

Teenagers commonly report such complaints as, "I never have time with my friends anymore, and I can't have my friends over because the noise upsets Grandma/Grandpa. I'm embarrassed to bring my friends over because of the way Grandma/Grandpa behaves and looks. They are always telling me what to do. We don't have enough money to go places because we are always spending it on them. It's not fair that I have to give up my room for people I hardly even know."

Another common complaint children voice about the caregiver (typically the child's mother) is, "You're always tired and in a bad mood now that you have to take care of Grandma, and you take it out on me." This complaint reinforces the notion that children would much prefer a rested and happy parent than a home-cooked meal.

Children are often "truth-sayers" who speak the unspeakable, and they can be brutally honest. However, they are often optimistic and hopeful. They often make light of situations and thus alleviate stress during difficult times. They remind elders that life goes on and that their life goes on with them. There is a wonderful multi-generational dimension added to families when elders and children are in the same home. Children often bridge the gap between generations. Children also bring a healing quality to life. When babies or small children

149

are present, the energy in the home seems to vibrate at a softer frequency. Just looking at or holding a young child brings joy to the hearts of most.

Even though it's important to observe your children and explore things they're concerned about with them, be careful that you don't make something an issue for them just because it's an issue for you. Children experience the same emotions we do. The only difference may be in the way they express their emotions.

I: How do children express emotions differently?
H: It is common for children to "act out" when they are scared, uncertain, or confused. Often this acting out manifests in overt, aggressive behaviors, like talking back, being disrespectful, challenging family rules, being especially mean to a younger brother or sister, or perhaps getting into trouble at school.

Some children act out in passive-aggressive ways, like conveniently forgetting to do chores or deliver messages, or perhaps by breaking something or throwing something away by "accident." Some children just close down altogether and won't talk at all. No matter how many times you ask them what's wrong, they just shrug and say, "Nothing."

It is very common for children of divorced parents to decide they want to live with the other parent when things change dramatically in their own home. I certainly cannot tell you how to handle each and every circumstance. You know your children and your family situation much better than anyone else.

However, I want to stress the need to keep communication lines open. Family members need to talk and talk, then talk some more, about all the issues involved in caring for an elderly loved one. The largest problem in the world could have been handled when it was small.

I: You have said before that it can be a positive experience for an adult. Is there a way to make it a positive experience for a child?

H: I believe children need to be given opportunities to do things for elderly relatives—to serve others. Ask your children what they think they could do to help out or if there is something they would like to do for their grandparents. Although I hated my assigned job of emptying my grandmother's bedpan, I enjoyed picking and bringing flowers to her because that was my idea. That was what I wanted to do. I also enjoyed drawing and coloring pictures for her. She always seemed pleased and would brag about what a good job I had done.

It seems comforting for us to have memories of things we have done for others to recall after they are no longer with us. I think this is also true for children. We need to convey to children the positive experiences we all have to gain from elderly individuals.

I: What would be some examples of that?
H: You might suggest to your children that they ask their grandparents to tell them about times when they were growing up. If you don't already have one, buy an inexpensive recorder so your children can record their conversations with their grandparents. This may be a source of comfort in the future not only for the children but for other family members as well.

You might also encourage your children to take photos of their grandparents and start a book of memories. Children get to know their grandparents naturally in most families just by spending time with them. However, if elderly relatives live in another state, or they are in a care facility and visits are infrequent, children might be helped to interact with them by thinking of subjects to talk about prior to their visits. Younger children may feel comfortable asking specific yet fanciful questions about favorite songs, favorite books, or favorite colors. They may ask their grandparents how they picked their mom's or dad's name. Other questions include but certainly are not limited to: "Who was your favorite president and why? Who was your hero? If you could change one thing in the world, what would you change?" Encourage children to form their own questions and write them down to take with them on their visits. It's especially useful to watch how elderly persons respond when they look back over eighty or ninety years. It is particularly interesting to note their response to the question regarding what they would change if they could.

By involving children, we give them an opportunity to see we all have much to learn from elderly folks. Adolescents and teenagers are an entirely a different topic. Typically, they feel more comfortable participating in adult conversations. However, don't expect them to lead the conversation or even to be particularly responsive.

There may be many things elderly people are still able to do, and they might enjoy teaching their grandchildren or great-grandchildren these things. Carl's mother taught me a lot about cooking, embroidering, and fishing. She also taught me how to dig for worms so that we would have fish bait. What's important is to recognize that children will have their own relationships with their grandparents and great-grandparents, so encourage them to participate in the caregiving process as much as they will, yet respect their feelings.

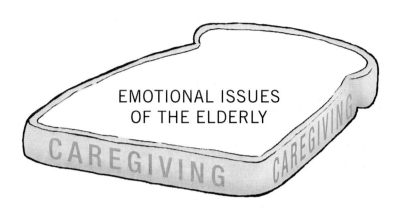

EMOTIONAL ISSUES
OF THE ELDERLY

All the art of living lies in a fine mingling of letting
go and holding on.
(Havelock Ellis)

I: Now that we've looked at the emotional issues for the caregiver and other family members, would you talk about the emotional issues and concerns of elderly persons?
H: Many individuals are in the ill-fated position of taking care of a spouse or sibling at the same time they are experiencing losses and fears associated with their own aging concerns. This might be an emotional overload for some, resulting in increased anxiety, panic attacks, and/or depression.

Many elderly folks that I've worked with report the transition from independence to dependence to be emotionally excruciating. As individuals experience multiple losses and become increasingly dependent on others, they often lose their sense of personhood and personal identity. I've heard it expressed this way: "I'm not even a person anymore. I'm just an old, broken down, sick body." Our culture is so geared toward work and productivity that many folks naturally identify themselves by their work.

Personal Identity

> Those whose work and pleasure are one...are...
> Fortune's favoured children.
> *(Winston Churchill, Nobel Prize, Literature, 1953)*

Often when we ask people who they are, they respond by telling us where they work or what kind of work they do. For example, "My name is Jane. I teach fifth grade at Miller Middle School," or "My name is Jack. I'm an artist." Where we work and the type work we do not only identifies who we are but also identifies our place in society. When individuals are no longer the teacher, the taxi driver, the doctor, the attorney, the nurse, or whatever their occupation was, many are at a loss as to who they are or how they fit into their communities or society in general. As I mentioned, my stepfather felt this way when he could no longer drive, since driving had been such a huge part of his life and identity.

Personhood

> I slept and dreamed that life was joy. I awoke and saw
> that life was service. I acted and behold, service was joy.
> *(Rabindranath Tagore, Nobel Prize, Literature, 1913)*

Personhood is partially defined by our roles in relationships. Part of who we are is tied up in whose son or daughter, whose wife or husband, whose mother or father, whose sister or brother, or whose friend we are. Personhood is further defined by our role in primary relationships. When roles change in primary relationships, the ways individuals relate to themselves and to others also change, and part of one's sense of personhood may be lost.

Personhood is further lost when individuals lose their ability to maintain control over their bodily functions and emotions or lose their ability to make independent decisions about their lives. The aging process is unkind and often leaves people with diminished eyesight, impaired hearing, and loss of cognitive functioning. Some lose their ability to walk and may lose control of their bladders and bowels in addition to other significant losses.

Loss of bodily functions is not only embarrassing and humiliating but usually means a loss of freedom. Many elderly individuals state they don't even want to leave their homes because they are afraid they'll have an "accident" and be embarrassed. Being confined to one's home often means a decrease in social interaction and sometimes loss of contact with friends and relatives.

This is also true when individuals are no longer able to drive and must depend on others for transportation. Many activities that helped keep them vibrant go by the wayside. Losing the privilege to drive often forces people into social isolation and reduces chances for intellectual stimulation and emotional validation, which further increases their risk of anxiety and depression. Losing one's ability to drive is disturbing and embarrassing for many elderly individuals.

Fears and Worries

The worst of all fears is the fear of living.
(*Theodore Roosevelt, Nobel Prize, Peace, 1906*)

Elderly people report many fears, which include fear of death, fear of the dying process, fear of losing everything they have worked for, and fear about not having enough money to sustain them. Some talk about their fear of losing their physical and mental faculties and having to live in a nursing home. Others talk about their fear of pain and debilitating illnesses.

In addition to their fears, many elderly people tend to

worry about many things. They worry about being a burden to their children and other relatives. They worry about what will happen to their spouse if they die first. They worry about what will happen to them if their spouse dies first. These are all real and valid concerns that may evoke tremendous emotional pain.

In order to avoid this emotional trauma, elderly people sometimes stay in denial and cling to their belief that they can still take care of themselves. As I said earlier, denial serves to protect individuals from pain associated with certain realities. What I observed with my own folks was that my mother's dementia was so pronounced that she didn't seem concerned about the moment, much less the future.

However, my stepfather moved in and out of contact with reality. During those times when he was lucid and aware of where he was, he verbalized nearly all the fears I mentioned. I remember sitting with him on many occasions while he cried about being in the nursing home and the realization that he and my mother would never live alone again.

I held him when he cried about not being able to work and provide for my mother and about not being able to drive or even tie his own shoes. My heart broke when I saw how embarrassed he was about wearing diapers and needing help to change them. This was once a strong and proud man. He worked hard and paid his taxes. He made a contribution to the world. He enjoyed life, especially driving.

My heart ached whenever I saw him in so much emotional pain. I was thankful when he would mentally go back to a happier time in his life and talk about things from his youth, like planting crops and feeding the mule. It was during those times he seemed to be free of physical as well as emotional pain. He expressed joy as he talked to me about the crop he'd just harvested.

At times he maintained the delusion that he and my

mother would once again live alone and he would be able to drive his truck again. Some days he even talked about getting a motorcycle, and this was a man who could hardly stand without support.

Delusions

> Men (and women) occasionally stumble over the
> truth, but most of them pick themselves up and hurry
> off as if nothing had happened.
> *(Winston Churchill, Nobel Prize, Literature, 1953)*

I: Dr. Haymon, when your parents talked about things that were totally unreasonable, like Carl riding a motorcycle, would you try to explain to them that was not possible? Or did you just agree with them?

H: That's a very good question. When elderly persons are delusional and operating from an entirely different belief system than we are, there are inherent communication problems. This often creates a double bind for us. On the one hand, if we agree with the delusion, we reinforce it. On the other hand, if we confront it, we risk driving the delusion deeper.

I: So how do we, as caregivers, find a balance between the two?

H: The important thing is to always show respect for the elderly person. Remember, not too long ago, these individuals were not unlike us. They were independent and managed their own lives, a task they've done far much longer than we have been alive. They deserve respect, understanding, and reassurance. Even if they had addictions and lived their lives differently than we've chosen to live ours, they still deserve respect.

The truth is that we all probably do the very best we can just to survive, and many of these people have survived eighty, ninety, maybe even a hundred years. So if you blatantly tell them they are never going to leave the nursing home, you risk insulting and scaring them, which creates unnecessary anxiety and tension for them.

However, you don't want to be dishonest with them either. So when an elderly person starts talking about leaving the care facility and moving back to her/his home or driving again, just try to remember the purpose of the delusion. That purpose is to protect them from emotional pain. It is very comforting for them to believe in something positive. That's true for all of us.

I: So how do we do that? How do we handle their delusions?

H: One way is to respond to the period in their lives the delusional comments represent. For example, when Carl would say something like, "As soon as your mother is better, we are going to take a trip. We'll probably drive all the way to California," I wouldn't agree with his delusion and say, "Yep. You'll probably drive the Winnebago all the way to San Diego." Neither would I confront his delusion by telling him Mother would never be able to take such a trip, and furthermore, he would never be able to drive again. I would just validate him by responding to that time in his life when he was strong, in good health, and independent. I would say something like, "You really enjoyed the trips you and Mother took a few years back, didn't you?" Do you see how I handled it? I responded to the period in his life that his comments represented. I never addressed whether he was actually going to California or whether he would ever drive again.

I: So you didn't argue or agree with him?

H: No, I just encouraged him to talk about those times in his life he enjoyed, and soon he'd have forgotten all about his notion of going to California. He'd be telling me about the trips he took when he was a young man.

My mother would often say she'd seen her sister, my aunt, Mae, who'd been dead for years. I wouldn't confront her delusion by telling her she had not seen Aunt Mae and reminding her that I took her to Aunt Mae's funeral. I also wouldn't agree with her delusion, lie to her, and tell her that I saw Aunt Mae leaving as I came in. First of all, I don't know whether she saw Aunt Mae or not. I personally believe the veil gets very thin as individuals near death. Perhaps loved ones from the other side do come to visit to help prepare them for the transition. At any rate, I would just respond to the purpose of the delusion. Mother was obviously missing her sister. I would say something like, "Mother, you really do miss Aunt Mae, don't you? Tell me again about the time when you and Aunt Mae were at that church social where you met Daddy." Soon Mother would be laughing and sharing numerous memories associated with her sister. Indeed, there is a fine line between reinforcing and confronting delusions.

Another way to handle delusional comments is to try to keep the person in the present. Instead of responding to what they have said, ask them what they did that morning or afternoon. Ask them what type of activities they've been involved in. Or here's a good one, ask them their opinion about something in your own life. Sometimes they surprise us by coming up with answers so simple they border on profoundness.

Empathic Presence

> Presence is more than just being there.
> (Malcolm S. Forbes, The Further
> Sayings of Chairman Malcolm)

Sometimes just feeling "heard" might be enough to reduce anxiety and lessen the person's distress. Therefore, it is vitally important to provide opportunities for your loved ones to talk about their fears and help them identify sources of comfort.

Engaging elderly folks in a review of their life and helping them affirm their personal contributions that added value and meaning to the lives of others may help them feel better about this stage in their lives. You might begin this process by simply asking them to tell you what they are most proud of or about the happiest time in their life. You might also ask them how they would like to be remembered.

My friend Gary recently told me that listening is an act of love. I know that's true. I feel most loved when another listens to me and when I feel truly heard. I think Gary was talking about something that is referred to as "empathic presence," which involves total engagement with the person to whom you're listening. Empathic listeners are relaxed but engaged at the same time. They ask questions and explore without prying. Empathetic presence includes providing a non-judgmental environment, which offers psychological permission to talk openly and honestly. The listener maintains appropriate eye contact and offers reassuring, appropriate touches if culturally acceptable.

Empathetic presence also requires listening beneath and beyond the spoken words for deeper meanings, acknowledging the other's suffering, and validating her/his feelings. Empathetic listeners may be required to admit when they don't have answers. Empathetic presence may also necessitate being happy and rejoicing in another's accomplishments at a level of genuine sincerity that conveys to the other person her/his importance.

Empathetic presence decreases feelings of abandonment and isolation. It may also allow individuals to come to terms with their own internal struggles while affirming their dignity, self-worth, and personhood.

You might also arrange for family members and friends to tell them how they've made a difference and how thankful they are to have them in their lives. However, the individual's own perception of whether her/his life was worth living is far more important than what others think.

Rituals

> We grow neither better nor worse as we grow old, but more like ourselves.
> *(May Lamberton Becker)*

Rituals also offer comfort and a sense of being in control at a time when there are few things within their realm of control. Certain rituals, like saying prayers each morning and/or night, may help some to feel a sense of normalcy. Even rituals such as getting her/his bath and eating meals at the same times each day may offer a sense of security and predictability. Having set days and times when you and others will visit them may also offer some sense of predictability. For some, religious or spiritual practices and traditions are comforting.

Unresolved Past Issues

> True reconciliation does not consist in merely forgetting the past.
> *(Nelson Mandela, Nobel Prize, Peace, 1993)*

Unresolved past issues may manifest in physical and psychological symptoms, such as anxiety, shortness of breath, panic attacks, restlessness, agitation, depression, insomnia, and nightmares. Generalized pain or pain that frequently changes location and is not alleviated with sufficient pain medication are other expressions of unresolved issues. Being afraid to die and concerns about afterlife also suggest individuals are unsettled about their past.

Sometimes individuals who are struggling with issues from

their past may have feelings of despair or feel that they have been abandoned by God, deity, or deities. They may refuse to take medicines secondary to the belief that they deserve to be in pain and to be punished. They may also refuse pain medications because they want to be alert and maintain some sense of control of their faculties.

Other behavioral signs of spiritual unrest or spiritual crisis may include self-injurious behaviors, constantly hollering out for others to help them, and frantically asking advice from others. Begging for pain medication or to be "put out of her/ his misery," repeatedly questioning "Why me?" withdrawing from others, and refusing to help with their own baths or with feeding themselves all suggest a lack of resolve. Anger outbursts and/or power struggles with family members or other caregivers further imply a lack of internal peace.

Spiritual and Religious Framework

> In every language, every culture, the most difficult words you have to say are: "I'm sorry. Forgive me."
> (Desmond Tutu, Nobel Prize, Peace, 1984)

Spiritual and religious frameworks offer a means of evaluating one's life. Individuals may search for ways to "make wrongs right." They may also seek ways to be forgiven so they might be released from guilt and shame. For some individuals, this might come only by means of formal "confession" to a member of the clergy. Therefore, you might ask your loved ones if they would like a private visit with a priest, minister, bishop, or other spiritual leader. They may also need to forgive others for perceived past transgressions.

When loved ones are angry, bitter, and resentful and seem unable to get out of their victim role, it might be helpful to encourage them to reframe their experience and look at their situation from a different perspective. In a loving way, you might suggest they focus more on what they *can* do rather than what they *can't* do. They may no longer be able to walk, but perhaps they can sit and write names on the backs of photos and put them in albums.

This time in life might provide a good opportunity to tell their life's story. They might want to write their memoirs or record their story on DVD so their heirs might have the opportunity to enjoy it. They might be able to make phone calls for a charitable organization, read to pre-school children, or help a child or an adult learn to read.

Thinking about, as well as creating a written list, of the things and people we are thankful for and the blessings and positive events in our lives releases neuro-chemicals, which help fight depression, boost the immune system, and enable us to feel better in general. I often suggest to folks that they write down something they are thankful for that begins with each letter of the alphabet every day and try not to use the same words two days in a row. Reframing one's situation often enables individuals to cope by finding meaning and value in their present situation.

Experiencing Life

> Look at everything as though you were seeing it
> either for the first or last time. Then your time on
> earth will be filled with glory.
> *(Betty Smith, A Tree Grows in Brooklyn)*

When some people become unable to participate in physical activities, they focus their energy, time, and attention on spiritual matters and personal reflection. Some who have "wandered from the fold" make a concerted effort to return to the teachings of their youth and renew covenants and religious practices and traditions.

Some request a picture or statue of Christ or other religious or cultural figures, or for rosary beads, prayer shawls, or prayer books to use when praying. Others may ask for scriptures or other religious books to read or to listen to, or for small altars or shrines to be constructed. Some may request particular objects or potions believed to have healing powers. Yet others may request that caregivers and family members pray with and/or for them. Some request that their names to be placed on prayer rolls so others might pray for them.

Research suggests humor (watching funny movies, television programs, or re-runs of funny episodes) and laughing releases endorphins that reduce pain and boost the immune system, as well as offer individuals a heightened sense of well-being. Other practices that might be beneficial in reducing internal unrest include relaxation techniques, listening to relaxing/classical music, reading, meditating, chanting, Shamanic treatments, herbal remedies, acupuncture, exercising, massages, and getting sunlight and fresh air. Caregivers might also encourage loved ones to do whatever they need to do in order to make amends or complete unfinished business in order to attain the peace they desire.

The Greek origin of the word "crisis" connotes opportunity and possibility. So it is with the final stage of life. Regardless of an individual's religious, spiritual, or philosophical framework, spiritual growth is possible for almost everyone, right up to the end of her/his life. Spiritual growth does not, however, necessarily diminish pain and suffering.

Fear of Death

It is only with the heart that one can see rightly; what
is essential is invisible to the eye.
(Antoine De Saint-Exupery, The Little Prince)

It has been suggested that unresolved issues and fear are the two most important factors in determining the level of resistance individuals will experience when facing death. Many individuals are terribly afraid to let go of the known and move into a realm of the unknown.

Fears about death itself vary according to individual frameworks. However, common fears have to do with the afterlife. Many report fearing the unknown and what may or may not await them. Some fear they will never be able to see their loved ones again. If that is an expressed fear, this might also be an indirect request to see family members they haven't seen for a long while.

When folks know their time is limited, they are sometimes willing to take emotional risks they have avoided in the past. You might ask if there's anyone they've been thinking about or anyone they'd like to see. Some might ask to see or talk with a family member they haven't seen in a while or an old lover or friend from their school years.

I was once asked by a 90-year-old client, Sarah, if I could use a computer to help her find out if her "first love," Danny, was still living. She had not waited for him to return from WWII. She'd married someone else and had one son. She'd spent sixty-five years wondering what her life might have been like had she waited and married her "true love."

Sarah had told me great stories during our therapy sessions about how she and Danny had met and the fun times they'd had. She told these stories over and over at every session. She'd always start with, "Have I told you about the time Danny and I...?"

I would always reply with, "I love hearing you tell that story." She was always quick to tell it again. She would laugh and recall their outings in vivid detail.

She loved coming to therapy because she felt she had no one else she could talk with about Danny. Having a memory and no one to share it with is perhaps one of the worst kinds of loneliness. Sarah's memories transported her to a place in time when she was young and vibrant. Her laughter released important neuro-chemicals, which helped fight her depression, boosted her immune system, and enabled her to feel better in general.

Her husband was in an Alzheimer's facility in another part of the state and no longer recognized her or their son. She almost never talked about him. She said that he had provided well for her, but he had been cold and hadn't make her laugh the way Danny had. Her husband died not long after I started seeing her in therapy, but his death was never a therapeutic issue.

She gave me Danny's full name and all the information she remembered of his last whereabouts in New York. I found his name through a Google search. It seemed ironic that she and Danny were both from New York, yet they had both moved to the South and had lived within a two-hour drive from one another for many years. Apparently neither knew the other was nearby.

According to the obituary, Danny was survived by his wife, three grown children, and several grandchildren and great-grandchildren. He had passed away in 1979. I printed a copy of the obituary and brought it for Sarah to read. She responded to the news of Danny's death as though it had just occurred. For her it had. She started dreaming about him, and we would discuss these dreams in therapy. She was always happy to have these "dream visits" from Danny. The central theme of these "dream visits" was that he still loved her and was waiting for her.

In these "dream visits," which she said sometimes occurred when she was not asleep, Danny would often be accompanied by her parents and her only sister, who had died when she was in her twenties. Sarah would talk about how happy she would be to finally be back with Danny and her folks. She died a few months after learning of Danny's death.

Views About Death and Spiritual Life After Death

> I believe that the difference between Heaven and
> Hell is not so much the climate as the company.
> Living in a world populated by people like themselves
> would, for many, be Heaven. And for others, it would
> indeed be Hell.
> *(Richard Paul Evans, The Gift)*

It is common for elderly folks to ask others what they believe about death. Often these types of questions are veiled attempts to clarify their own beliefs. A good way to help them gain clarification is to turn the question back to them or ask other self-discovery questions. For example, you might ask these or similar questions: "What have you been taught about an afterlife?" "What do you hope happens after death?" "What have you envisioned it might be like after death?" "Is there some thought about death that brings you comfort?" "Where do you turn for strength?"

Views about death itself and spiritual life after death depend largely on cultural and/or religious teachings, as well as individual frameworks. Some cultures and religions believe the quality of existence after life depends in part on how the person died. For example, some believe a person who dies a violent death, is murdered, or takes her/his own life might not go to the same spiritual place or enjoy the same quality of spiritual life as one who died a peaceful death. Some also believe the spiritual, mental, and emotional state of individuals at the time of death directly impacts their transition to the spirit world, as well as their life in that realm.

Customs and rituals performed by the living for the dead are thought by some to also influence the transition of the person from this sphere into the next. How others care for the body of the deceased is thought by some to improve the quality of afterlife for that person. Certain rituals of cleansing and special preparation of the remains, as well as prayers for those believed to be in purgatory, and emotional chants of the bereaved, are all customs believed to impact the quality of afterlife.

Funeral and burial customs, as well as the way people mourn, may be as varied as the people mourning. Mourning periods may be as short as a few hours or go on for years. There is also a myriad of beliefs about the bonds or ties between the living and the dead. What a person believes about these relationships has great bearing on her/his grieving process.

Fears about the dying process are different from fears about death itself. Common fears about the dying process include fear of being left alone, fear of losing control of one's bodily functions, fear of losing one's mind, fear of pain, and/or fear of suffocating. Sometimes elderly people report a sense of choking, which increases their anxiety and often results in full-blown panic attacks.

The status of an individual's physical, mental, and emotional health plays a huge role in her/his level of fear and anxiety. Those who have multiple health problems are more likely to experience higher levels of fear and anxiety than those who are relatively healthy. Plus, through the lens of depression, life regrets are often magnified, which in turn increases death anxiety.

When elderly loved ones have a fearful, anxious response to their losses, it is important to show empathy and help normalize their responses. Although every person's pain and suffering is unique, it is often helpful for them to hear that their response is considered normal and they are not "crazy." Normalizing their experience as well as their response may build trust by conveying knowledge that they are not the first nor the only ones to go through similar trials. It may also diminish their fear and anxiety and offer hope that they too can make it through this unfamiliar territory.

It is also not uncommon for family members to hold conflicting views about dying, death, and what happens after death. It is absolutely essential to respect others' views about these sacred topics and ensure their beliefs are held in highest regard, even when we may have a totally different perspective.

Another aspect associated with end-of-life concerns is the reality that for the caregiver, these issues are on the horizon. By helping others prepare for their death, we are also helping ourselves prepare for our own. Fear of death may also undergird the caregiver's feelings of anxiety and depression.

Goals for the Last Stage of Life

> There is no better way to clothe one's grief than to
> celebrate another's joy.
> (Sheldon Glashow, Nobel Prize, Physics, 1979)

There are many reasonable goals for the last stage of a person's life, such as the alleviation of emotional pain by reconciling relationships, finishing unfinished business, and/or coming to terms with past regrets. Feeling joy is also a worthwhile goal—joy experienced in laughing about old times with friends and loved ones, looking at old photos, and celebrating one's life. Also, having friends and relatives share in one's fears and grief, as well as having an opportunity to say good-bye, seem to be worthwhile goals that bring comfort and closure for many individuals, as well as for family members and friends.

CLOSURE—SAYING
GOOD-BYE

CAREGIVING CAREGIVING

Now he has departed from this strange world a little
ahead of me. That signifies nothing. For us believing
physicists, the distinction between past, present, and
future is only an illusion however persistent.
(Albert Einstein, Nobel Prize, Physics, 1929)

*I: Dr. Haymon, we've talked about the emotional issues of the care-
giver, other family members, and for the elderly. Inevitably, the
time comes when our elderly loved ones die. Please talk to us about
this final phase of caregiving and how we might move through the
grieving process.*

H: In order for us to understand where we are in any process,
it is often helpful to start with a historical perspective. As I
mentioned earlier, when we look back to when the majority
of people in our country farmed and two or three generations
lived on the same farm, maybe even in the same house, families were expected to take care of their elderly. That was part
of life. Because there were usually lots of family members to
help out, it didn't seem such a burden.

Being old and dependent was as much a part of life as
being young and independent. Illness and poor health for the
elderly were viewed as being as natural as strength and vitality
for the young. There was no denial about death.

There was respect for life because death was understood as part of the process of living. People died at home with dignity. Their family and friends surrounded them to support them in the next step of their eternal journey. It was common for family and friends to prepare the body for burial. The body then remained at home for two or three days so loved ones and friends could visit and pay their last respects.

For the most part, work stopped for those few days. Family and friends gathered and in their own ways celebrated the person's life and the parts of it they'd shared. Often they sat in the room with the casket and told one story after another. I experienced this when my own grandparents died when I was young. It seemed to me the deceased person's spirit remained and shared in the closure taking place. As I look back on those memories, I see the benefits of that process.

When I was a little girl, probably not much more than three years old, my great-uncle died. I remember sitting in the front room of my grandmother's home. The casket was in that room, and lots of family members sat around. Relatives told stories and laughed.

During that period in time, it was common for families to sit up all night with the deceased person's body. They sort of took shifts. A few family members would sit with the body for a while, then they might leave and take a break while other family members would come to sit. People just wandered in and out, but there was always someone sitting near the body.

It reminds me of a custom of the Aborigines. When a baby is born, every tribe member comes by and says, "I'm happy you're here and support you in your journey." Then, when someone dies, everyone in the tribe comes by and says, "I'm happy for you and support you in your journey." As I look back on our family rituals, which took place when I was a child, it seems as though we were all there supporting our relatives in this next step of her/his spiritual journey.

I didn't really know my great-uncle. I had only seen him three or four times in my life. I was quite young and he did not live nearby. "Nearby" meant within walking distance because most of my relatives on my maternal grandparents' side (us included) all lived on the same street.

What I do remember are the stories. What immortalized him in my mind was not what I actually remembered about my own interactions with him, but what I remembered from the great stories other relatives told. There were lots of wonderful and funny stories, things about his kindness and his sense of humor. Then one of my great-aunts said she remembered when she got into this squabble with him. She relived the event as though it had been the day before.

What those stories did for me was to normalize his life and help me realize there are good and bad in everyone. For every person who would change us, there's someone who loves us just the way we are. It also seems to me that as unique as we truly are, we're really not very different from one another.

I was almost four when my mother's father died. My mom had told me, "If you kiss a dead person bye, then you won't have nightmares or bad dreams about them." So she held me up, and I leaned over the casket. I looked at my grandpa, and when I leaned over to kiss him on the cheek, my mother said, "Be sure you don't kiss him too hard because you will bruise him." So very gently, I leaned over and kissed my grandpa good-bye. His cheek was very, very cold. I remember pulling back a little and thinking that was strange. Then I just lightly kissed him again.

I: But you weren't frightened by that?

H: Oh, no, I wasn't frightened at all. The coldness of his face just seemed a little strange to me. I remember a while back when one of my little cousins was at the funeral of his great-grandfather and a similar thing happened. I smiled as I watched his mother hold him up to kiss his grandpa good-bye.

He kissed his grandpa and said, "Oh, Grandpa's cold. I'll get him a blanket." That scene brought back very positive memories for me.

There was closure in my experience. I was able to kiss Grandpa and tell him good-bye. It was all very positive. I'm also very thankful for the stories other relatives shared while we were sitting with our deceased relatives' bodies. If not for their stories, I wouldn't remember some of my relatives at all.

> We have to recognize that we are spiritual beings
> with souls existing in a spiritual world as well as
> material beings with bodies and brains existing in a
> material world.
> *(John Eccles, Nobel Prize, Medicine, 1963)*

I: From a psychological standpoint, does it help people to participate in the dying process of others?

H: I believe it may help us come to some realization about our own mortality. For many, those moments of quiet introspection remind them that in the end relationships may be all that really matter. I remember those who died while struggling in relationships of disharmony, needing others to be wrong so they could be right. There was tremendous sadness. There seemed to be a cloud of heaviness in the realization that they had died without resolving their own internal struggles. They lacked self-acceptance. It now seems to me that the only ones who feared death were those who were dissatisfied with their lives.

For others who resolved their internal conflicts as they journeyed along life's path, there seemed to be a peace about their death that was reflected in others. There was appropriate sadness without hysteria and joyfulness in the privilege of having known them.

I: So, Dr. Haymon, you're really advocating that the entire fam-

ily—from the youngest to the oldest—get involved in the final process.

H: Yes, I am. It seems taking part in a loved one's dying process provides an opportunity for us to work through lots of tender emotions.

However, getting back to a historical perspective, as history was being written, we moved from a rural way of life into what would become known as the Industrial Revolution. For those who did not have transportation, it became necessary to live near the towns and the factories. Many of the older people refused to leave their farms, so families separated. Physical distance created emotional distance.

Life during the industrial period continued to accelerate. Soon there was hardly time for death, much less for the dying process. Many people died without their loved ones with them to support them in their final hours and minutes. Relatives and friends were notified in person or by phone, telegram, or letter that their loved ones had passed.

Families were hardly inconvenienced at all. This was the first generation in our history to delegate responsibilities associated with the death of loved ones to total strangers. Funeral homes would take care of everything.

Families could spend a couple of hours receiving guests and friends at the chapel, which was conveniently located in the same building where the body was prepared for burial. Paying last respects would be done in the evening. The funeral could be scheduled for the following afternoon so people wouldn't have to miss any more work than necessary.

Close friends and family could come by the designated house right after the funeral for a bite to eat, and everyone could still be home to catch the ten o'clock news then go back to work the following morning. If people moved really fast, they could deny death had occurred at all. Weeks later, some would think about dropping by the nursing home for a visit. Then some faint part of their memory would remind them their loved one was gone. They would vaguely recall the funeral and scratch their heads in confusion as to how it had all happened so fast, as though it had been a dream.

Feelings of emptiness would be attributed to their sense of loss. They'd convince themselves that what they really needed to do was to stay busy so they wouldn't have to think about it. Many would do exactly that. By staying preoccupied with other things, some could postpone emotional pain. They could forfeit the occasion to celebrate the deceased person's life or to assess their own and abort any chance of closure. It seems to me that we've lost something in this evolutionary process, which seems to constantly accelerate. Recently I attended the viewing and funeral of a friend. Both were held at night, so folks wouldn't have to lose time from work.

The last several funerals I've gone to, I've seen no children, and I knew the people had grandchildren. Some even had great-grandchildren. I wondered how these children were being taught to say good-bye and bring closure to relationships. When I asked the adults where the children were, I was told things like, "Well, I didn't see any need in taking them out of school," "I was afraid they would make too much noise," or "I didn't want them to get upset." There is great therapeutic value in children taking part in rituals and ceremonies and being allowed to feel. It's natural to be upset and sad when someone dies. How will they learn to deal with their emotions if they're not allowed to feel them? It also seemed to me that some of the adults were robotically going through the motions of the burial ceremony, not even allowing themselves to feel.

> There is no distance on this earth as far away as
> yesterday.
> *(Robert Nathan, So Love Returns)*

Many of my clients come for counseling because they're depressed. I often learn they have never grieved the losses of significant relationships. They often deny a particular rela-

175

tionship was important to them because it was negative, unre-solved, or filled with anger and resentment. Some people pre-tend only positive relationships are meaningful.

The irony may be that relationships that have unresolved anger and resentment are the very ones from which we have the most to learn. If our relationships with others are, in fact, mirrored reflections of our relationship with ourselves, then we have at least as much to learn about ourselves from our so-called negative relationships as those we refer to as positive.

I: But how can we resolve issues with someone who has already passed away?

H: When my biological father died on July 10, 1981, I was still angry with him. Enraged would be a better word. Not only had he been alcoholic, he had been criminally abusive to me and my sisters, and perhaps my bother. I don't remember much about my brother because he left home and joined the Navy when I was just three years old. There were many times when I feared for our lives. As a child, I hated my father, and I used to pray that he would die, just so the abuse would stop. But he didn't die until I was thirty-one years old. Even though I didn't see him often those last few years, I still harbored much anger, resentment, and I guess maybe even hatred for him.

So during the few days between the time he died and the time he was buried, I didn't know what to do with my anger. While I was processing my feelings, trying to sort all this out, I recognized that my worst fear had been realized. Remember-ing that anger is only one layer up from fear, I looked under my anger and saw my fear.

My worst fear was that he would die before things changed, and I would never have the father I wanted. That had hap-pened! When I looked around, I also realized I had lived through it. I had lived through my worst fear; he was gone, I was still here, and I never had the father I wanted.

I was so sad. I sat down and wrote him a letter. I told him

how much I had always wanted a good relationship with him. I told him how much I had wanted us to be a happy family and how sad I was we'd never been able to. I told him that I hoped, somewhere in time and space, we would be given the opportunity to have the love and happiness we had not had here. I told him how sorry I was that he had been in so much emotional pain that he'd had to use alcohol to anesthetize himself.

While finishing the letter, I noticed my anger was gone. I had forgiven him. I felt so light I wasn't even sure I was touching the ground. Then I felt something that felt very strange at first, and I wasn't sure what it was. I was sitting there very quietly, just allowing myself to feel whatever this was, when the strangest notion came to me. Underneath all that, I loved him.

Although I didn't know about it until I was grown, he'd had a horrible childhood himself. I remembered the story my great-aunt told me about my grandmother getting pregnant with him when she was only fifteen, and her folks had made her and her baby live out in an old cookhouse with no heat because they were ashamed of her. Our society is much more accepting of illegitimate children now than it was a hundred years ago. Back then, a child born out of wedlock was not referred to as an illegitimate child. He or she was referred to as a "bastard" child, with all the shame such a title would carry. He'd lived the first few years of his life being shunned and shamed for a mistake he had nothing to do with and the rest of his life trying to ease the emotional pain he'd inherited from it.

He didn't know how to let go of his anger and resentment, so he took it out on us. I then concluded the letter by telling him how much I loved him and that I hoped one day I'd be given the opportunity to show him that love. I also told him I hoped he would now be in peace and out of his pain. I took the letter to the funeral home the morning of his funeral, and I placed it inside his coat pocket, right over his heart. Then I kissed him and said good-bye on July 12, 1981.

I remember looking in the rearview mirror as the procession traveled from the funeral home to the cemetery. There were headlights as far back as I could see. There must have been a hundred cars.

I did not know at that time how many lives he'd touched, how many folks he'd befriended, or how many families he'd helped out. I would later hear stories of how he'd chopped wood for his brother's widow so she and her children could have a fire to keep them warm. I learned he'd dropped off food many times for my mother's sister, whose husband had left her with twelve kids to feed.

I listened while person after person told stories about a man I called my father but they called their friend. I realized there was a side of him I'd never known. I wondered why it's often easier to be kind to those outside your family. I pictured him as a little boy confused, trying to understand why members of his own family would be so unkind to him.

Sandra's biological father, Pat Haymon,
waiting to go on dialysis, 1981.

I: Dr. Haymon, thank you for sharing that story with us. I know it
was not easy, and I hope others will benefit from your willingness

178

to share it. What about situations where we still have unresolved anger and resentment with relatives that perhaps died many years ago? Can we still come to this kind of letting go, many years past their death?

H: Writing a letter to someone you have unresolved issues with or you haven't brought closure to is a very old technique. It is also very effective. Even if the person's been gone for years, go ahead and write the letter. Say all the things you wish you had said while she or he was living or maybe need to say now.

Vent whatever anger and frustration you might have, then try to look underneath the anger for the fear. You may have to look closely, but it's there. When you see your fear, look around and see that you have lived through it. Sometimes emotional pain is so great that we're afraid if we acknowledge it we might not live through it. When you realize you have in fact lived through perhaps your worst fear or your worst nightmare, close your eyes and feel the peacefulness that comes with that realization.

In my case, I felt so light I wasn't sure I was still sitting in the chair. I felt much lighter because the anger and fear were gone. It truly is amazing to me, even as a psychologist, when I consider this phenomenon. People come to my office, and they're so burdened. They're heavy with anger and fear. Then weeks or maybe months later, when they've worked through some of their anger and fear, when they've forgiven and let go of it, they look physically lighter.

Their countenance changes, and the energy field around them becomes clearer and brighter. For me, it was a wonderful feeling. You'll know when your anger and fears are gone because the heaviness leaves. When that happens, take a couple of deep breaths and enjoy the peace and positive feelings that replace the anger and fear.

Then write about your new feelings in your letter. If you need to say you're sorry, that you forgive them, or that you love them, then do so. Remember, you've already written about your anger, hurt, disappointment, and/or other negative feelings. Once you've looked past all that, write whatever else you feel. Put everything you feel in the letter. Then put it into an envelope and address it to that person, "somewhere in the universe." Don't put a return address on it, but put a stamp on it and mail it.

I: Do I actually need to mail it? Couldn't I just write the letter then tear it up and throw it in the wastebasket? Wouldn't that have the same effect?
H: I believe there is closure in mailing it. You might choose to keep a copy of it, but part of the catharsis is in sending it to them. Who knows? They might receive it.

I: Wouldn't this also work with someone who's still living?
H: I think it's just as important to write letters from your heart to people who are still living. It's similar to a dress rehearsal, with a chance to say what you really want to say. Sometimes, we psychologists use what is called "The Empty-Chair Technique."

We suggest individuals pretend the person they want to talk to is in the chair and say whatever they want to say. That is often very effective in allowing persons to vent their feelings and say things they've perhaps kept bottled up for a long time.

But letter writing is something you can do just for you. Nobody else is listening. You can write down everything you want or need to say to the person. You can release your anger, frustration, resentment, and other feelings. This is often painful. Emotional pain is just as real and can be just as painful, if not more so, than physical pain.

I: But if they're living, would I still send it to them?
H: Wait a few days or weeks after you've written it to allow yourself to process what you've written and to see how you feel. You may decide to mail it, or you may decide you'd rather talk to the person face-to-face.

It is also very valuable to write letters to individuals who've been a positive influence in your life—parents, grandparents, teachers, neighbors, and friends. It's important to tell others all of the wonderful things you've never said but wished you had. Or maybe you just want to remind them of how you feel. Maybe you've said "I love you" a million times, and you just want to tell them once again.

Most people, especially elderly folks, love to get notes and cards validating their contribution to someone's life. My friend Debbie, who owned and managed a retirement facility for years, told me nearly all the folks who live in retirement homes look forward to two things: meals and mail.

Another friend told me she wrote a letter to her mother after she and I had talked about this exercise. She said she wrote down very positive feelings she had for her mother but had been unable to tell her. She said she told her mother, in the letter, how much she meant to her. She included things that made her mother special to her. She said it was a wonderful experience for her, and her mother loved it! Although it's been several years, her mother still carries the letter with her in her purse.

> You don't get to choose how you're going to die, or
> when. You can only decide how you're going to live.
> Now.
> *(Joan Baez)*

My stepfather's dying process and death was an entirely different experience for me than my biological father's death had been. Carl had been in the final stage of Alzheimer's disease for about a year before he died. During this stage, patients usually lose their ability to talk. This was true for Carl. His communication had been reduced to mostly grunts, other monosyllabic sounds, and pointing.

Three days prior to his death, he was standing with Sandi,

181

a certified nurse practitioner (CNP), just looking up at the ceiling. When Sandi asked him what he was looking at, in a voice clear and audible, Carl replied, "I can see the light, but I can't get in it." Here was a man who had not spoken an intelligible word for over a year responding as though there was nothing wrong with his cognitive processing or his ability to speak. He never spoke another word.

I spent the last day of his life with him. When I arrived shortly after lunch on Friday, his eyes had closed for the last time although he was still conscious. He seemed to recognize my voice because his head moved in my direction as I spoke to him. I placed cool, moist cloths on his forehead, Vaseline on his lips, and held his hands while the nurses put morphine sublingual tablets under his tongue.

I talked with him about the good times we'd had, about all the fish we'd caught and the great vegetables he'd grown in his gardens. I told him how much I loved him, how much he'd meant to me, and how much I appreciated him being there for me when I was a kid after my biological father had been so abusive. I told him how much I appreciated him being there for my mother and loving her all those years. I read to him from his favorite Scriptures—the Psalms and the Book of John. I told him Mother would be fine and that I would take good care of her.

He would squeeze my hand so tightly my rings would hurt my fingers. I would gently squeeze his hand back. I wanted him to know I was there with him. I think he knew I had come to say good-bye and to help him during these last moments. I told him Mother and I would join him one day, and when he was ready, it was okay for him to move toward the light. I suggested he not look back but stay focused on the light.

It was nearly midnight, and I had not left his side except for a couple of minutes for a bathroom break. Mother had sat near his bed most of the day, although she didn't seem to understand what was happening. Hours earlier, a CNA had put Mother into her bed, which was next to Carl's. As I stood holding Carl's hand, I looked over at her. She was sleeping soundly.

My mind was like a kaleidoscope. Memory fragments swirled around, overlapping one another—a scene from a cruise I took them on years ago when a belly dancer danced in front of Carl and Mother got jealous, one of the two of them holding up long stringers of fish, Mother driving their small boat with an outboard motor while Carl sat up front, Carl walking with me around his garden and showing me the new biddies that had hatched out and newly born rabbits, Carl coming to pick me up from the local skating rink in his taxi, all of us sitting in church together, Carl and his mother standing on a bank fishing side by side, Carl showing my friend Patty how to throw out her fishing line, Patty and her mom with Carl, Mother, and me on Fisherman's Wharf in San Francisco.

I had flashes of Carl being in the hospital after he had gotten his left arm caught in a plywood press. I was only eight years old, but I would ride my bicycle to visit him in the hospital every day after school, and I helped put clean dressings on his arm after he came home. I saw him, Mother, and Patty at all my graduations. I remembered Carl's generosity. Whatever he had, if someone else needed it, he would hasten to give it or take it to them.

I saw fish fries, cookouts, and Mother and him dancing. They loved to dance, and I loved watching them dance. Mother always led and Carl just danced along. I remembered crying as Mother and Carl would leave me at the airport when I would fly back to my home in California. He always asked if I needed any money. I would thank him and assure him I didn't. Only after I'd boarded the plane would I find twenty or forty dollars stuck in the side of my purse. Neither he nor I would ever mention it. He wanted to think he had gotten away with something, and I allowed him that joy.

My heart broke as I watched the replays of a lifetime with a stepfather who was about to board a plane that would take him to a place where I would not be able see him or to talk with him. Had I told him often enough how much I loved him? What else did I need to say? What else did I need to do? How would I tell Mother? Would she be able to understand?

Carl & Mildred just prior to Carl's death in 1998.
Both suffered from Alzheimer's Disease.

I was not aware I had begun to cry. A nurse quietly handed me some tissues and suggested I go home for a while and get something to eat. I leaned over and kissed him on the forehead. He squeezed my hand for the last time. I had hardly gotten into my house when the phone rang. The kind nurse who had handed me the tissues said that when I left, he left. I immediately drove back to the nursing home. On the drive there, my mental kaleidoscope continued. I knew he had waited for me to leave so he could leave. It was just too hard for him to leave while I stood holding his hand. Carl died in the early hours of Saturday, May 30, and was buried the following day—May 31, 1998. The sun was setting as I drove home.

*Sandra's mother with the pastor who
preached Carl's funeral, 5/31/1998.*

I remembered listening to many heartbroken clients as they described staying with their loved one in a hospital for days and only leaving the bedside long enough to go to the bathroom, and when they returned, their loved one was gone. Others recalled sitting at their loved one's side day and night. Then they happened to doze off for a few minutes, and when they awakened, their loved one would have also dozed off for the last time. Most reported feeling guilty for leaving their loved one's side or for dozing off, as if somehow had they remained close by and alert, they could have prevented her or his departure.

Remembering their stories comforted me as I thought about not being there at the very moment Carl left. I believed Carl, like those in the stories I'd heard, left when he needed to, perhaps when it was not so difficult for him or for me.

I told myself that the end happens the way it is supposed to. Just as with Carl, I think it is often too painful for people to leave while family members surround them. I also think it's important to give them permission to go. However, five years after Carl's death, when Pat, one of my dearest friends for more than twenty years, died from cancer, I didn't remember the things I had learned about death and people leaving when they needed to.

Sandra in a beautiful Saree with her husband when they lived in India.

My husband and I had just gotten back to the United States after living in India for nearly eighteen months and were visiting with Pat when she was diagnosed with cancer in both kidneys. Although she lived 2000 miles from me, we visited several times during the following year. We would often spend weeks together. She knew she only had about a year left, so we processed her impending death. We talked about what it might be like on the other side. We talked about how we might communicate with one another once she was gone. She said I would feel her presence and know she was near. She also said that sometimes I would know she was nearby because I would remember our times together as vividly as if she were present or I would say something she might say and know she was part of the conversation. We talked every day, sometimes several times a day, on the phone.

Several friends and I wrote Pat letters and cards telling her how much we loved her. I, along with about a hundred other folks, wrote stories describing memories of joyful times with her. We compiled these stories into a scrapbook complete with photos and gave it to her for Christmas 2002—the last time I saw her alive.

Sandra's dear friend Pat Russell the year before she died.

Since I had not seen Pat for nearly two months, I had planned to visit her on Valentine's Day. I had already purchased my airline ticket. However, unbeknown to me at the time I made my plans, my oldest sister, Nita, was coming to Tallahassee to visit us during that same time period. She asked if I would postpone my trip to see Pat by one week so I could be on the same flight as her return trip to help her with her bags and to accompany her should she fall or have some other mishap. I agreed to do this and changed my ticket to fly out with Nita on the morning of February 22. However, Nita fell on February 12, the morning she was to fly from San Jose to Tallahassee, and injured her back. Thus, she was not able to make the trip after all.

Pat and I decided I should keep my flight arrangements as planned. We continued to talk every day and even the night before my flight. Then, while I was loading my luggage into the car that Saturday morning, Pat's husband called to say she was gone. I was really upset. I couldn't understand why she wouldn't have waited just a few more hours. I flew out anyway because I wanted to be there for her funeral. Plus, she had requested her mother and I dress her in her burial clothes. I was still angry when the plane landed.

I was angry with Nita for asking me to change my plans to accommodate her. I was angry with myself for not listening to my own internal voice that whispered I needed to keep my plans to fly out on Valentine's Day. I was angry with Pat for not waiting until I got there so I could say good-bye in person. I was angry that the hospice team didn't know with greater accuracy when Pat's time would be up. After all, I had talked with several of them and asked them to let me know if they thought the end was near so I could change my ticket and fly there immediately.

I was angry, and the fear driving that anger was that Pat would die before I had a chance to see her one more time and tell her in person what a great friend she had been and how much I loved her. I blamed the *Law of the Harvest,* the *Law of Attraction,* and every other law I could blame. I knew with greater clarity than I wanted that our greatest fears will always materialize if we hang on to them long enough. I was reminded that fear has no life of its own. Fear is parasitic in nature, and as long as we allow it to hang on and drain energy from us, it not only lives but thrives and one day becomes the monster that consumes us. Another of my worst fears had once again come true. Pat was gone, and I was left feeling very, very sad.

Pat had only one brother. Since she had no sisters, I'd become the sister she'd never had. I felt I had let her down. I was the closest thing she had to a sister, and I was not by her side to support her on her journey. I cried and cried.

I had known Pat's mother, Agnes, for as long as I had known Pat. She was a very wise and spiritual woman. The morning we drove to the funeral home to dress Pat, I talked to her about my feelings. She invited me to reframe my experience, although she didn't use that word. Agnes told me Pat didn't want me to see her the way she was just before she died. She said Pat had lost about seventy pounds in the couple of months since I had seen her, and her hair had turned completely white although she was only sixty-one years old. Agnes attributed it to the chemotherapy.

Agnes assured me that Pat knew how much I loved her. She said Pat had related many things we'd talked about and said how helpful it had been for her to have someone who wasn't afraid to talk with her about her impending death. Agnes told me how much she admired my strength and how glad she was that I could be there for Pat at a level that extended beyond physical presence. She said, "Sandra, you *were* there with Pat. The bond of spiritual sisterhood you two shared was not limited by time and space."

Agnes went on to tell me that whether I had arrived on the fourteenth, the tenth, or the twentieth, Pat would still have gone before I arrived. She said Pat had already talked with her about how painful it would be to see me again, knowing it would for be the last time. She said Pat wanted to remember our last day together when we sat on the deck of her winter home in Florida, watching the sunset on the Gulf of Mexico. She told me Pat had said to her on more than one occasion, "Mama, it will be too hard for Sandra to see me like this."

Our conversation expanded the half hour drive to the funeral home. Pat's stepdaughter, Cathy, was waiting for us. The director took the three of us into the room where Pat's remains waited for us to dress her, put on her wig (Pat always wore wigs), make up her face, and polish her nails, the last things we could do for her. She would have hated the fact she could not do something in return for us.

The director walked the three of us to the table and pulled the sheet from her face. I quickly explained to him that we were in the wrong room. I was embarrassed that we were standing over the remains of an elderly woman we did not know. I then pulled the sheet back over the elderly woman's face and reiterated to the director who we were there to dress. The director looked directly at Pat's mother. Agnes put her arm around me and said quietly, "Now do you see why she left before you got here?"

I had not recognized my own dear friend. I knew her voice had grown weaker, but I could not have envisioned what I saw before me. I *did not* understand how she could have changed so much in just a few short weeks. What I *did* understand was that the words Agnes had said to me were true. Pat's funeral was February 25, 2003. It started to snow as we left her grave.

Pat visiting Sandra's mother at an Alzheimer's facility, 2002.

Mother died on June 26, just four months after Pat passed away. I was driving to work when my cell phone rang. I answered, and the woman on the other end identified herself and simply said, "I'm calling to let you know your mother has expired." The word "expired" stuck in my ear. My only association with that word was related to my car license plate and my driver's license.

Expired—the coldness hit me on that summer morning in Florida. Couldn't she have said, "I'm sorry to have to tell you, but your mother has passed away," or "I'm so sorry to inform you that your mother died early this morning." She could have said anything but *expired*. I thanked her for calling and assured her I would be right there. My sister Wanda worked at the psychiatric hospital on the same campus where I worked in the outpatient clinic. Since I was nearly there, I drove to my office, informed the staff my mother had passed away, and then went to the psychiatric hospital and waited the few minutes until Wanda arrived. The moment she saw me, she said, "What's wrong?" In a much kinder way than I had received the news, I told her Mother had passed away. We cried together, and then she followed me as I drove to the nursing home.

I tried to reach my husband. The phone rang and rang, but there was no answer. I later learned the phone in that part of our house had been unplugged. I called our next-door neighbor to go over and ask my husband to call me on my cell phone. I knew it was only 5:00 in California, but I had to talk with my friend Patty. So I picked up my cell phone.

Friends can call friends at five o'clock in the morning when their mothers die. My mother had been like a second mother to Patty. Patty was another daughter to my mother. Patty, like my friend Pat, didn't have a sister. She didn't even have a brother. Consequently, just as I had been to Pat, I was and still am the sister Patty never had. I completely understood why she would not be able to come for the funeral. She had two kids in summer school and was caring for her own elderly mother. We talked and agreed to get together later. It was comforting just knowing she was there grieving with me.

I had visited with Mother the previous Sunday afternoon. Looking back, I saw that all the signs were in place, alerting me something had changed, but once again, I was in denial and overlooked them. For a long time prior to her death, Mother had also been in the final stage of Alzheimer's disease and had not talked for a long time. I always asked her how she was and never got so much as a grunt. She had not known who I was for years. Many times, before she lost the ability to speak, she would ask me if I thought Sandra was coming to visit her.

Yet that Sunday afternoon, when I came into her room and asked her how she was doing, she shocked me by saying, "I'm feeling some better." That Sunday she was sitting up in her bed, and I fed her ice cream. I asked her if she knew who I was, and she smiled as though I was teasing and said, "Why sure. You're Sandra." I was thrilled she was doing so well. Our visit was short because I had a church commitment. When I started to leave, I kissed her and told her I loved her. She grinned and said, "You do?" We both laughed, and she said, "I love you too." Those were our last words.

I called all three of my sisters the following day to let them know of Mother's remarkable improvement. Not one of us connected the dots.

As soon as I got the ice-coated phone call telling me she had *expired*, it all started to make sense to me. Why hadn't I realized the same thing was happening with her that had happened with Carl? How could I have just assumed she was "remarkably better?" I knew enough about dementia to know that wasn't possible. Something else had to be at play. Yet I somehow accepted the impossible as possible and explained it that way to myself and to my sisters.

Why hadn't I at least suspected it was the beginning of the end? If I had, I would certainly have stayed with her rather than attend the function at church. No, I don't think I could have prevented or even postponed her leaving, but I could have enjoyed a much longer visit with her. If I had connected enough dots to realize that visit was significantly different than the previous hundred visits, I would not have left until she did.

How had I explained in my own head her ability to speak and to know who I was? I knew of other stories where the light got brighter just before it went out, just as a candle flickers its brightest before it dims for the last time. How could I not have seen it for what it was?

The only time she had spoken a full sentence in years had been in February, four months prior to her death. She was coming out from under anesthesia from her leg being amputated, and she said, "Where's my leg?" I'd nearly fainted. She had not said anything else until that infamous Sunday except for moaning sounds, communicating the pain she apparently felt.

Ever since her leg had been amputated and she had appeared to be in so much pain, we as a family, had prayed God would be merciful and allow her to be free of her physical body. We prayed he would allow her to return home to him. So when our prayers were being answered, why had I not seen and understood it? Instead I danced the dance of denial with my mother for the last time.

Sandra with her mother when Sandra was about four years old.

I presented the eulogy at her funeral. I talked about the dash in her life. The dash between the time we are born and the time we die is our life. My mother's dash existed between 11/3/1913—6/26/2003.

Sandra's mother (Mildred), 1956

I knew her better than anyone else knew her. I wanted her great-grandchildren and others who missed the chance to know her before the alcoholism and Alzheimer's disease claimed her to know this amazing, incredible human being.

I wanted them to know of the special relationship she had with the earth. She loved the earth and loved being on the earth. She had a reciprocal love relationship with all of God's creations. She loved every plant and every animal, and they loved her in return. She would stick a leaf in a can of dirt, and it would grow into a beautiful plant and bloom as though seeking her attention and approval.

She loved to pick blackberries, blueberries, and every other kind of fruits and vegetables, and they loved her. It seemed they would eagerly drop from their bushes and trees into her pail, rejoicing she'd chosen them for canning or baking, some-how knowing she would magnify their brilliance and flavor.

She loved to fish and fish loved her. She always caught a stringer full when no one else could get as much as a nibble. It was as though they too knew she would prepare them with the utmost care and cook them to perfection, allowing them to do what they'd been created to do. Thus, they willingly grabbed her bait and hung on until they were safely out of the water.

Sandra's mother showing off her catch of the day.

Sandra's mother and biological father
(Pat Haymon). What a catch!

She taught me to never use the word *can't*. That was a "four-letter word." Her motto was, "Where there is a will, there is a way. And, if you look long enough and work hard enough, you will find the way."

She expanded that motto to include not allowing me to claim anything was too *hard* for me. *Hard* was another "four-letter word" I was not allowed to use. Even now, I don't stop to consider the level of difficulty of any project I'm called to do. I just start figuring out *how* I'm going to get it done.

In her eulogy, I shared the things she had taught me that helped me keep my life simple. She taught me to share. No matter what she had, she always shared. Sometimes people have too much to share. They're afraid to have others visit or stay with them because they're afraid their stuff will get messed up. We never had too much to share. The more we shared the more we had to share.

She taught me to be honest. Her rules were simple. She would say, "If it's not yours, don't touch it."

She taught me not to procrastinate. She said, "You'll never have more time than you have now. So just go ahead and get it done." It never mattered what "it" was.

She also taught me to do my best at whatever I did. She believed if you didn't have time to do it right, you surely would not have time to do it over.

She taught me to live within my means. That rule was simple also. If you can't afford to pay cash for it, you can't afford it. Buying on credit was not an option.

She taught me to be frugal. She'd adopted an old pioneer motto from her own parents, which she lived by and expected us to live by: "Use it up. Wear it out. Make it do. Or do without." It seems she found a use for everything.

Sandra's maternal grandparents, Laura Anna
Trawick and Daniel Nathan Reeder, at their
fiftieth wedding anniversary, 1951.

She taught me to be thankful. She understood the importance of having an attitude of gratitude. She'd say, "Why do
you think the Lord would bless you with more if you are not
thankful for what you already have?" I am richly blessed and
very thankful for everything I'm blessed with.

She also taught me to take care of the things I've been
blessed with. She'd say, "Getting something is only half of it.
Taking care of it is the other half."

She taught me the value of work. Very early in life, I
learned from her that I could have anything I wanted if I was
willing to work hard enough and long enough for it. That lesson also helped me learn to prioritize how I spend my time,
energy, and resources.

She taught me to respect other people and other people's
stuff. She said, "If you can't say something good about people,
then don't say anything at all." To this day, I say "Ma'am" and
"Sir" to those older than me, to those in authority, and even
younger folks in positions worthy of respect. I don't walk on

my neighbor's grass, litter, or throw gum on the ground where someone else might step on it.

She also taught me not to whine. I have little tolerance for whiners.

I think practicing my mother's simple lessons about life not only enables me to keep my life simple, it makes my life easier. I've understood the *Law of Attraction* since I was a child. Although I never heard it called that until a few years ago, I clearly understood that the way you treat others is the way you'll be treated, and if you think about negative things, negative things will come into your life. I was glad Mother taught me to think about positive things and to keep my mind focused on the things I wanted.

I talked about her love of life, her Irish temper, and her great faith. I did not talk about her alcoholism. She had out-lived that, and besides, I didn't feel qualified to talk about something I knew only from an outsider's point of view. I can only hope in my own eulogy someone will be able to talk about the valuable lessons I have taught, the risks I have taken, and the joys I have known.

We all have imperfections and Mother was no exception. I think about her when I think about the piece of marble from which Michelangelo carved his famous statue of David. That particular marble stone was so flawed that many other artists had refused to even consider using it. Michelangelo was able to see beyond the flaws and create a masterpiece from a very flawed stone.

Mother was indeed a masterpiece. We buried her on June 28, 2003. It started to rain as we left her grave. I'm sure the heavens were crying, sad that she would no longer be here to help take care of the earth.

Since my mother was Irish, I want to share this Irish Blessing with you. The author is unknown to me.

Sandra's mother, June 14, 1996. Mildred was
seventy-three years old and still very lovely!

Irish Blessings

I wish for you not a path devoid of clouds,
nor life on a bed of roses,
not that you might never need regret,
nor that you should never feel pain.

No, that is not my wish for you.

My wish for you is:
That you might be brave in times of trial,
when others lay crosses upon your shoulders,
When mountains must be climbed,
and chasms are to be crossed;
when hope scarce can shine through.

That every gift God gave you might grow along with you,
And let you give the gift of joy to all who care for you.

That you may always have a friend who is worth that name,
Whom you can trust,
and who helps you in times of sadness,
Who will defy the storms of daily life by your side.

One more wish I have for you:
That in every hour of joy and pain you may feel God close
to you.
This is my wish for you and all who care for you.
This is my hope for you now and forever.

SECTION FOUR:
MAKING CHOICES AND DECISIONS

CAREGIVING   CAREGIVING

MEDICAL CHOICES AND ADVANCE DIRECTIVES

LIVING ARRANGEMENTS

ASSISTANCE PROGRAMS

MEDICAL CHOICES AND
ADVANCE DIRECTIVES

(State laws differ from state to state. Therefore, I
highly recommend you go to the World Wide Web
and verify documents specific to your state. This
information is not intended to be legal advice.)

What you don't know can hurt you!

*I: Dr. Haymon, you mentioned there are many end-of-life medical
decisions that we may have to make and advance medical directives we'll need to ensure our wishes are carried out. Will you tell
us more about our choices and the necessary directives?*
H: First of all, I want to state clearly that I am not a medical doctor, and I am not an attorney. I am a psychologist.
So the information I share with you is based on my personal
experience and on my own personal grasp of these medical
decisions.

It is interesting to note that among other "firsts" for baby
boomers, we are the first generation to be faced with so many
medical choices. Most of the heart-wrenching decisions we
have to make have to do with hospitalization, CPR, and feeding tubes. These are all extremely difficult decisions, and they
cause spiritual, emotional, and moral struggles for most of us.

My intent here is not to persuade individuals one way or
another. These are very personal decisions that must be made

on an individual basis. The only point I want to make is that we do have choices. However, we only have choices if we make these decisions *in advance.*

I: Just for clarification, what is an advance directive?
H: It is a legal document that allows individuals to make their own medical decisions while they are competent to make them. One of the first choices I want to talk about is CPR.

I: I didn't even know we had a choice about CPR.
H: Neither did I, nor did I know administering CPR to frail, elderly patients is often actually harmful to them.

Cardiopulmonary Resuscitation and DNR Orders

I: Tell us about CPR.
H: CPR is the acronym for cardiopulmonary resuscitation. For the past fifty years standard CPR procedures consisted of chest compressions with artificial respiration. However, in March 2008 the American Heart Association, along with the European Resuscitation Council, approved the effectiveness of chest compressions without artificial respiration for adult victims of cardiac arrest. There is evidence that some form of CPR was used even thousands of years ago. Some believe the Hebrew prophet Elisha performed CPR in Old Testament times, as recorded in the II Books of Kings (4:34) when a dead child returned to life after Elisha warmed the child's body and "put his mouth upon his mouth."

Dr. H.R. Silvester, developed "The Silvester Method" of artificial respiration in the nineteenth century. His method of helping individuals resume breathing entailed laying persons on their backs, raising their arms above their heads to facilitate inhalation, and then pressing against their chests sixteen times per minute to aid exhalation.

Fast forward to the early 1900s when a Danish colonel, Holger-Neilson, described another method of artificial respiration. His technique was basically the same as the Silvester Method, except individuals were laid face down, head to the side, and then the person administering the technique would lift the individual's arms and press on their backs. This technique of trying to get individuals to resume breathing was utilized well into the mid 1950s until Dr. Peter Safar, together with Dr. James Elam, rediscovered the mouth-to-mouth technique of forcing air into the airway.

Safar and Elam are credited with pioneering modern cardiopulmonary resuscitation. They also convinced a Norwegian doll manufacturing company to design and manufacture mannequins to be used in CPR training. However, this modern procedure of tilting the head, lifting the chin, and blowing air into the victim's mouth was not promoted in the U.S. until the early 1970s.

CPR entails establishing an effective airway so the person can breathe as well as maintain cardiac output, which may require the assistance of ventilators and cardiac massage. CPR was never intended to be used in cases of end stage illnesses, such as advanced heart disease, lung cancer, kidney failure, or multiple medical problems where death was expected. Research suggests resuscitation in those cases might represent violation of a person's right to die with dignity. Rather, CPR was developed as a means of preventing sudden, unexpected death in cases such as drowning, electrical shock, or cardiac arrest.

The brain normally sustains damage after the flow of blood has been stopped for about four minutes and suffers irreversible damage after seven minutes. Consequently, CPR is usually only effective if successfully performed within six to seven minutes after the blood ceases to flow to the brain. There is only about a 5–10% survival rate among the general population, with very few complete recoveries without serious complications. That percentage drops drastically, to about 2%, for elderly patients.

The techniques used in CPR are extremely aggressive and may result in painful and harmful injuries, especially to frail, elderly people. Ribs may be bruised or broken or a lung might be punctured, and brain damage could occur due to lack of oxygen for too long a time.

In addition to all that, if the person is transferred to an emergency room, treatment usually becomes even more aggressive. Unless individuals have documents prohibiting the use of artificial life support, they could receive treatment that includes electrical shock to the heart or injections of medications intended to stimulate the heart, and they could be placed on mechanical respirators, even though they might not have wanted that.

I: I really had no idea.

H: I think most people have no idea of the complications associated with CPR. Frail, elderly patients usually never recover from the complications of cardiopulmonary resuscitation. Using CPR on those patients can be emotionally and physically traumatic for them, plus it significantly reduces the possibility of them dying a normal and peaceful death. Even when physicians are on duty around the clock with the most advanced cardiac life support (ACLS) equipment and medications, frail, elderly patients rarely survive to be discharged from the hospital.

Those who do survive almost always have a *Do Not Resuscitate (DNR)* order placed in their medical records afterward. Neither they nor their families feel the trauma and complications associated with CPR are worth the very slim chance they will survive. They also recognize the reality that quality of life is even further diminished after receiving CPR. Thus, they choose not to go through that again.

CPR is a choice. However, for frail, elderly individuals, it may not be the best choice, and it is only a choice as long as that decision is made ahead of time.

Please remember, neither paramedics, nor nurses, nor physicians, will make this decision for you, no matter how seriously ill the patient is. So for those who decide they would rather not go through the trauma and risks of CPR, they must have a *Do Not Resuscitate (DNR)* order placed in their medical records. Sometimes this is also called a No Code, No CPR, or DNRO (Do Not Resuscitate Order).

Some facilities prefer using a *Do Not Attempt Resuscitation (DNAR)* order to avoid or lessen the implication of success that might be construed from a simple DNR. Patients who have a DNR order have implied they also want a *Do Not Intubate (DNI)* order, since CPR requires establishing an airway for effective breathing. They may also designate a person to speak on their behalf in the event they are unable to speak for themselves. In this case, they need to fill out and sign a *Durable Power of Attorney for Healthcare* (DPOAHc).

Some states have standard forms. In other states, a physician has to actually write an order. The bottom line is that if you don't want to go through the trauma of CPR, there has to be an advance directive in your medical records that prohibits CPR from being administered. This document not only needs to be in your medical records, but your emergency contact person also needs to have a copy of it.

I: As we conclude our discussion on CPR, you have told us how to avoid having CPR and heroic measures. What if you do want heroic measures? Do you have to fill out advance directives?

H: Normally not. However, there is a Physician Orders for Life-Sustaining Treatment (POLST) document now being used extensively in Oregon. Even without advance directives or a POLST, the medical community will ensure that every possible effort is made to keep the person alive unless she/he has signed directives to the contrary.

Intubation and DNI Orders

I: Dr. Haymon, you mentioned a DNI order. DNI is a term I have not heard before.

H: Do Not Intubate (DNI) orders are not used as frequently as DNR orders. The medical term intubation most often refers to tracheal intubation (TI) but may also refer to endoscopic procedures. Tracheal intubation is used when a flexible plastic tube is placed into a person's trachea to provide a means of mechanical ventilation and to protect their airway. The most common intubation is orotracheal intubation. This procedure is performed using a laryngoscope.

An endotracheal tube is passed through the mouth, the larynx, and vocal cords into the trachea. A bulb is then inflated near the distal tip of the tube to help secure it in place and to protect the person's airway from secretions, blood, or vomit. Another type of intubation is nasotracheal intubation. This procedure entails passing a tube through the nose rather than the mouth, then through the larynx, vocal cords, and into the trachea.

DNI orders are sometimes chosen by patients with chronic, progressive lung diseases, who do not want a ventilator even if the machine could possibly save their lives. Individuals whose wishes do not include artificial life-sustaining procedures and equipment (where there is no reasonable probability of a meaningful quality of life) would need to complete a Living Will Declaration.

Emergency Medical Information Kit

I also learned during my turn that many paramedics are trained to look on the refrigerator door for emergency medical information. That just made common sense to me. So, over twelve years ago I created *The Medical Emergency Information Kit,* which I included in my last book. It is a clear plastic envelope with a magnet on the back of it and includes a card for basic emergency information as well as a Living Will Declaration, a Durable Power of Attorney, a Consent to Withhold CPR, a Health Care Surrogate Designation, a Do Not Hospitalize Order, and a Medical Information Release form. These advance directives have been standardized to be used in states that recognize advance medical directives, and most states do. The magnet on the back allows it to stick to the refrigerator door so that emergency information is readily available. The *Medical Emergency Information Kit,* which includes the above Advance Medical Directives, may be ordered online at www.babyboomerssandwich.com.

I: That is a great idea! I know my mother has filled out some forms with her specific requests written out. She has probably even filled out a Living Will, but her documents are in an old trunk, under three old quilts at the foot of her bed where paramedics would never find them.

H: In reality, it doesn't matter what documents your mother has filled out. If nobody has access to them and they are not part of her medical records, technically, she doesn't have any documents. I am sure you are aware of the recent landmark case involving Terri Schiavo, who was only 26 years old when she experienced respiratory and cardiac arrest at her home. She suffered brain damage, which led to fifteen years of institutionalization and a diagnosis of persistent vegetative state (PVS).

She had been sustained by artificial feeding for more than fifteen years when the feeding tube was removed by court order, following over seven years of legal battles between her husband and her parents. This dispute involved politicians, as well as pro-life and disability-rights advocacy groups. The questions raised in these battles received extensive national, as well as international, media coverage. Sadly enough, even after the feeding tube was removed, it took nearly two weeks for the dying process to complete. Terri was pronounced dead on March 31, 2005.

I would not attempt to try to address the pain felt by her husband, parents, and other family members and friends. I only use this as an example of the possible complications that could occur if individuals have not completed appropriate advanced medical directives and made them available to medical professionals involved in their care.

Ironically, I had written about the importance of having necessary medical directives in *My Turn*, which included the *Emergency Information Kit* years before these issues ever became headline news. As I stated in 1996, I believe everyone needs to have her/his emergency medical information on her/his refrigerator door. It's also a good idea, if you are responsible for an elderly loved one, to get copies of emergency medical information and keep those with you. For months, I carried every document I thought I would need for my parents in the glove compartment of my car because I never knew when I would have to meet paramedics at an emergency room. If your parents are living alone, you might insist they give a copy of their emergency information to their next-door neighbor, as well as have it on their refrigerator door. The bottom line is that we want to ensure that no matter what a person's wishes are, those wishes will be carried out.

Hospitalization and DNH Orders

I: Dr. Haymon, can we now talk about the choices we have regarding hospitalization of elderly individuals? Why wouldn't an elderly person want to be hospitalized?
H: I suppose I was naïve, but honestly, at the time, I didn't know we had a choice as to whether my parents would be hospitalized. I had assumed, regardless of their condition and

no matter what the prognosis for recovery, they would go to a hospital. However, during my turn, I learned that a *Do Not Hospitalize Order (DNH)* actually protects individuals from automatically being hospitalized without first carefully considering their state of health. I also learned there are certain traumas and risks associated with hospitalization.

Infections one might contract in a hospital are more resistant to antibiotics and can be much more difficult to treat than infections we might get at home. For example, methicillin-resistant *Staphylococcus aureus* (MRSA) is rapidly spreading worldwide, with millions already infected. This drug-resistant bug is spread by contact with infected people and/or contaminated objects. Persons with weak immune systems and living in nursing homes, hospitals, or other healthcare centers are most vulnerable. It can cause infections in various parts of the body, which may be serious, and some can be life threatening. MRSA kills more people in the United States each year than HIV and AIDS.

My own mother contracted MRSA when she went to a wound care center for debridement of dead tissue in her big toe. She also had peripheral artery disease (PAD), which is a painful and dangerous disease caused by blockage when the arteries are clogged with plaque. Clogged arteries slow the supply of blood to the legs. Consequently, it was difficult for the antibiotics to reach her foot. The combination of PAD plus MRSA resulted in the amputation of Mother's right leg. That was another extremely painful and heart-wrenching decision I had to make for my mother.

In addition to being vulnerable to possible infections, many elderly people become confused when they go to hospitals or other unfamiliar environments. When hospitalized, they are surrounded by nurses, orderlies, aides, and other strangers. This is not only confusing for them, but they often become fearful, anxious, and combative. This is especially true for demented patients who may already be disorientated. If they become agitated and combative, there is a greater likelihood that they will be restrained or sedated.

When an individual is hospitalized, there is also an increased possibility of receiving more aggressive treatment, which might include diagnostic testing the person might not have wanted. Diagnostic tests are often invasive and may be frightening and painful to elderly people. So when you know you wouldn't treat any condition these tests might reveal, it just seems kinder not to put them through the trauma.

Many patients are able to receive appropriate pain control and treatment in their own familiar environment, whether in their own homes, nursing homes, or other care facilities. This would prevent the trauma of hospitalization. So individuals who prefer treatment in their own homes or care facility will need to fill out a Do Not Hospitalize Order (DNH). This will eliminate unnecessary hospitalizations yet allow patients to be hospitalized after they, or the person who has been given authority to make medical decisions for them, have talked with the attending physician, and hospitalization is deemed to be absolutely necessary. Then and only then are they admitted to a hospital. Also, many nursing homes and other long-term care facilities now allow a *Do Not Transfer (DNT)* order, which ensures that the individual's wish not to be transferred to an acute care hospital is honored.

Feeding Tubes and Living Wills

I: Dr. Haymon, there is a lot of controversy about feeding tubes. Are there special considerations we should take into account when making a decision regarding feeding tubes where the elderly are concerned?

H: This is another heart-wrenching decision that must be made on an individual basis. Once again, I am not trying to persuade individuals one way or the other, but as you know, I am a strong proponent of making informed decisions. Therefore, it might be helpful to review the different types of feeding tubes and discuss the pros and cons of this most difficult decision, especially as it relates to the elderly. There is no question that thousands of patients' lives have been prolonged with artificial feeding, especially younger, healthier patients. However, once placed on artificial feeding, frail, elderly people almost never regain the ability to take in food and water by mouth. In the United States today, there are approximately three million people who depend on the nation's 16,000 nursing homes to provide life-saving care at some point during any given year. The sad part is that thousands of these individuals are unable to make any purposeful response to their surroundings, yet they are maintained on feeding tubes for years, much like Terri Schiavo.

I: You say there are different types?

H: Yes, there are several ways to provide nutrition and medications artificially. As I mentioned earlier, one way is through nasogastric tubes. In this procedure, the tube is inserted into the person's nose, down through the esophagus, and into the stomach. Another way is through gastrostomy tubes, which are surgically inserted into the stomach wall. With both the nasogastric and the gastrostomy tubes, fluids can either be poured in or pumped in mechanically. The third means, and probably the one most familiar, is commonly referred to as an IV, technically known as artificial intravenous hydration. This method enables individuals to receive nutrition and medicines through a needle inserted into a vein. Just as with CPR, there are certain risks associated with artificially feeding frail, elderly patients, no matter which procedure is used.

I: What are some of those risks?

H: Should the tube become displaced or if regurgitated fluid enters the lungs, there is the risk of the person developing pneumonia. Also, ulcers and infections may result from certain feeding tubes. Agitated patients may have to be sedated or restrained in order to keep them from removing the tubes. Immobility also causes problems for the elderly, including bedsores and joint contractures.

It is also common for patients on artificial feeding to get diarrhea, which may further increase the likelihood of bedsores. Sadly, patients on feeding tubes often become more isolated, simply because there is less need for contact with caregivers. When individuals can still take in food and water by mouth, even if they have to be hand fed, there is interaction with other people at least three times a day during feedings. That is not the case with tube feeding. This isolation may be difficult for some elderly individuals to tolerate. Many of them are already extremely anxious and fearful.

Many don't even know where they are. This is especially true for patients suffering from dementia. Besides these obvious risks, there is another factor that needs to be considered for patients who are coherent. Even though these patients are being fed artificially, they may perceive they are being allowed to starve because they are not offered food. Many have also reported that the smell of food causes them to experience severe hunger, which is agonizing.

I: I have heard withholding or withdrawing artificial feeding causes a painful death.
H: Pain control is a real concern; however, withholding artificial feeding results in dehydration before starvation. Consequently, pain and certain discomforts associated with starvation would not be experienced.

Artificial hydration is accomplished by giving the patient fluids intravenously. In the past, dehydration was thought to cause a painful death. However, current research purports that gradual dehydration is not painful but actually diminishes the patient's level of awareness about her/his condition.

Additional research indicates there is a release of natural, pain-relieving chemicals as the body dehydrates. Consequently, pain the patient may be feeling from other illnesses, like cancer, actually might be lessened. Decreased awareness, along with decreased pain, would allow the person to slip into death naturally and without unnecessary discomfort.

Intravenous hydration at the end of life could, in reality, prolong the dying process rather than prolong the person's life. Patients who are under hospice care are not normally given artificial hydration when they have begun the dying process or when they are close to death. However, pain secondary to cancer or other end-stage illnesses would still be treated.

The primary physical sensation reported during dehydration is dry mouth. This sensation is more effectively treated with good oral care rather than with IV fluids.

I: This is such a difficult topic, but I am also wondering if there are any other benefits besides the natural, pain-relieving chemicals associated with dehydration?

H: Yes. Without feeding tubes, frail, elderly patients may have the opportunity to die a more peaceful death, because as the person dehydrates, there is less fluid in the throat and lungs. Consequently, there would be less need for suctioning and less congestion, which might make it easier for them to breathe. Since fluids would not be continually pumped in, the patient would urinate less frequently and be less disposed to diarrhea, which might lessen the risk of bedsores.

I: Even with all of this information, however, there are still those who believe we should do absolutely everything we can—any heroic measure to keep people alive.

H: You're right. There are two sides to this coin. As with all controversial issues, there are always different ways of looking

at the same question. Often these perspectives are diametri-
cally opposed. On one side of the coin, there is the contention
that food and water are basic human rights, and no matter
what the chances of recovery are, everything possible should
be done to prolong life.

On the other side of this same coin is the contention that
artificially feeding a person does not prolong life but in fact
prolongs the dying process and is much like using a respirator to force air into the lungs of the patient. Many view the
inability to take in fluids by mouth as a terminal medical condition. Their conviction is that withholding artificial feeding
is to allow a natural death to occur.

*I: Is there a general feeling or agreement among members of the
medical community regarding feeding tubes?*
H: Medical evidence is quite clear that dehydration in the
end-stage of any terminal illness is a very compassionate and
natural way to die.

I: Is our choice a limited yes or no regarding feeding tubes?
H: Not always. In many states, people actually have several
choices. They may choose to introduce a feeding tube for an
indefinite period of time once the patient can no longer take
in fluids by mouth. They may also choose artificial feeding
on a time-limited basis, or individuals may make conscious
choices not to introduce artificial feeding at all. I encourage
individuals to check with their doctors and find out what
choices their state permits. I also recommend that people talk
with their primary care physician to find out how she/he feels
about feeding tubes.

Some physicians refuse to withhold feeding tubes. If the
person's choice is not to introduce a feeding tube but the doctor is of an entirely different opinion, then they will probably
need to change doctors and find a physician who honors the
patient's wishes regardless of the doctor's personal opinion.

It also seems emotionally more difficult for some family members and physicians to withdraw a feeding tube rather than to withhold it in the beginning. Once the tube is in place, it is often very difficult to make the decision to remove it. In fact, many medical doctors are reluctant to withdraw a tube once it has been introduced. Even when it was introduced on a time-limited basis, they are still reluctant to remove it. We can certainly understand why. Not only does this have to do with moral issues, there may be some legal implications in this instance. It is most important that you discuss options with medical professionals then encourage your loved ones to make decisions for themselves in advance.

Hospice and Comfort Measures Only

I: Dr. Haymon, where does the hospice approach fit in with these end-of-life medical decisions?
H: Hospice care is an approach to care that focuses on preserving the dignity of terminally ill patients. It specifies a general philosophy of care rather than a particular place or facility. Thus, the hospice approach may be provided to individuals whether in their own homes, a hospital, a nursing home, or other facility. Hospice focuses on the patient's quality of life when she/he is faced with a life-limiting illness or disease and was designed primarily for end-stage cancer patients. Hospice care offers a holistic approach and treats the whole person rather than just treating the illness or disease. The primary goal is to keep patients as comfortable as possible. This includes relieving physical pain and/or emotional and spiritual suffering. Consequently, it is a specialized form of palliative rather than curative care. Hospice care does not hasten or prolong the dying process.

At this time, it might be helpful to review the three primary but distinct goals of medical treatment. These goals are cure, stabilization, and comfort. When a cure is the goal, the prescribed treatment is intended to cure the pathology, the illness. With the goal of stabilization, the intent of medical treatment is to stabilize the pathology. When comfort is the goal, it is often understood there is no cure and no means of stabilization. Therefore, the goal is to keep the person comfortable and to help prepare her/him for a natural and dignified death. This last goal is the goal of hospice programs. This is commonly referred to as a comfort measures only approach. The emphasis of this approach is on management of pain and other symptoms and on quality of life rather than length of life. If the person opts for this approach, it does not mean we stop treating or caring for her/him. It simply means we allow her/him to die naturally instead of prolonging the dying process.

The hospice approach offers care provided by an interdisciplinary team usually comprised of physicians, nurses and nursing assistants, a pharmacist, a psychologist, a social worker, a nutritionist, a physical therapist, a chaplain, and volunteers. Therefore, hospice is able to address the needs of the family as well as care for the patient. Hospice teams offer an invaluable service. Workers and volunteers assist with physically taking care of the patient—bathing, dressing, and giving medicines. They also assist the family with transportation, respite, and handling insurance forms, among many other things. Hospice teams are often available twenty-four hours a day, seven days a week, for support, consultation, and visits.

For individuals who wish to remain in a nursing home or other care facility, the hospice team may become an adjunct to the staff, advising, teaching, observing, and providing extra equipment. Many communities provide in-patient hospice facilities, which incorporate the entire hospice philosophy into a unique setting with specially trained staff.

I: What kind of care would be offered in a hospice setting?

H: Often comfort measures include but are not limited to medications to reduce pain or fever, oxygen to make breathing easier, routine nursing care, such as keeping the patient clean and dry, and providing emotional and spiritual support as patients face coming to terms with the end of their lives.

I: Is medical treatment a choice or an option?
H: Certain medical treatments are optional. Radiation and chemotherapy would not be administered in an effort to cure but might be used to relieve pain. Antibiotics would also be used to control infection but not in an attempt to cure. Since cure and stabilization are normally ruled out prior to opting for comfort measures only, there would be no need for diagnostic testing. Therefore, the person would be protected from unnecessary, painful, or invasive procedures. Feeding tubes would not be started. Intravenous lines would be used to administer pain medication but not as a means of prolonging the dying process. Surgical procedures would be performed only if necessary to enhance the person's comfort.

I: Is there an advance directive for this choice?
H: Individuals for whom a cure is not realistically possible and those who desire a high quality of life for their remaining time may decide on the *comfort measures only* (hospice care) approach. In these cases, the patient or person responsible for making medical decisions would need to discuss this option with the attending physician. A comfort measures only order would then be placed in the patient's medical records.

I: So is palliative care different from hospice care?
H: Palliative care is any form of medical care that focuses on reducing the symptoms of a disease, preventing and relieving suffering, and on improving the quality of life for patients diagnosed with complex and serious illnesses. However, unlike hospice care, patients are not necessarily in the end-stage of their illnesses. Therefore, palliative care may be offered in con-

junction with curative and other types of medical treatment, although the goal of palliative care is not to provide a cure.

Living Will Declarations

I: Dr. Haymon, would you talk with us about living wills?
H: Most states have now passed a *Natural Death Act.* Some states refer to this as a *HealthCare Decisions Act,* which provides for living will declarations. In most states, this document must be prepared while the person is competent, and the person's signature has to be witnessed. As I mentioned earlier, most living wills only address the issue of artificial life support, so individuals who do not want to be placed on artificial life support when there is no hope of them recovering might consider a living will. However, I want to remind people that a living will is not effective until it's delivered to their healthcare provider.

I: You say the primary purpose of living wills is to prohibit the use of artificial life support, but could the person include other wishes in this document?
H: Yes. There are a number of requests individuals might include in their living wills. They might want to name a person to carry out their wishes should they become unable to do so. Another point about living wills—they don't necessarily prohibit the use of all life-prolonging procedures. Individuals may want to specify particular procedures to be used, when those procedures are to be withheld, and when they're to be withdrawn. They might also want to address other issues should they become terminally ill. For example, what role will their religious preferences play in decisions related to their care? Those wishes could be included in a living will.

I: What if a person fills out a living will and then later changes her or his mind?
H: It's important to make a note of everyone to whom you've

given a copy of your living will, so if you should change your mind and want to amend or revoke it, you can recover all copies.

I: Are most living wills fairly straightforward?

H: Usually they are; however, as with most legal documents, there can be problems with living wills. So if you have any reason for concern, you should seek advice from an attorney. For example, living wills must be understood by the patient as well as the physician.

Some common questions in regard to a living will are: What constitutes the definition of the term "artificial"? What constitutes a terminal condition? What defines a life-prolonging procedure? Who determines when there's no hope of recovery? The point here is that due to the possibility of misinterpretation, it is extremely important that living wills be explicit and leave as little room as possible for subjective interpretation.

I: Dr. Haymon, what if individuals have a living will and then become unable to make decisions for themselves, and their family members believe differently? Can family members override a living will?

H: Not normally, except under certain circumstances, as may be set forth by state law. The whole purpose of making these decisions for yourself in advance is to ensure your wishes, and not your family's wishes, are carried out.

I: You said earlier that individuals may change their living wills. What if they simply don't want them anymore?

H: People who are competent may revoke their living wills in a number of ways. They may physically destroy their living will by tearing it up. They just need to be sure they destroy all copies. They may also orally state their intent to revoke their living will in the presence of witnesses. This situation might occur while they're in the hospital. Perhaps they don't have their living will with them, but at the last minute, they say, "No, no, I changed my mind." If they're competent when they say that and there are a couple of witnesses, their living will is revoked at that time.

Another way is to write "revoked" on the face of their living will and sign and date it. However, all copies need to be treated the same way. They may also write their intentions to revoke their living will, date and sign the form, and get a couple of people to witness their signature. Living wills are also revoked by means of a subsequently executed living will that materially differs from the preceding one. If you write out a living will today and later decide you want to make significant changes to it, then the new living will takes precedence over the old one.

Healthcare Surrogate

I: Dr. Haymon, I'm not familiar with the term healthcare surrogate.
H: Sometimes there are no advance directives, and the individual becomes incompetent. As with other legal documents, state laws may differ. However, in many states, competent individuals may name a *healthcare surrogate* to make medical decisions for them should they become incapable of making their own informed decisions. Normally this document must be in writing and signed by two witnesses. In many states, only one witness may be the spouse or a blood relative. Customarily, the named surrogate may not be one of the witnesses.

I: Are there special requirements in order to be named a healthcare surrogate?
H: Not normally. Customarily, any competent adult may be named healthcare surrogate. However, some states require the named surrogate to agree in writing to accept those responsibilities.

I: When would a surrogate need to take over?

H: Surrogate directives usually become effective only when the attending physician determines the patient no longer has the capacity to make informed decisions and give informed consent. Here's a side note; usually a judge is not needed to declare an individual incompetent to make medical decisions. However, most states require that the patient be examined by two physicians to determine capacity. The results of these examinations are then placed in the patient's medical records.

I: So what would a surrogate caregiver be expected to do?

H: The functions of healthcare surrogates also differ from state to state. In some states, healthcare surrogates may do a number of things. They might be able to review the patient's medical records, consult with the patient's doctor, give medical consent for treatment, apply for medical benefits on behalf of the patient, and exercise other rights set forth by state law.

I: Are there things a surrogate caregiver is not allowed to do?

H: Yes. Many states prohibit certain functions of healthcare surrogates. For example, in some states, the healthcare surrogate is prohibited from giving consent to electroshock, sterilization, psychosurgery, or voluntary admission to a mental hospital. Sometimes they're prohibited from giving consent for experimental treatment.

I: What happens if the person recovers and can handle her or his own affairs?

H: Should the individual regain competency, the healthcare surrogate would then cease to act on behalf of that person. However, I strongly recommend that you check with an attorney in your state for accurate information regarding healthcare surrogates.

Healthcare Proxy

I: This may be the worst of situations, but what if a person becomes unable to make her or his own decisions, there are no advance directives, and they have not named a healthcare surrogate? What would happen then?

H: Unfortunately, this situation occurs quite frequently.

I: *Is that because people just don't plan ahead?*

H: Well, that's the obvious answer. On an even deeper level, many elderly people are not even aware they have all these choices. People who are 75, 80, or 90 years old grew up long before we even had CPR. The medical technology we have today was not available then.

The good news is that some states have provisions for the situation you described. In the event a resident in a healthcare facility has not named a healthcare surrogate, or maybe a surrogate has been named but for some reason can't act on behalf of the individual, then a *healthcare proxy* may be named. In this case, the facility would find a competent person willing to act on behalf of the patient as the healthcare proxy. However, many state laws require healthcare proxies be appointed from a priority list.

I: *Who would be on that list?*

H: State laws are different, so the priority list for healthcare proxies may or may not follow this order, but customarily, the first person on the list would be a judicially appointed guardian of the patient who has been authorized to consent to medical treatment on behalf of the patient—that is, if a guardian has been appointed. Next would be the patient's competent spouse. Third would be the competent adult child of the patient or a majority of competent adult children who are reasonably available. Next might be a competent parent of the patient.

I: *If we're talking about elderly people, their parents probably wouldn't be an option, would they?*

H: Probably not in most cases. However, many people who are in their 60s and some who are in their 70s still have parents who are living. Sometimes parents are in better health than their adult children.

I: I hadn't really thought about that.

H: If none of these people are available, a competent adult relative who has exhibited special care and concern for the patient might be appointed, or perhaps a competent friend of the patient.

I: You told us earlier that a healthcare surrogate normally has to agree to accept these responsibilities. Is that also true of the health-care proxy?

H: Yes. Usually proxies are notified in writing and may be required to convey their agreement in writing.

I: Why would a healthcare surrogate not agree? Walk me through a situation so I can better understand.

H: Okay. Let's use you as an example. Let's say you decide you want to name your sister as your healthcare surrogate, or perhaps she is chosen as your healthcare proxy. Yet nobody has asked her if she would be willing to accept this responsibility. Then let's say you get into an automobile accident, and you're comatose. Someone from the hospital calls your sister and starts asking her all sorts of questions—whether CPR is to be administered if necessary, whether you are to be placed on a respirator, whether you have advance directives, and who will be paying for your care. She says, "Excuse me, but nobody even asked me if I would be willing to make these decisions. The truth is, I don't want this responsibility. Call somebody else." As you can see, this is not a decision to be taken lightly. It is very important to discuss this subject and allow the potential healthcare surrogate to accept or reject the responsibility.

I: So that's another choice then—who will carry out these decisions for you, even though you may have filled out advance directives ahead of time.

H: Once the healthcare proxy agrees to accept this responsibility on behalf of the person, then she/he must comply with the provisions of the surrogate law for that particular state. Healthcare proxies, as well as healthcare surrogates, are required to make healthcare decisions they believe the person would make for herself or himself. Furthermore, should the decision to be made involve life-prolonging procedures, most healthcare facilities require the surrogate or proxy to show clear and convincing evidence of the patient's wishes.

I: How could you prove that?
H: Well, normally valid living wills are accepted as standard of proof. However, each case is determined upon its particular circumstances. As I've said, I'm not an attorney, and I'm not trying to give legal advice here. I just want people to be aware of these issues. I strongly urge individuals to check with an attorney in their state should they have questions.

Guardians

I: Let's talk about guardians for a minute. You stated that one of the first people to be appointed as a healthcare proxy would be a guardian. Do we need to know more about guardianship as well?
H: There are situations where a guardian may be appointed. However, these situations tend to be very complex and must be handled on an individual basis. Consequently, people need to contact an attorney in the event their loved one should need a guardian. A guardian is someone who has been appointed to handle a person's affairs. Guardians may be given full power to make all decisions for the individual. They may be given power over just the person, over just the person's property, or any combination of these. They may only be allowed to make emergency medical decisions for the person. Though most states provide for the same types of guardianship, there are specific laws pertaining to these provisions, and filing must be done by an attorney.

Durable Power of Attorney (DPOA and DPOAHc)

I: A friend of mine has a Durable Power of Attorney for her mother, and it sounds complicated.

H: In most states, a *Durable Power of Attorney* (DPOA) specifies exactly the powers the patient is giving to the person holding the power—their agent. Power may include consent to arrange for a number of things. For example, agents may be given power to make medical decisions for the person. They may be given power to make therapeutic and surgical decisions. Agents may be able to decide which drugs would be administered. They also might be able to transfer property for the person, borrow money, or even manage bank accounts. There are any number of specific or general powers the person holding Durable Power of Attorney may have.

I: Who can hold Durable Power of Attorney?

H: Customarily, any competent adult named by the person to act as her/his agent may hold Durable Power of Attorney in those states that have such provisions. If the person is a relative, the relationship customarily has to be stated. The person holding the power of attorney cannot delegate that authority to another person. Also, just as with surrogate caregivers and healthcare proxies, persons holding power of attorney must attempt to carry out the patient's wishes.

I: This is a complicated question to me. Does a Durable Power of Attorney remain effective should the patient become mentally incapacitated?

H: It is a complicated question. That's why at the beginning I recommended individuals go online and look up medical advance directives for their specific state. Having set forth that disclaimer, I'll attempt to answer your question. Should a petition be filed to determine the patient's mental capacity, the Durable Power of Attorney is normally suspended at that time.

However, in some states, the Durable Power of Attorney may remain effective should the patient become functionally incompetent. I'm told this must include language that clearly states the power is not affected by the individual's mental disability except as provided by statute. I want to emphasize the importance of your attorney wording this document to communicate clearly the intent of the patient to this effect. When so worded, the Durable Power of Attorney would then give the designated person—the agent—authority to make healthcare decisions, or perhaps other decisions on behalf of the patient, should she/he become incapacitated until and unless a guardianship is created. Then those legal provisions would apply.

I: Could a person delegate power to make only medical decisions?
H: Yes, in some states. In this case, the designated person is only authorized to make medical decisions on behalf of the patient. This is normally handled with a *Durable Power of Attorney for Healthcare* (DPOAHc).

I: When would a Durable Power of Attorney expire?
H: Normally a Durable Power of Attorney expires in three ways. It expires, of course, at the death of the patient. It would expire at the time the patient revoked the power. It would also expire if the patient were judged incompetent by a court of law, unless otherwise stated in the Durable Power of Attorney.

I: So do I hear you saying we need an attorney to fill out a Durable Power of Attorney?
H: In some states you may have to, but in most states, there are standard forms, which may be downloaded from Web sites.

Case Law

I: Dr. Haymon, what if the person has no advance directives, and no one has been appointed to make medical decisions?
H: In the event the patient has not initiated any of the docu-

ments I've discussed and no guardian has been appointed, there are methods an attorney might use to assist in carrying out the patient's wishes, but this is very risky. In fact, the courts may have altered a portion of Case law that affects such decisions, even the night before. It may be important that someone in your family or a close friend discuss this matter with a private attorney in the event the patient has no advance directives and no agent has been named.

General Discussion

I: Dr. Haymon, thank you for helping us understand more about advance medical directives and the many legal issues. You've really taken some complicated material and presented it in a way that most of us can understand. I have a couple of simple questions. For instance, is a living will different from a Last Will and Testament?

H: Absolutely. A living will addresses a person's healthcare—what happens to his or her body while they are still living. A *Last Will and Testament* addresses what happens to their material possessions after they die.

I: Would the differences compare to those between, for instance, the executor of an estate and a guardian?

H: Yes. If you're asked to handle a person's estate and make decisions after the person has died, then you're primarily dealing with real property, bank accounts, and other legal issues. However, if you're a guardian for that person, you will be making decisions that will affect the person while she/he is living.

I: Regarding the end-of-life decisions and advance directives, we've talked about, I feel so much more aware now, but if I were to call my 85-year-old mother tomorrow and say, "Mother, you need to do this, this, and this," I'm not quite sure what those things are. What should I tell my mother she needs to do? Can you summarize that for me?

H: I guess we're going to assume she doesn't have any documents, or advance directives filled out. We'll assume she has done nothing, right?

I: She's got her Last Will and Testament, and she's appointed my sister as the executrix of her estate. She thinks she's done everything she needs to do.

H: First, you'll need to talk with her about the choices she has. She's 85 years old. She probably doesn't know she has a choice about CPR or a choice as to whether she will be treated in a hospital. She may know a little about living wills, but she may not understand that in a living will she can specify any number of wishes. Your job would be to talk with her, explain that there are choices regarding CPR and other medical decisions, and then discuss possible choices with her. Give her an opportunity to think about the choices you've discussed. I wouldn't ask her to fill out any forms that day. Give her a few days to process the information.

This is a lot to comprehend, so you might not want to talk with her about all of her choices at one time. You don't want to overwhelm her. To do so might engender such anxiety that she becomes immobilized to do anything. Help her to come to some understanding about how she feels about certain choices. When you've talked with her and she understands her choices, encourage her to fill out appropriate medical advance directives to ensure her last wishes are carried out.

I: Can one person serve as guardian and surrogate caregiver?
H: Yes, there can be just one person. You will need to be sure, though, that you have the appropriate documents to cover all that. One document I might recommend would be a Durable Power of Attorney (DPOA). Specify in the DPOA all the powers you want the named person to have, such as the authority to make legal, medical, and perhaps even life-prolonging decisions for you. Remember, specific powers have to be clearly

spelled out. Also, be sure the person you name is willing to accept this responsibility and signs accordingly.

I: Dr. Haymon, thank you for helping us wade through all this legalese and, to borrow your phrase, "decode this bowl of alphabet soup." I have one last question. Should we, as younger people, complete these forms?

H: Absolutely, and sooner rather than later. Later might not come, as was the case for Terri Schiavo. These issues do not pertain just to old age. Death is not reserved for the elderly.

LIVING ARRANGEMENTS

Home is a place you grow up wanting to leave, and
grow old wanting to get back to.
*(John Ed Pearce in Louisville
Courier-Journal Magazine)*

*I: Dr. Haymon, when we recognize that our parents need help,
what should we do?*
H: For those of you who live in the same town with your
elderly loved ones, occasional companionship may be all they
need in order to feel supported. However, your responsibilities
may require you to do a number of other chores in addition
to regular phone calls and visits. You may need to help them
with grocery shopping or meal preparation. You may have to
help with their laundry or do it for them. You may need to
help with yard work or with minor home repairs. You may also
need to help them pay bills, make medical appointments, or
complete insurance and Medicare forms, which seems like an
endless job. You may need to ensure they take medications as
prescribed. Remember the problems I had with my folks and
their medications? There are many tasks that may require your
time and attention, so if you or your folks can afford to hire
someone to help, I highly recommend that you or they do so.

I: I was intrigued with the ingenuity you used for the pill problem.

Were there other adjustments you made around their home to make it more comfortable for them?

H: One problem that comes to mind had to do with lamps. Due to arthritis in their hands, it was difficult for them to switch lamps on and off. So I replaced all their lamps with touch-on lamps. Instead of having an on/off switch, it is designed so that touching it anywhere on the base turns the light on or off. This was especially helpful when they needed to get up and use the bathroom in the middle of the night. These lamps are also helpful for people who can't see well. Touch lamps enable them to have light in order to find their glasses. There are adapters that convert regular lamps to touch capability.

Something else that helped was getting a telephone for them that had about one inch numbers. That not only enabled them to see the numbers but also enabled them to dial without pressing two numbers at the same time or inadvertently pressing the wrong number. It was also programmable, so I pre-programmed emergency and frequently called numbers and put a large sheet of paper identifying the buttons next to the phone. Then all they had to do was press the #1 button to get 911, #2 to reach me at work, and #3 to reach me at home.

Also, since they were hard of hearing, I purchased an amplifier to make the ringer on their telephone very, very loud. Later I had to put an adapter on their phone, so not only was the ringer loud but a light would flash on and off so they would know when their phone was ringing.

Carl had a great deal of trouble with the remote control for their television set. Mother didn't even try to use it. While Carl was watching his favorite television program, he would decide to turn the volume up. However, he would touch the wrong button, which would change the channel. He wouldn't be able to return to his program and would frequently miss the conclusion. I bought a remote control with large buttons, but that didn't solve the problem. On the right side of this particular remote control were power buttons, as well as those for volume and channel control. All the other buttons were on the left side of the remote. So I taped the entire left side of the remote control with adhesive tape. This prevented him from inadvertently changing channels yet permitted him to turn the TV on and off, increase or decrease volume, and move channels up or down. This significantly reduced the probability that he would lose the channel he was watching.

I: That's a great idea. It almost sounds like you were Grandma and Grandpa-proofing the house—similar to childproofing. Yet it made a huge difference in helping them to be more comfortable.
H: Most caregivers learn to be very creative, but all these challenges take time and energy. As I mentioned earlier, if you can hire someone else to do some of their chores, like yard work or house cleaning, by all means do so and save your time and energy for chores only you can handle.

Some elderly individuals may need help with their activities of daily living (ADLs), such as bathing, shopping, and/or preparing meals. If so, you might ask their doctor to make a referral for these services.

I: What are your recommendations for those who are looking for someone to care for their parents in their own home?
H: Should you need to hire someone to come into your parents' home, be sure they are bonded or the company they work for has them bonded. That may offer you some recourse if theft or something else occurs. Also, be sure the company carries workers' compensation insurance on their employees. Then, if they are injured while working on your property, they are at least covered by workers' compensation.

It's common for workers to get back injuries when they are caring for elderly people. Sometimes, the caregiver has to pull the elderly person up to help them out of bed, or the elderly person may be about to fall, causing the caregiver to reach out to catch her or him. The likelihood of someone getting injured is fairly high when dealing with elderly people.

I: If you bring in an adult sitter, will your home insurance cover you against that liability if they don't have workers' compensation?
H: That's a good question. I recommend that you contact your homeowner's insurance company and ask whether persons whom you hire to come to your parents' home or to your home are covered if injured. You might need to specify *injured* because an *accident* might be covered, whereas an *injury* might not be.

For example, a worker might fall down the stairs and break a leg; that might be covered. But if a back injury results from helping the elderly person out of bed, that might not be covered by homeowner's insurance. Also, specify that you have actually *hired* the person, because sometimes insurance policies will cover people who are *visiting* in your home and have an accident or become injured but won't cover people who are actually *working* in your home.

I also recommend that when you contact a home health-care agency, you specify exactly what you want the caregiver to do. Don't assume they will use common sense. I don't mean this in a derogatory manner, but you'll need to be very, very specific from the start. I recommend preparing a detailed list and describing exactly what you want the caregiver to do.

You should specify that you want them to help your loved one get up and walk around the room three times a day for exercise or actually help her/him to the bathroom. If you aren't specific, the caregiver might just put a bedpan underneath her/him. Write down all services your loved ones are in need of.

When interviewing a company to provide home-health care services, discuss exactly what you want them to do, then have an agent of that company sign and date your list. Then, if you learn that your mother hasn't gotten out of bed for three days or that her hair hasn't been shampooed in a week after you specifically requested these services be performed, you can contact the company, and they can't say they didn't know that you wanted those services. Do you see where I am going with this?

I: Yes, I do.

H: Don't let them intimidate you. Remember, you're the one purchasing services from them. You have every right to know what you are paying for and every right to expect them to provide the services you've purchased.

You will also need to ensure the company has backup personnel. It might surprise you to know that many companies have none. In that case, you could get a phone call early one morning telling you the caregiver cannot be there that day. At that point, it becomes your problem. So ask the company how they handle it if the assigned caregiver is unable to work.

Another important factor is to ensure that the person assigned to your loved ones is compatible with them. Being aged and infirm, maybe even bedridden, is stressful enough without having to spend hour after hour with somebody you really don't like or with someone who's incompatible.

You will want to make surprise visits to ensure the caregiver is doing what you hired her/him to do and to observe interactions with your loved ones. Talk to your folks and ask them if they like the caregiver. Sometimes, they won't like anyone you bring in, but you'll know when that's the case. You'll know when they just don't want anybody in their house, but you can make a better assessment after your observations.

You might also need to check your loved one for bedsores. I don't know how to emphasize this strongly enough. Bedsores are a common problem and can be extremely painful. Far too often, elderly individuals are in so much pain already, they may not even notice when there is additional pain caused by bedsores. Many elderly people rarely complain about anything. So even if they don't want to roll over, even if it's embarrassing, put your embarrassment aside, roll them over, and look to see if they have bedsores. If so, seek medical treatment, talk with the caregiver, and be very clear about how unacceptable this is.

I: I didn't realize that kind of assistance is available.
H: The shift is now away from expensive institutional care. Consequently, the entire home healthcare industry is expected to expand because it is much less costly. There are many agencies that provide custodial (skilled) and/or supportive (unskilled) care.

Skilled services are normally provided by medical home-health agencies and offer nursing care, respiratory, speech, physical, and occupational therapy, as well as social services and hospice care. These skilled services can often help patients avoid unnecessary hospitalizations or shorten their hospital stays. In-home skilled care may also enable patients to stay in their own homes during acute illnesses or while convalescing from an accident or illness. Normally these services are ordered by a physician and are provided on an intermittent basis to homebound patients only. Skilled care is usually offered by licensed skilled providers. However, certified home health aides may also provide personal care for patients under the supervision of a skilled nurse or therapist.

Supportive services do not require certified healthcare providers. Most of these services are provided by non-medical home care agencies. They offer such services as assistance with bathing, dressing, and meal preparation, as well as light housekeeping and shopping. They may also offer assistance with medications, exercise, and ambulation. Sometimes, transportation to medical appointments is provided.

Custodial and/or supportive services can be arranged for up to and including twenty-four hours every day for an extended period of time. There are also government-funded programs that provide transportation to community centers, where elderly individuals may go several times a week for meals and other social activities.

However, depending on the person's level of functioning, you might want to contact an organization that actually brings meals to their home. As I mentioned earlier, I dealt with all of this with my parents. The main objective is to help elderly people remain in their own homes for as long as they want to and are able to. Many of these programs provide the necessary support to enable elderly people to maintain their independence and stay in their own homes for years.

I: Do most states have these organizations?
H: Yes, they have toll-free help lines that provide information, as well as referral services. These phone numbers are usually listed under Elder Affairs in the white pages of the telephone directory. Besides state agencies, there are other resources that might be able to help. For example, many churches and synagogues, as well as civic organizations and some social groups, offer similar assistance through volunteers.

Also, the American Association of Retired Persons (AARP) provides an invaluable amount of information. Because the need for assistance in caring for elderly people has become so great, there are a number of public and private companies that have begun to develop local and national care manager programs. In many states, elder care divisions have programs that provide case assessment, as well as case management, which also includes some placement services.

Some states presently offer Medicaid-waiver programs that enable elderly individuals who are disabled to continue living at home by providing nursing home-level care. Medicaid will not normally pay for custodial care. However, when elderly people are enabled to stay in their own homes, it not only delays the loss of independence for them, it also delays the need for a much more costly care program. For people who can't afford to hire in-home care, I highly recommend contacting these agencies.

I: Are there private companies that offer help, or is it primarily through state programs?

H: There are hundreds of private companies, and charges range anywhere from $10 to $85 per hour. It just depends on what you hire them to do and whether they work as an individual contractor or through an agency. The national average rate of pay for non-certified but licensed in-home services is $17.46/hr., and skilled in-home care is $32.37/hr.

Corporations are gradually recognizing that, like childcare, elder care is a corporate issue because it affects performance and absenteeism. Sometimes, when employees are worried about their elderly loved ones, they often have to leave their jobs to go check on them. I know from personal experience it really can interfere with work.

To address this, some corporations have already created programs that include seminars, support groups, and telephone help lines. Most companies now have Employee Assistance Programs (EAPs), and a few companies provide elder/adult day care. I was just thrilled when I learned a number of companies are moving in this direction. I think that, within the next decade, we are going to see more and more companies providing that for employees.

Some people may not be familiar with it, but we do have a *Family Leave Act*, which was passed in 1993. It allows individuals to take leave time from their jobs to care for their family members without having to worry about losing their jobs. They are guaranteed to have a job when they return. However, there are certain criteria that must be met. So I would recommend that individuals either refer to the Act itself or seek professional advice before they apply for leave. Most companies would have a copy of the *Family Leave Act* in their personnel office.

I: But what about those of us who live in one part of the country while our parents live in another? I think we are called scattered families.

H: There are many companies that will find a care manager to actually take care of your loved ones for you. These care managers will serve as advocates, counselors, coordinators, and/or liaisons. They will also monitor other services your loved ones may need in order for them to stay in their own home. You might look online under home healthcare agencies to find a list of agencies in the particular city and state of interest.

I: What if elderly parents need more than just daily assistance?

H: In addition to assistance programs, there is also the option of hiring someone to move into their homes to help care for them. This is usually quite expensive, and finding someone they would be compatible with and whom you trust may be difficult, but you do have that option. There are certain companies that also provide assisted-living services. Most charge anywhere from $1,500 to $3,000 a month or more.

I: Let's face it—at some point, unless they die first, there will probably come a time when elderly people can no longer stay in their homes. What then?

H: Unfortunately, this is true. More often than not, other people usually recognize when that time comes long before the elderly person does. At that point, somebody has to make a decision as to where the elderly person is going to live. This is often a very difficult decision.

I: Where do they go when they can't go home? Should we just move them in with us?

H: To move an elderly loved one into your own home is a major decision. Since it affects everybody involved, it might be helpful if we discuss certain aspects that need to be considered before making that decision.

The first consideration is whether our elderly loved ones

even want to move in with us. This sounds very simple, I know, but some families never bother to ask. They make the decision for them, start packing, and move them in. If your elderly loved one would rather not live with you, then you need to consider other options.

I: Gee, I'd think most elderly people would rather live with a daughter or son than go to a care facility.

H: That's not always true. Some elderly people think they would be a burden on their family, and so rather than wake up every day feeling like they are a burden, they would rather live in a care facility. Some individuals realize they would have more opportunities for companionship and to socialize with people their own age if they lived in a facility. Sometimes family relationships have become so strained over the years due to unresolved family or personal issues that the elderly person may not want to live in the same house with a daughter or son. There may be young children in the home, and some elderly folks get anxious from the noise often associated with children. For that reason, individuals may not want to live with a relative. Maybe the elderly person doesn't even know why she/he doesn't want to live with relatives. They just don't want to. That's okay too.

I: There are so many things about all this that I've just never thought of. What if they do want to move in with you, and you want them to?

H: In that case, there are a number of considerations. Is your present home large enough to accommodate another person or perhaps two? If your house isn't large enough, then you may have problems that are inherent in expanding your present home. Or maybe you'll have to find a larger home. Either of these options could be quite costly.

There are also subtle expenses that occur after you bring another person into your home, such as increased utility and heating bills. Some people are on tight budgets, yet they don't think about added expenses beforehand. Then budgets are stretched, money gets tight, and stress levels go up. Financial stress often causes relationship problems. People often get into emotional difficulty because they didn't think decisions through prior to making them.

Here's another consideration: If you have to move to another neighborhood, because you have to get a larger house, and you have children, you will need to consider how moving will affect them should they be required to move from their school and their friends. Also, what effect will moving have on other family members? Will there be added burdens associated with increased driving times, larger fuel bills, and wear and tear on vehicles? In some rural areas, people choose to place a mobile home or build a small house next door to their own home for their elderly loved one(s) to live in if they have enough property to do so. This usually occurs only in very rural areas. Whether you expand your present home, buy or rent a larger house, or put a mobile home or small house next door to you, there are still many other considerations.

I: What are some examples?

H: One of the first considerations might be whether it is safe to leave the elderly person alone, and if so, for how long? In situations where it is unsafe for elderly persons to stay at home all day by themselves, you might need to hire someone to stay with them while you work. Even if you work at home, you may still need someone to care for them so you can get your work done. There may also be the option of taking them to day care during the day and providing in-home care for them at night so you can get necessary sleep and rest.

However, even if you are capable of taking care of your loved one in your home, there are still going to be times and situations when you are going to need help. I recommend that you have a back-up person, maybe a friend or a relative, who would be willing to take care of the elderly person in the event that you become ill or need to be out of town. You also need to schedule vacation time away from your caregiving responsibilities.

I: What about safety issues in the home?

H: When trying to decide whether to move your loved one(s) in with you, there are many safety hazards you might not normally think about. Providing a safe environment for elderly people is actually quite involved.

For example, you will need to ensure that there are no rugs they could trip over or water on the floors that could cause them to slip. You need to ensure there is no body powder on the floors, especially in bathrooms. Powder creates a real fall hazard. You might need to place support handles on the bathtub, raise the level of the toilet seat, or perhaps buy a toilet chair that fits over a normal toilet seat and provides arm rails for support.

You may need to install special wheelchair ramps both inside and outside your home. You may need to widen door openings to accommodate walkers and wheelchairs. If the individual is disabled or blind, there are even more safety factors that must be considered. While research does indicate the value of elderly persons having pets, some pets present a safety hazard, especially dogs and cats that like to jump and play around people's feet. Besides safety issues, remember the other problems I had with pets?

I: I sure do. I could probably handle the pets, Dr. Haymon, but I would have no idea where to get equipment such as raised toilet seats.

H: Medical supply businesses normally carry these. Check the yellow pages under *Medical Supplies.* There are also catalogs and Web sites that specialize in all sorts of equipment and gadgets for elderly people.

You also need to think about meals, medications, and transportation. Many elderly people require special meals, especially if they are diabetic or require that their food be pureed. They may also take numerous medications, several times a day. If they are unable to prepare their own meals, eat without supervision, or dispense and take their own medications properly, then you'll need to decide how this will be handled.

There is also the problem of getting them to and from medical appointments. If they are unable to take public transportation, then someone will obviously need to drive them. If they are not competent to manage interacting with healthcare providers, then someone will need to accompany them to discuss their health issues.

If she/he is on dialysis, you will need to decide how transportation to and from dialysis will be handled several times a week. If they are to be dialyzed at home, how will this be managed? So you see, the decision to move an elderly person into your home may appear fairly simple at first but may, in reality, be quite complicated.

I would certainly not try to persuade anybody one way or the other, but before you make the decision to move an elderly loved one into your home, I would encourage you to talk with all family members this will affect and get their input. I also recommend that you talk with your loved one's healthcare providers and with a social worker. It's also a good idea to find someone who has experienced this and talk with her/him. It may be that moving an elderly loved one into your home is not the best option. Although you may want to and really wish you could, bringing your parents or other elderly loved ones into your home may not be realistic. You may wrestle with guilt and other emotions about not being able to do so, but it just may not be logistically possible.

In most families, both the husband and wife work out of necessity. Therefore, it may not be feasible for either one of them to quit their job in order to stay home and care for their loved one, even though they may wish they could.

I: So if it is not possible for your loved ones to live with you, how do you decide where to place them?

H: The type of care facility depends on the individual's required level of care. Once that is determined, there are many options available. Placement alternatives include adult foster homes, which are similar to foster homes for children.

There are also congregate community living facilities (CCLFs); these offer apartments or small cluster homes where individuals live independently. They do most of their own cooking and shopping, yet a nurse or an aide comes by and checks on them every day to ensure they are taking their medications and eating properly, as well as to take their vital signs. These facilities usually coordinate medical appointments and provide transportation. They may also provide transportation for shopping, attending church, and other personal errands. Most offer ongoing educational talks on nutrition and medications, as well as motivational talks. Some provide church services and spiritual guidance.

Sometimes these facilities assist with insurance forms and bill paying. There is often a clubhouse, where residents can visit with other residents, play cards or shuffleboard, or participate in arts and crafts and other social activities. Some even provide driving ranges for golfers. Usually, there are planned outings to movies, plays, ball games, and events of that nature. The services provided by many of these congregate community homes are endless. It just depends on how much money you have and want to spend.

There are also adult congregate living facilities (ACLFs). This is the type of facility in which I first placed my mother and stepfather. ACLFs are quite similar to community cluster homes, but instead of residents living in free-standing apartments or individual homes, ACLFs offer quasi-apartments, which are contained within a larger building, much like suites in a large hotel. These quasi-apartments normally have one or more large bedrooms, walk-in closets, and a large bathroom. The facility prepares all meals, and residents eat together in a large dining room. Residents are often given menus so they may order what they want to eat in advance. However, as I learned when my mother was interviewed, residents must be able to bathe, dress, feed, and toilet themselves.

At least one nurse is normally on premise around the clock. Medications are dispensed to residents because they are not allowed to keep medications in their rooms. ACLFs also offer planned social activities, both inside and outside the facility. Some even provide space for individuals to plant flowers and vegetable gardens. The primary goal is to encourage individuals to remain as independent as possible while still being monitored. The national average monthly cost for a one bedroom unit in 2007 was $2714, which equates to a daily rate of $89 and an annual cost of $32,572.

There are also care facilities that provide care for individuals suffering from Alzheimer's as well as other types of dementia. A psychiatrist friend once said: "Dementia is dementia—whether you diagnose it as Dementia Alzheimer's Type (DAT), senile, vascular, or alcohol dementia, the bottom line is the person experiences thought confusion and disorientation, which may or may not include hostile, aggressive acting-out behaviors."

Since individuals with dementia tend to wander, they live in units that are contained because they are not allowed to go to other areas without an escort. These facilities provide skilled nursing twenty-four hours a day, and medical doctors, including psychiatrists, make rounds frequently. Patients eat their meals under supervision and with assistance, if needed. There are planned activities inside the facility, including some form of regular exercise. Often there are fenced patios or gardens, so residents may safely go outside. Beauty and barber shops are often located in the same unit where residents live. Even with a diagnosis of dementia, residents are encouraged to function at their highest levels.

Another option in long-term care is nursing homes. Current predictions are that 35% of Americans over 65 will need nursing home care before they die. About 18% will live in a nursing home for at least one year, 7% for more than three years, and 5% for at least five years. Nearly half of all nursing home residents have dementia, and more than half are confined to a wheelchair or bed. Over 80% require help with four or five ADLs (activities of daily living), such as eating, dressing, toileting, transferring, and/or bed mobility.

Nursing homes provide twenty-four-hour-a-day skilled nursing care. Medical doctors, including psychiatrists, make regular visits. These facilities provide care for individuals ranging anywhere from those who are incontinent and need assistance bathing, dressing, and feeding themselves to people who are in persistive vegetative states and on feeding tubes. Although many of the services provided by nursing homes are also provided by hospitals, it is less costly to care for individuals in nursing homes.

A word of caution—there is limited space in all the facilities I've just mentioned, and waiting lists are usually quite long. So it is not a good idea to postpone the decision regarding where your loved one will live until the need is urgent, as you may find there is "no room in the inn."

I: I had no idea there were so many choices.
H: You actually may not have as many choices as you might think. Each facility has its own admissions criteria. That is why it is so important for the individual's true level of functioning to be accurately assessed before you start looking for a place for her/him to live. If you place them in the wrong facility, you will end up moving them. As I've already mentioned,

this can be physically and emotionally distressing not only for the elderly person but also for the caregiver.

I would like to discuss a couple of other facilities. One is adult day care, which I mentioned earlier. These centers provide day care for individuals who are highly functioning. They usually do not accept people with dementia, and some will not accept those who are incontinent.

There are also rehabilitation centers. These usually offer physical, occupational, and speech therapy, as well as other types of rehabilitation programs for individuals who may have had strokes, surgery, or are perhaps recovering from broken hips or other injuries. Usually, rehabilitation centers are short-term, length of stay is determined by need, and a doctor's order is required.

I: Dr. Haymon, what happens if one of your parents is functioning pretty well, but the other needs a lot of assistance?
H: That's a really good question. There are additional concerns when an elderly couple has to be separated because they function at different levels and require different levels of care. One scenario occurs when a couple has been living independently on both Social Security incomes and/or other combined pensions. Then, one becomes dependent, requires skilled nursing care, and also needs Medicaid financial assistance to help pay for nursing home care. Yet her/his spouse is still capable of remaining in their home. What you might learn at this point is that in order for one to receive Medicaid, they may be required to dispose of most of their mutual assets. This leaves the other spouse with virtually no funds to live on.

In other cases, both may initially qualify for the same level of care, enabling them to live in the same facility. Then, weeks or months later, one becomes more disabled than the other. Consequently, she/he has to be moved to a facility that provides greater care, or perhaps she/he requires skilled care then gets better and has to move because she/he no longer qualifies for skilled care.

In most cases, as an individual's level of care changes, so does the provider of that care. Since the level of care does not follow a straight line, it is not uncommon to experience the need for change in care facilities several times a year. It might be helpful to visualize a staircase with children playing on it. They start at the top stair and hop down a couple of steps. Then they jump back up a step then hop down three. They go back up one, hop down two, and so on and so forth. That is commonly the way it goes with level of functioning once individuals decompensate to the point of needing assistance or supervision. As I mentioned earlier, I had to move my stepfather ten times and my mother eight times in the first eighteen months.

I: Dr. Haymon, I can't even begin to imagine what a drain that must have been on you and them. Why did you have to move them so many times?

H: The first move was when I moved them from their home into a townhouse to be near me. The next move occurred that infamous Valentine's Day when Carl had to go to the hospital, and my mother had to go to an assisted living facility the following day. Then Carl was dismissed from the hospital to a nursing home that provided twenty-four-hour skilled nursing care. He was there for less than two weeks when he improved enough that skilled care was no longer needed. So he was discharged. He then went to a rehabilitation facility. Three days after moving him there, my mother fell and broke her hip.

Consequently, she had to go to a hospital. After hip surgery, she was released to a rehabilitation facility. Fortunately, and I do mean fortunately, I was able to get her in the same rehabilitation center where Carl was. I can assure you that due to limited bed space and long waiting lists, that was, again, the exception rather than the rule.

My mother was in the rehabilitation center for nearly three weeks. During that time, I was sent a notice that the Adult Congregate Living Facility (ACLF), where she had been living, was only allowed to hold her room for thirty days after she left. She had been hospitalized for several days prior to going to the rehabilitation center. Those days counted. Consequently, she had been away from the ACLF for over three weeks when I got the certified letter stating they were only allowed to hold her room for thirty days. That meant I had to get her functioning at a high enough level for her to go back to the ACLF within less than ten days! So we beefed up all rehabilitation efforts, and I talked her doctor into releasing her to go back to her residence facility. In retrospect, a better decision might have been to allow her to remain in the rehabilitation center and just allow things to take a natural course. The truth was, rather than going back to the ACLF, my mother really needed to have been placed in a nursing home. However, as I've admitted several times, I was still in denial.

About two weeks after I moved Mother back to the ACLF, Carl was also discharged from the rehabilitation center. Thank goodness, I was able to move him into the same ACLF where Mother was living. However, I had to move Mother from the room she shared with another female resident into a room designated for couples so she and Carl could be together. Obtaining a room at the same facility for both of them was, once again, the exception rather than the rule. I felt very, very fortunate that I was able to get Carl into this facility with my mother. Since women normally outlive their husbands, most rooms and bed spaces are for females only. There are usually a few for men only and even fewer for couples.

Carl and Mother stayed together at that ACLF until the incident involving alcohol, when Carl left the facility pushing Mother in her wheelchair and I was asked to move them. That's when I moved both of them to a nursing home about forty-five minutes from where I lived because there were no vacancies in any of the local facilities. If you recall, that was when Carl was no longer able to obtain alcohol.

Well, he was in the nursing home for only a couple of weeks when he went into withdrawal and had to go to a psychiatric hospital. He stayed there for a couple of weeks then returned to the nursing home.

He was there for two more weeks and had to return to the psychiatric center. He developed a bladder infection while he was there, so he then had to be admitted to a hospital, where he underwent minor surgery. He was discharged a few days later.

However, I was told at that time that he was no longer appropriate for nursing home care. So I had to move him to an Alzheimer's unit.

Once again, there were no beds available in any of the local facilities. Consequently, I had to move Carl to an Alzheimer's facility in another part of the state. My mother remained in the nursing home. After a couple of months, I was able to move Mother to the Alzheimer's care facility with Carl, which was a ninety-minute drive from my home. They lived there for about two years before Carl passed away, and I was able to move Mother back to Tallahassee to be closer to me.

Eighteen moves in eighteen months. The number of changes for these two people was inconceivable. Many times, I thought I would literally lose my mind. I used to make jokes about "who's on first."

These moves created a lot of distress for them. Distress was not only associated with their own moves, but they became stressed each time the other one had to move. Each and every move was also extremely stressful for me.

As I mentioned earlier, level of care is dynamic and moves in both directions. That's why I used the analogy of children playing on the stairs. The early changes seemed to be sudden, and then they would level off. This would be followed by another spurt of rapid changes. Every time there is a change that requires elderly people to relocate, it usually creates anxiety and disorientation for them. They often become fearful and agitated.

Since I had not been through this process nor had I ever talked with anyone who had, I could never have anticipated the steps that inherently followed every crisis. I was continually in a state of anxiety. I certainly had not conceptualized the notion that there would be many times when they would not be able to live together because they were functioning at different levels.

This is certainly not the worst-case scenario, but it is a real life scenario. I have had people talk with me after I've spoken at seminars, and my story pales in comparison to theirs. The point here is the first placement will probably be followed by many others, especially if initial placement is not appropriate to their needs.

I: I will be honest with you. I am overwhelmed just listening to this. I can't imagine what it must have been like living it.

H: Like I said earlier, there were times I thought I would literally lose my mind. Perhaps if I had not been in denial or at least if I had gotten some input from others, some of the changes my folks had to endure could have been prevented. Because denial influences decisions and sometimes paralyzes people from taking any action at all, I strongly encourage people to solicit input from others. It is very difficult to accurately assess the level of functioning for someone you love and care about. Your desire for them to maintain their independence may distort your perception. Hopefully my experience will help others see how choosing an inappropriate living arrangement could easily result in numerous moves that could probably be avoided if their loved ones are placed in the proper care facility at the outset.

Regardless of how great a care facility is, inevitably, there will be conditions and circumstances you and your loved ones might like to see changed or improved. It is vitally important to use a rational approach when registering complaints and suggestions. When patients and/or family members are difficult to deal with, rude to staff, or even hint at contacting an attorney, they might be asked to move to another facility. At best, they might be allowed to stay until discharged by their physician, but it is highly unlikely they would ever be readmitted under any circumstances. Concerns certainly need to be addressed, but there are appropriate ways of doing so. Please be reminded the waiting lists for most facilities are long, and administrators can afford to be choosy.

There is an old saying: "You catch a lot more flies with sugar than you do with salt." This is absolutely true when dealing with individuals who work in care facilities. Staff members in many assisted living and long-term care facilities are overworked and underpaid. Their responsibilities include unpleasant tasks most of us would be reluctant or perhaps unwilling to perform. They often rely on intrinsic value, appreciation, and validation of their work to help compensate for the deficit in their hourly wages and the lack of glamour in their work environments. There were many CNAs, nurses, orderlies, and housekeeping employees that took such loving care of my folks that I was sure they were angels in disguise. The most powerful words in any language are "please" and "thank you." Use these words sincerely and generously. Small tokens of appreciation reap large benefits of gratitude. Remember the *Law of The Harvest.*

ASSISTANCE PROGRAMS

Another's person secret is like another person's
money: you are not as careful with it as you are your
own.
(E. W. Howe)

*I: Dr. Haymon, you have told us how expensive elder care is. When
you say nursing home care could cost as much as $75,000 a year,
that's scary. I hear horror stories where elderly people simply do not
have enough money to pay for nursing home care, yet they have too
many assets to qualify for government programs. What assistance
is available?*

H: First, let me say any government program I discuss is subject to change. Congressional leaders are presently arguing
about whether to turn billions of federal dollars over to the
fifty individual states and allowing them to decide how to
provide for their elderly. Thus, many of these programs may
change or be eliminated altogether in the very near future.

However, at this time, Medicare and Medicaid are the
two main government programs. Currently, over 100 million Americans participate in these two programs. Approximately 45 million Americans are enrolled in Medicare, nearly
57 million in Medicaid, and more than 7 million are classified
as Medicare dual-eligible. This means they qualify for both

Medicare and Medicaid. Currently, 41 million of the 45 million people who participate in the Medicare program are 65 or older. Medicare expenditures are expected to exceed $386 billion in 2008. In just over two decades, by 2031, when over half of the baby boomers are fully enrolled, this participation is expected to reach nearly 90 million, with an annual cost of over a trillion dollars! Medicare's long-term debt is projected at $32.4 trillion, which includes 8 trillion dollars associated with Part D (drug entitlements).

Although Medicare and Medicaid pay for much more than nursing home care, these two programs pay approximately 78% of the $90 billion annual bill for the nation's 16,000 nursing homes. This translates into over $70 billion a year. Medicaid pays about 60% ($54 billion), while Medicare pays about 18% ($16 billion). This leaves only 22% ($20 billion) of nursing home expenditures to be paid by private long-term care insurance, out-of-pocket, or by other private and/or public sources. Medicaid alone pays about 43% of the total bill for all long-term care, which includes other facilities in addition to nursing homes.

Medicare

I: Dr. Haymon, could you give us a brief overview of the Medicare Program?
H: Medicare has become so complicated I'm not sure anyone fully understands it in its present state. In general, Medicare is our nation's health insurance program and is administered by the United States federal government. It was originally signed into law by President Lyndon B. Johnson on July 30, 1965, as an amendment to Social Security. Former President Harry S. Truman was enrolled as the first Medicare beneficiary. President Johnson presented him with the first red, white, and blue Medicare card at the bill-signing ceremony.

Medicare was originally created because many older people could not afford to purchase healthcare insurance. However, Medicare is available to individuals, whether they can afford healthcare insurance or not. This point was poignantly illustrated by issuing a former U.S. president the first Medicare card. Benefits for Disabled Americans were added to the Medicare program in 1972.

Individuals are automatically enrolled in Medicare when they turn 65 if they or their spouse previously worked for at least ten years in Medicare-covered employment and are citizens or permanent residents of the United States. Younger individuals may also be eligible if they are disabled or have end stage renal disease. However, they must have been receiving disability benefits for at least twenty-four months from either Social Security or the Railroad Retirement Board before they are automatically enrolled in Medicare.

The Original Medicare Program had only two parts: Part A (Hospital Insurance), which covers inpatient medical services, and Part B (Medical Insurance), which pays for outpatient services provided by approved healthcare providers, as well as approved durable medical equipment. In January of 2006, Medicare Part D (Drug Benefit Program) went into effect. Currently, Medicare is divided into these three basic parts, and although it provides for basic healthcare, it does not cover all expenses.

Part A (Hospital Insurance)

Medicare Part A provides hospital insurance coverage. Part A is partially financed by payroll taxes paid by workers and employers and taxes paid by self-employed individuals. These taxes are mandated by the Federal Insurance Contributions Act (FICA) and by the Self-Employment Contributions Act of 1954 and are deducted from every paycheck. The FICA deduction from your paycheck is your contribution to our national healthcare insurance program.

All individuals 65 or older qualify for premium free Medicare Part A if they are getting Social Security or Railroad Retirement. Even those who are not getting Social Security or Railroad Retirement but have worked long enough to qualify for those benefits could still be eligible.

Although there are no monthly premiums for Part A, there are deductibles and co-payments. In 2008, Medicare Part A beneficiaries were required to pay an inpatient hospital deductible of $1024 for each benefit period; no hospital co-payment for days 0–60; $256 per day for days 61–90; $512 per day for days 91–150; and all costs for each day beyond 150 days of a hospital stay as part of their limited Lifetime Reserve Days. There is also a deductible for the first three pints of blood needed in a calendar year, unless donations are made to replace the blood.

After deductibles are met, Medicare will pay its part for covered services and supplies. Participants are responsible for their deductibles and co-payments unless they have supplemental insurance that pays for these and other covered costs not paid by Medicare.

Individuals 65 or older who do not qualify for premium free Part A may purchase this coverage, which is presently $233 a month for individuals with 30–39 quarters and $423 a month for those with less than thirty quarters of qualified employment. However, they must also purchase Part B at the standard rate of $96.40 a month.

Long-Term Care

Medicare does not pay for long-term care. Part A will pay for up to one hundred days of prescribed skilled nursing home care per benefit period. Presently, Medicare pays 100% of the first twenty days following a hospital stay of at least three days. After twenty days, recipients must pay a co-payment, which is currently $128 per day for days twenty-one through one hundred each benefit period. Medicare will pay the remainder for an additional eighty days. Beyond one hundred days, Medicare Part A pays nothing for skilled nursing care.

It gets to be a real Catch-22 for folks living in assisted living facilities. Even though Medicare Part A allows one hundred days of skilled care, most residential facilities will only hold a room or bed space for a predetermined number of days.

For example, when my mother broke her hip, she had to be admitted to a hospital. Several days later, she was discharged from the hospital to a rehabilitation facility. Medicare would help pay for one hundred days, as long as she was improving.

But here's the catch. It wasn't practical for her to stay the entire one hundred days because her assisted living facility would only hold her room for thirty days unless we agreed to pay out-of-pocket. My mother actually had one hundred days of coverage, which she needed in order to fully recover, but her room would only be held for thirty days from the day she left her assisted living facility. If she had stayed in the rehabilitative center the full length of time, she would have lost her room. She would have then been placed at the end of the waiting list, which technically would have left her out in the cold.

To help patients and families negotiate this maze, many hospitals provide social workers who help with arrangements for the patient's specific needs at discharge. Social workers often arrange for transportation, long-term care, or perhaps recuperation assistance. I also need to mention that when individuals are in a rehabilitative center, once their progress stops and the physician sees no improvement in ability to function, Medicare coverage stops.

Part A helps pay for psychiatric hospital stays, hospice care, and for inpatient services provided by Medicare-participating

Christian Science sanatoriums. It also pays for approved durable medical equipment and supplies for an unlimited time, as long as the individual meets Medicare requirements.

Part A will also pay for part-time or intermittent home health care for people who are confined in their homes, provided a physician writes an order for these services. Of course, the home health care agency has to be Medicare-approved.

In those cases, Medicare Part A normally covers services, which might include medical supplies and equipment, speech, physical, and occupational therapy, medical social services, and part-time skilled nursing care. Part A does not pay for custodial care, such as help with bathing, dressing, or going to the bathroom, if that's the only type of care the person needs.

I: How does skilled nursing care differ from non-skilled nursing care?

H: In order to qualify for skilled nursing care, the patient must have a diagnosis from a medical doctor for treatment that requires a registered nurse or other licensed personnel. Non-skilled nursing care does not require a registered nurse or licensed personnel. For example, an IV would require skilled care, but catheter care probably would not.

I: Are waiting lists for nursing home placement different for individuals who are dependent on Medicare Part A or Medicaid compared to private pay patients?

H: Many facilities report as many as one hundred patients on their waiting lists at any given time. Plus, the wait may be as long as six to nine months for individuals who do not come directly from a hospital. Most facilities prefer patients who have not used all of their one hundred covered, skilled nursing days because Part A pays more than Medicaid or private pay individuals. Thus, if they have covered days remaining, they usually get preferential treatment as far as bed space is concerned. Facilities are often quick to acknowledge they prefer individuals who have days covered under Medicare Part A and continued care provided through Medicaid because there is no limit to the number of days covered under Medicaid.

The irony is that although Medicaid is considered a last resort for coverage, the Medicaid program finances the largest portion of nursing home bills. As I mentioned, Medicaid paid some $54 billion dollars in nursing home charges last year. Yet many nursing homes, who acknowledge they couldn't operate without Medicaid funds, still give Medicaid patients lowest priority. Some Medicaid patients remain on waiting lists for months or even years.

I: What are your recommendations for ways to pay for nursing home care?

H: I highly recommend that individuals purchase long-term care (LTC) insurance. LTC insurance helps defray some of the cost when you or your loved one needs skilled nursing care. The provisions of these policies vary from short periods of supplemental coverage to an indefinite period extending until the person dies or no longer needs long-term care. Premiums vary accordingly.

Also, if you're purchasing a long-term care policy several years before you expect to use it, then you need to ensure it has an inflation rider. The daily rate in most nursing homes is presently about $200, and according to the national average, these rates will steadily increase about 5% per year for a private room. Many policy inflation riders increase the value of the coverage 5–10% a year.

DRGs

I: Dr. Haymon, what are DRGs?

H: This is the acronym for Diagnosis-Related Group Decisions. DRGs are classifications of specific conditions. Medicare Part

A will pay a flat fee for each patient hospitalized under those classifications unless there are extenuating circumstances.

I'll use the example of when my mother fell and broke her hip. Broken hips fall into a specific classification, and the amount Part A will pay for hospital stays secondary to broken hips is based on the DRG for that classification. The DRG outlines the flat amount Medicare Part A will pay for a broken hip. Hospitals and other inpatient facilities maintain current lists of DRGs and thus know exactly how many days as well the dollar amount Medicare will pay for each diagnosis.

Hospitals are driven by money. Therefore, it is in their best interest, financially, to discharge patients when the number of days and/or the dollar amount allotted by the DRG has been used. Whether patients are ready to be discharged or not, most hospitals are not likely to allow them to stay beyond the amount of time for which the hospital will be reimbursed. Consequently, when the dollar amount allocated by the DRG has been consumed, patients must go somewhere else. They may be discharged to a rehabilitative center or to a homeless shelter, but when the amount allocated by the DRG is used, they *will be* discharged from the hospital. Individual health-care providers really don't have a choice. They must abide by DRG decisions.

I: Do patients have the right to appeal a DRG decision?
H: Normally patients are given notice as to the last day Medicare Part A will pay for. Then, unless they have a supplemental policy that picks up where Medicare leaves off, they would be required to personally pay for all additional days. If they disagree with the DRG decision, they could call the Professional Review Organization (PRO) by noon the day after they are given notice. At that point, they would not be liable for any covered hospital charges until the Professional Review Organization informs them in writing of their decision. However, the PRO might not rule in their favor. They would then be

liable for all charges incurred after the last day of Medicare coverage. Individuals may contact the Professional Review Organization by calling Medicare Customer Services.

If I had known then what I know now, every time my mother or stepfather was admitted as an inpatient, I would have asked up front, "What's the diagnosis? How long can she/he stay? What will Part A pay?" Asking those questions ahead of time also gives the caregiver some idea as to when their loved one will be discharged, so they can make arrangements ahead of time.

Part B (Medical Insurance)

I: Dr. Haymon, what is Medicare Part B, and how does it different from Part A?

H: Medicare Part B is optional medical insurance, which was part of the Original Medicare Program. About 75% of Medicare Part B is funded by the federal government. The remainder is financed by monthly premiums paid by individuals who elect to participate in this program.

Normally, anyone 65 or older may enroll in Medicare Part B by paying a monthly premium, which is presently $96.40 for taxpayers whose AGI (adjusted gross income) is greater than $82,000 or $164,000 for those filing joint tax returns. Participants are also required to pay a yearly deductible of $135 (in 2008) and a co-payment of 20% of the Medicare-approved amount for all services covered by Part B. Members are also responsible for all unapproved charges—that is, unless they have a supplemental insurance policy, which pays for deductibles, co-pays, and/or other costs not covered by Part A or Part B. Deductibles, monthly premiums, and co-payments for Part B are separate and distinct from those required by Medicare Part A. These are two separate insurance policies.

After the monthly premium is paid and the deductible

is met, Medicare Part B pays 80% of the amount *allowed* by Medicare for all approved charges. However, should you receive outpatient services at a hospital, your portion of the bill could be 20% of the actual hospital charges rather than 20% of the amount Medicare approved.

I: Would I enroll in Part B at the same time I become eligible for Part A?
H: Yes, if you want to pay for that coverage.

I: Can anyone buy part B, even if she/he has a pre-existing medical condition?
H: Yes, but they have to be enrolled in premium free Part A or purchase Part A at the same time they purchase Part B. As I mentioned, individuals who do not qualify for premium free Part A may purchase only Medicare Part A as long as they qualify for it. But they can't purchase Part B without getting Part A.

I: But there is no pre-existing condition limitation?
H: No. However, there may be a waiting period if they don't sign up during their initial enrollment period, and their premiums may also be higher.

I: Why is that?
H: We are talking about elderly people. Many of them are frail and have medical problems. Let's say you did not enroll in Medicare Part B at age 65. Now you're 80 and just found out you have some serious medical disorder. You decide to enroll because you need coverage immediately. It would be too costly to allow people to do that. When you purchase private medical insurance, it is common for there to be a waiting period of thirty, sixty, or ninety days before coverage begins, even for healthy individuals.

I: Is there any reason a person might not enroll in Medicare Part B during the initial enrollment period?

H: The primary reason people don't buy Part B is because they are already covered under another insurance program that pays for medical services. Sometimes people just don't have the money to pay the monthly premium.

I: What if individuals already have private medical insurance and also have the money for Part B premiums? Would they still need to buy Medicare Part B?

H: That's a very good question, since every insurance policy is different. Part B is basically for people who either do not have medical insurance or are retiring from a job that will not offer medical insurance once they retire.

Some organizations continue to provide insurance for their retirees, but the premiums may be higher. In that case, individuals need to compare the coverage and monthly premium of their private insurance policy with the coverage and monthly premium for Medicare Part B. Then decide whether they need to purchase Part B in addition to or in lieu of their present insurance.

I: So you could have private insurance and also have Part B?

H: Yes, and I highly recommend that people who are eligible for Part B and not totally covered by some other insurance program purchase Part B. When you consider the benefits compared to monthly premiums, Medicare Part B is an absolute bargain!

I: Does Part B pay the doctor and other providers directly, like Part A does?

H: Yes. However, the amount of co-insurance the patient would be responsible for depends on whether the medical provider accepts assignment from Medicare. Medical providers who accept assignment agree to accept the 80% of the Medicare approved amount plus the patient's co-pay of 20%. In cases in which doctors or medical suppliers do not accept assignment, they are allowed by federal law to charge an additional

15% over the Medicare-approved amount. This means the patient would actually be responsible for 35% of the charges. Some providers also require patients to pay the full amount at the time of service. Then, after the claim has been filed and approved, Medicare would pay 80% of the approved amount directly to the patient.

I: Do most providers accept assignment?
H: I don't know about most, but some do although they are not legally obligated to. It is always a good idea to know what the medical provider accepts, as far as Medicare is concerned, before receiving treatment.

I: What services are normally covered by Part B?
H: Outpatient services rendered by a medical doctor and determined to be medically necessary are normally covered, regardless of whether the person receives them in a doctor's office, medical clinic, nursing home, hospital, or in her/his own home. Also, services provided by some specially qualified practitioners may be covered.

Medicare Part B policies typically cover outpatient hospital services and ambulance transportation; blood (after the first three pints per calendar year); flu, pneumonia, and hepatitis B immunizations; artificial limbs and eyes; breast prostheses following a mastectomy; anesthesia, x-rays, and laboratory tests; radiology and pathology services; physical, occupational, and speech therapy; arm, leg, neck, and back braces; certain home healthcare services, durable medical equipment prescribed by a medical doctor, such as walkers, wheelchairs, hospital beds, and oxygen equipment; pap smears, mammograms, and some prostate tests.

In addition, kidney dialysis and kidney transplants are normally covered, and under certain conditions, liver and heart transplants received in Medicare-approved facilities may be covered. Surgical dressings, splints, casts, colostomy bags, and other medical supplies are presently covered. Outpatient mental health services are also normally covered.

As you can see, it is vitally important for people to have either Medicare Part B or some other medical insurance that will cover outpatient services. Supplemental insurance may also be helpful in covering certain outpatient services that are not covered by Part B, such as custodial care. Remember services such as bathing, dressing, toileting, and other services that could be provided by non-skilled medical personnel are not usually covered by Part A or Part B.

There are private insurance policies that cover those services. Here again, you need to check each policy to see what is and is not covered. Medical care received outside of the United States is not normally covered by Medicare Part B. However, if you are in the U.S. when a medical emergency occurs and a Canadian or Mexican hospital that can treat the emergency is closer than a U.S. hospital, that might be covered.

Also, if you are travelling through Canada without unreasonable delay when a medical emergency occurs and a Canadian hospital is closest, that might be covered. There are many services and equipment that Part B will not cover. Therefore, I suggest individuals consider their personal medical needs when deciding which policy to enroll in.

Part C (Advantage Plans)

Medicare Advantage (MA) plans, also known as Medicare Part C, are the way of the future. The number of plans has more than doubled in the past couple of years. There are presently more than 600 Medicare Advantage Plans. These plans provide coordinated care plans, which replace Original Medicare coverage, although individuals remain enrolled in Medicare and maintain all rights and protections.

By law, Medicare Advantage plans must cover at least the

same fees and services as Original Medicare. However, most Medicare Advantage plans offer benefits not covered by Medicare for little or no additional cost. They also eliminate much of the paperwork involved in medical care.

Advantage plans are approved by Medicare but are run by private insurance companies. Many of these plans offer lower deductibles, premiums, and co-pays than the Original Medicare program. Thus, out-of-pocket costs may be significantly less. However, some have networks and require participants to utilize health care providers and facilities who belong to their plan or are in their network. This limits the participant's choice of medical providers. Some plans may also require referrals to see specialists. Advantage plans also include Medicare Managed Care Plans.

Medicare Managed Care Plans (HMOs, PPOs, and POSs)

Medicare managed care plans are quite different from Medigap plans. Managed care plans provide basic Medicare coverage in addition to all other benefits needed to fill the gaps in Medicare, whereas Medigap policies cover only the gaps in Medicare coverage. The additional coverage beyond basic Medicare, monthly premiums, and amount of co-pays are all controlled by the managed care plan itself, not by Medicare. So are the decisions as to whether a claim will be paid. The basic premise of managed care is that the member agrees to receive care only from a specified list of doctors, hospitals, and healthcare providers in order to get reduced healthcare costs. Specified healthcare providers are referred to as a network.

The two most popular are: Health Maintenance Organizations (HMOs), which are the least expensive and most restrictive, and Preferred Provider Organizations (PPOs), which are similar to HMOs with a point-of-service plan. Most HMOs and PPOs provide Part A (hospital), Part B (medical), and Part D (prescription drug) coverage for their participants.

Eligibility for some HMOs and PPOs requires participants to be enrolled in Medicare Part B and continue to pay Part B premiums. However, beneficiaries would not have to pay Medicare's deductibles or co-insurance amounts.

Most HMOs and PPOs will not cover individuals who are already receiving care in a Medicare certified Hospice Program or who have a diagnosis of permanent kidney failure. Each plan has its own medical network of doctors, hospitals, skilled care facilities, home health agencies, and other medical providers. Primary care physicians are chosen from a list of approved providers. The primary care physician is responsible for managing insured's medical care.

Participants are allowed to change primary care physicians as long as they choose one from an approved list. Usually participants must live within the service area of the HMO/PPO and are required to get all services from providers within the network. Some HMOs and PPOs have restrictive enrollment policies, and pre-existing conditions may be excluded.

All plans that have contracts with Medicare are required to have an advertised, open enrollment for at least thirty days each calendar year. Once participants are enrolled, they may stay in the plan as long as the Advantage plan has a contract with Medicare.

There are also different types of Medicare contracts: Risk, Point-of-Service (POS), and Cost. Risk plans have lock-in requirements, which means participants are locked into receiving all covered medical care through that plan or from referrals made through that plan. Normally, if participants receive services not covered under that plan, neither the plan nor Medicare will pay for those services, unless the services are due to an emergency.

Under the Point of Service (POS) plan, participants would

be permitted to see physicians and other health care providers as well as receive certain services outside the network. Members could also see specialists without being required to go through their primary care physician. Monthly premiums are higher than standard HMOs. The plan would pay as much as 80% of the charges. Participants would be responsible for the remaining 20%.

Cost plans do not have lock-in requirements. Therefore, participants have the option of going to medical providers within the plan's network or receiving treatment from providers outside the network. Although the plan would not pay for services received out of network, Medicare would pay its share of approved charges. Participants would then be responsible for Medicare deductibles, premiums, and co-payment amounts, as well as all unapproved charges. However, Cost plans may be a good choice for individuals who travel a lot or live outside the plan's area part of the year, especially since other plans usually provide coverage for a fixed period of time for travel. Therefore, coverage would be limited to those times.

Medicare Medical Savings Account Plans

There are two Medicare Medical Savings Account Plans: a Medicare Advantage health plan with a high deductible, and a Medical Savings Account into which Medicare deposits money to be used to pay costs until the deductible is met. Any money left in this account rolls over to the next year.

Medigap

Medigap is a Medicare supplemental insurance policy that is normally purchased through a private insurance company. Medigap works alongside Medicare. Medical charges are sent to Medicare and to the Medigap insurer, and each pays their portion of the approved charges.

There are presently twelve standard Medigap plans designed to help pay healthcare expenses either not covered or not fully covered by Medicare, such as long-term care. Medigap plans normally require a monthly premium in addition to the monthly premium charged by Medicare for Part B coverage. However, these plans typically eliminate deductibles and co-payments.

Just as with HMOs and PPOs, there is an open enrollment period that normally begins six months from the date participants become enrolled in Medicare Part B. Individuals cannot be turned down or charged higher premiums due to poor health if they buy a Medigap plan during this initial six-month period. However, once this Medigap enrollment period ends, you might not be eligible to purchase the plan of your choice.

Medicare Special Needs Plans

Special Needs Plans (SNPs) are available in some parts of the country. SNPs were created to help coordinate services needed by people who have certain chronic diseases and conditions. They offer all the coverage of Medicare Part A (hospital), Part B (medical), and Part D (prescription drugs), plus additional benefits and lower co-insurance payments.

Part D (Prescription Drug Coverage)

Medicare Part D went into effect January 1, 2006. It is part of the Medicare Prescription Drug, Improvement, and Modernization Act (MMA) of 2003, signed into law by President George W. Bush. Unlike other Medicare services, individual states partially finance this benefit.

Part D offers a more comprehensive prescription drug program than has ever been offered in the past. It subsidizes the costs of prescription drugs for individuals enrolled in Medicare Parts A and B. Medicare Part D is actually administered by private insurance plans and reimbursed by the Centers for Medicare and Medicaid Services (CMS). $1 billion was appropriated by Congress to the CMS for start-up administrative costs associated with implementing Part D. However, twelve months later, by the end of December 2006, CMS had already expended over 90% of the $1 billion. About $735 million was paid to about 250 private contractors.

Individuals may obtain the Medicare Drug benefit through two types of private plans, which are independent of Parts A and B. They could join a Medicare Advantage plan with prescription drug coverage (MA-PD) that covers inpatient and outpatient medical services, as well as prescription drugs. Or they could opt for a Prescription Drug Plan (PDP), which provides only drug coverage. These plans are approved and regulated by the Medicare program but are actually designed and administered by private health insurance companies.

Unlike the Original Medicare Program, Part D coverage is not standardized. Private prescription drug plans offer lower drug costs through a system of tiered formularies. Consequently, these plans choose which drugs and/or classes of drugs they will or will not cover and at what level they will cover them. However, Medicare specifically excludes from coverage such drugs as barbiturates, benzodiazepines, and cough suppressants. Plans that choose to cover excluded drugs are not allowed to pass those costs on to Medicare.

It should be noted that for beneficiaries who are dual-eligible (Medicare and Medicaid eligible), Medicaid will pay for excluded drugs not covered by Medicare Part D, including benzodiazepines, which are commonly prescribed for anxiety disorders. Participants who have both Medicare and Medicaid are automatically enrolled in a random Prescription Drug Plan (PDP) in their area. If they were already enrolled in a Medicare Advantage plan (MA), they would automatically be removed from the MA plan upon enrollment in the Prescription Drug Plan.

Medicaid

> You can't get rid of poverty by giving people money.
> *(P. J. O'Rourke)*

Medicaid is a joint state and federal program provided through Title XIX of the Social Security Act and was signed into law July 30, 1965, the same day Medicare was enacted. Medicaid was created to provide healthcare for low-income individuals of all ages, including children and seniors who have no medical insurance or poor healthcare insurance. Eligibility is determined by income. Individuals who qualify for Medicaid have incomes at or below the poverty level. Therefore, Medicaid requires only a minimal cost-sharing contribution from the people who qualify. One way to distinguish between Medicare and Medicaid is to think of the Medi as representing medical for both. Then add *care* or *caid.* Medicare is medical care and Medicaid is medical aid.

According to the Kaiser Commission, enrollment has increased over 40% since 2000. *Medicaid enrollment is now greater than any other single healthcare program in America, including Medicare.* There are currently about 57 million recipients of the Medicaid program. Forty-eight percent (27.4 million) are children, 27% (15.4 million) are low-income adults, 16% (9.1 million) are blind and/or disabled, and 9% (5.1 million) are seniors 65 or older.

The seven million elderly people who are dual eligible, and thus on the rolls of both Medicare and Medicaid, account for more than 40% of total Medicaid spending because they tend to be frail with substantial health problems in addition to being very poor. They are also a huge burden to state budgets because not only are their long-term needs and prescription drugs paid for, but states also pay for their Medicare premiums and co-payments.

Expenditures for Medicaid have tripled in the past twenty years and are up over 60% in just the past five years alone. This is partially due to an increased number of employers opting not to provide healthcare insurance for their employees. Consequently, many working poor have to turn to government programs. Medicaid programs now account for nearly 25% of state budgets when federal funds are factored in. Unfortunately, the growth of Medicaid spending is crowding out funding for other state programs, including education, transportation, and corrections. Medicaid is the largest source of funding for medical services for people with fixed and extremely limited financial resources.

At this time, state and federal governments together spend over $350 billion annually on Medicaid programs. In attempts to curb Medicaid spending, all states have reduced payments to nursing homes, doctors, and other healthcare providers. Most states have also tightened eligibility requirements, as well as tightened prescription drug payouts.

In reality, Medicaid is not one program but fifty different programs, with each state administering their own Medicaid programs using broad federal guidelines and federal funds. However, the Centers for Medicare and Medicaid Services (CMS) establish requirements for eligibility and services in addition to monitoring the state-run programs. The federal government matches state expenditures at various rates.

Matched funds range from 50% to 80%, depending on the state's per capita income. In some states, counties also contribute to the funding of Medicaid. However, since Medicaid is the greatest source of federal revenue to individual states, even the slightest variation of the matched percentage has a huge impact on a state's budget.

Medicaid programs offer a much wider range of healthcare services than Medicare. There is a variety of mandatory benefits for elderly Medicaid recipients including but not limited to inpatient hospital services, laboratory tests, X-rays, medical doctors, and other approved healthcare provider visits, as well as preventative outpatient services, diagnostic testing, and rehabilitative services. Medicaid also pays for home health and nursing home care. Many states provide optional benefits, including hospice care, medical equipment and supplies, wheelchairs, eyeglasses, hearing aids, and dental services. Prescription drug coverage and ambulance transport are listed as optional; however, all states offer both.

Medicaid for the Medically Needy

Most states offer additional state Medicaid programs, such as Medicaid for the Medically Needy. These programs are designed for people whose income is too high for them to qualify for regular Medicaid but too low to be able to pay additional medical bills. The assistance provided by these programs is based on a month-to-month need for help to pay medical bills.

Qualified Medicare Beneficiaries (QMBs)

Many states have Qualified Medicare Beneficiaries (QMBs) assistance programs. QMBs provide assistance for individuals unable to pay the deductibles, premiums, and co-insurance amounts required for Medicare Parts A and B.

Institutional Care Programs (ICPs)

Some states offer Medicaid programs referred to as ICPs

(Institutional Care Programs), covered under spousal impoverishment policies. ICPs help individuals pay for nursing home care and provide assistance to the wife or husband who remains in the community while her/his spouse resides in a care facility.

State Funded Programs

Beyond the worlds of Medicare and Medicaid, there are other state assistance programs for the elderly. Many of those pay for services not covered by Medicare Parts A, B, or D, or by Medicaid. However, as I mentioned earlier, every state has its own specific programs. Therefore, individuals need to contact the Department of Elder Affairs, the Area Agency on Aging, or the Health and Rehabilitative Services within their own state to learn what assistance programs are offered and eligibility requirements.

Optional State Supplemental (OSS)

Many states provide programs often referred to as OSS (Optional State Supplemental) assistance. The purpose of these programs is to supplement the income of individuals who reside in an adult congregate living facility or who live in a foster home or other specialized living arrangement that accepts state clients. Other states provide what may be referred to as SS (State Supplements). State supplements are customarily intended to be used for room and board and certain other services provided by authorized facilities.

State Children's Health Insurance Program (SCHIP)

Since many folks are raising grandchildren and perhaps even great-grandchildren, I want to briefly discuss State Children's Health Insurance Program (SCHIP) since this might be helpful in getting insurance coverage for minor children. This federal program was created in 1997 to provide health insurance coverage to children whose families were too poor to pay for private health insurance but made too much money to qualify for Medicaid. In 2007 family income had to be less than $41,000 annually. Federal funds are matched with state funds to provide healthcare coverage to children typically 18 years of age and younger. States might apply for a waiver from the federal government to cover people other than children aged 18 and younger and families who exceeded the income limit. States are typically given the option of creating new, individualized state healthcare programs which they administer, funding private insurance programs, providing healthcare coverage by expanding their Medicare programs, or perhaps a combination of these three.

According to the Congressional Budget Office, approximately 7 million children and about 1 million adults receive coverage. It is estimated another 6 million children are eligible for SCHIP or for Medicare. In 2008, $7.6 billion was budgeted for SCHIP.

Supplemental Security Income (SSI)

Unlike Social Security, which requires recipients to make contributions before they are eligible for benefits, Supplemental Security Income (SSI) is a federal welfare program that does not require that any contributions be made by recipients in order to be eligible. Immigrants, as well as U.S. citizens, are equally eligible thanks to President Nixon, who signed this into law on October 30, 1972. SSI was designed to assure that persons who are 65 or older, disabled, or blind have a minimum level of income. However, all individuals who live below the poverty level may apply for SSI benefits and receive a monthly cash amount that will bring them at least up to the poverty line if they qualify. Individuals would need to contact their local Social Security office to inquire as to whether they are eligible.

Food Stamp Program

The Food Stamp Program is designed to guarantee an adequate diet to individuals who are living on low incomes. Food stamps are issued free of charge, and age is not a factor. People don't necessarily have to be destitute to get food stamps. I recommend that individuals contact their local Food Stamp office to find out if they qualify.

Department of Veterans Affairs (VA)

The Department of Veterans Affairs, previously known as the Veterans Administration, was established in 1930, and benefits include pensions, nursing home care, hospitalization, and outpatient medical treatment, as well as disability benefits and services for the blind. VA benefits also customarily pay for prosthetic appliances and a clothing allowance for those who have prosthetic devices. Alcohol and drug treatment is also provided. Death benefits such as burial flags, burial in a national cemetery, and a grave marker, as well as reimbursement for burial expenses, may also be provided. Life insurance is often provided for survivors of disabled veterans. Some benefits are available to all veterans, while other benefits are available only to veterans who served during specific periods of time. Individuals who want additional information should contact the Department of Veterans Affairs.

Federal Income Tax

Persons who need help in filling out their income tax forms may contact the Internal Revenue Service (IRS) or the American Association of Retired Persons (AARP) in their area. In addition to personal exemptions, individuals 65 or older are eligible for an additional deduction. If they are blind, they are eligible for yet a third deduction. Persons 55 or older who sell their primary residence may be entitled to a one-time exclusion of a percentage of the gain realized on the sale of their property. Also, income from Social Security, Supplemental Security Income, and certain other public assistance programs customarily is not taxable. However, it depends on the person's total income. Therefore, I suggest that individuals check with the IRS for clarification.

Property Tax Reductions

There are also special reductions on property taxes for elderly people. Many states offer elderly people the benefit of paying reduced taxes on their property. Nearly all states offer a homestead exemption that allows the homeowner to deduct some pre-determined amount from the taxable value of her/his home. In addition, some states allow exemptions for disabled persons, veterans, and for widows and widowers. Many states exempt persons with certain disabilities from paying property taxes.

For example, persons who are legally blind, confined to a wheelchair, paraplegic, or quadriplegic may be exempt from property taxes in some states. In order to determine if individuals are receiving all of the exemptions they are entitled to, they need to contact the local tax appraiser's office.

Reverse Mortgages

Individuals who want to remain in their own home but can't afford to live in it because they can't afford utility bills, repairs, or upkeep might consider a reverse mortgage, which is similar to a normal mortgage except in reverse. Normally, the home has to be paid for or at least have substantial equity in it. Individuals actually borrow money on their homes. This money is divided into equal payments and is paid to them on a monthly basis. The monthly amount is deducted from the equity in the house. They are allowed to live in the home until they die or need to move to a care facility. This means they no longer have a house payment and in fact may have a steady income stream that allows them to remain in their own home. Should the time come when they're no longer able to live in the home or at their death, family members have a choice to refinance and keep the house or allow the bank to sell it and accept the balance after the debt is satisfied. I actually have two sisters who have already chosen reverse mortgages for their homes and are quite happy with this arrangement.

Let me offer a word of caution here, however. Eligibility for some government programs, such as Supplemental Security Income, Food Stamps, and Medicaid, might be negatively affected if the person has a reverse mortgage. Monthly income from a reverse mortgage increases total income, therefore, she/he might not be eligible for certain programs.

If you are already receiving benefits, or if you think you might need Medicaid in the near future, I would at least check with those agencies to find out what effect, if any, a reverse mortgage would have on eligibility for those programs. There always seems to be a rippling effect with every choice and with each new decision.

I know from experience that figuring out where to go and who to talk with concerning assistance programs can be confusing, frustrating, and overwhelming. Consequently, I have included addresses, phone numbers, and Web sites of over 250 agencies and organizations in the *Resource* section at the end of this book. Hopefully, these resources will help others have a much less frustrating experience than I had when it's *their turn* to figure this out.

SECTION FIVE:
PREPARING FOR RETIREMENT

BABY BOOMERS RETIRE

SILVER TSUNAMI EXPECTED TO
HIT WITH A VENGEANCE

ARE THERE ENOUGH EGGS IN YOUR BASKET?

A DRESS REHEARSAL BEFORE YOU RETIRE

WHERE WILL BOOMERS CHOOSE TO LIVE?

BABY BOOMERS RETIRE

So Many of Us—So Many Concerns, So Many Needs

A Nation is a body of people who have done great
things together in the past and who hope to do great
things together in the future.
(F. H. Underhill)

We've been labeled at every stage of our lives—*baby boomers, hippies, flower children, yuppies,* the *sandwich generation,*
and now *America's silver tsunami.* Throughout the life cycle of
our generation, we have presented enormous challenges for
the economics of our country. Beginning in 1946, the birth
of so many of us within a short period of time created a huge
increase in the demand for housing. In the early 1950s, as we
approached school age, we challenged our country's educational systems by necessitating tremendous investment in
the construction of thousands of new schools and the largest
demand in history for elementary school teachers. The same
thing happened as we moved to the secondary level. Then in
the 1960s and 1970s, we created the greatest demand for higher
education our country had ever known when we enrolled in
colleges in record numbers. After graduation, we presented an
even greater challenge to the U.S. economy as tens of millions
of new workers had to be absorbed into the national labor

force. Now we pose perhaps the greatest challenge yet to our country's economy—a tsunami of spending related to the rising costs of health care, along with millions of us retiring at about the same time. The annual *trillion* dollar question is: "How will these mega costs be funded?" especially given the uncertain future of Social Security and Medicare.

On Monday, October 15, 2007, the first baby boomer (those born between 1946 and 1964) applied for Social Security benefits over the Internet. Kathleen Casey-Kirschling, a teacher in New Jersey, who was born one minute after midnight January 1, 1946, was eligible for benefits when she turned 62 on January 1, 2008. Another 3.2 million boomers (365 every hour) will also turn 62 in 2008. It's easy to see that the boat she's in is getting crowded very fast.

Kathleen Casey-Kirschling, the first baby boomer to receive a Social Security retirement check, 1/01/2008.

According to the U.S. Census Bureau, in 1950, only 10% of the population was over the age of sixty-five. By 2030 (the year the youngest of the baby boomers turns 66), it is estimated that 20% of our nation's population will be sixty-five or older. This represents twice the present number. In fact, over 75 million baby boomers (approximately 10,000 a day) will become eligible for Social Security benefits over the next two decades.

By 2030, approximately 84 million people will be receiving Social Security benefits—an increase of 34 million from the present caseload of 50 million. Social Security presently represents 2% of the economy. By 2030, it will have increased to 6% of the nation's economy.

The first wave of Boomers will turn 65 in 2011 and will then be eligible for Medicare. At that time, the number of Medicare recipients will increase from 45 million to nearly 80 million and increase from 3% to 11% of the economy. How the costs associated with this record number of retirees will be covered is certainly an open question.

In my previous book and earlier in this book, I discussed the sobering reality that the number of people over 65 had more than tripled since 1900, yet the number of people to take care of them dropped from 14:1 to 4:1.

A similar phenomenon has happened with Social Security. This phenomenon contributes to decreasing the base in the ultimate Social Security pyramid game. It is also such an emotionally charged issue that people are often unable to process the numbers.

In 1945, just ten years after it was signed into law, the ratio of workers paying into Social Security for every person drawing benefits was 42:1. Today that number has dropped to just over 3:1, and this ratio is projected to go down to 2:1 by 2030, when boomers retire in big numbers. This change in ratio has occurred primarily because boomers have not produced enough children to replace themselves. The "baby boom" was subsequently followed by a "baby bust."

Social attitudes started to change drastically by the mid 1960s with the legalization of abortion and the development of birth control pills. These changes in social attitudes led to a sharp decline in birth rates. During the baby boom era, the U.S. fertility rate was 3.8. This dropped to 2.43 in 1970 and to 1.77 by 1975. In order for the population to remain stable, the fertility rate needs to be at least 2.1; however, the rate stayed far below this level until about 1990. Since then the U.S. fertility rate has stayed around 2.1. Consequently, the generation of workers behind the baby boom generation will be experiencing much slower growth. This could spell disaster for the present pay-as-you-go system of Social Security.

Throughout human history, people have feared the uncertainties brought on by illness, disability, unemployment, becoming too old to work, and/or the death of primary breadwinners. Prior to the 1930s, many elderly Americans faced these uncertainties as well as the fear of becoming impoverished should they become unable to work and provide for themselves. Unfortunately, this was highly probable for some. In 1934, over 50% of elderly Americans lacked sufficient income to support themselves, yet state welfare pensions remained virtually non-existent.

Financial support for disabled and retired individuals was mostly handled by family members (to the extent resources allowed) and was more of a concern at the local and state levels, which resembled England's "Elizabethan Poor Law of 1601" rather than a matter for federal involvement (with the exception of veterans' pensions). England's Poor Law of 1601 declared that members of poor families were responsible for one another. Thus, elderly folks were expected to live with their adult children. It also stated that expenses related to caring for the poor were the responsibility of local parishes (churches), which were also responsible for the administration of this law. Basically, this is what was being practiced in the United States.

However, nationwide suffering left in the wake of the stock market crash of 1929 and the Great Depression of the 1930s not only brought attention to this national dilemma, it also brought support for several proposals for a national old-age insurance program as part of President Roosevelt's "New Deal."

The idea of a national economic security system was not "new" at all. Nearly 160 years prior to the Social Security Act of 1935, the first national pension program for soldiers was passed in early 1776 prior to the signing of the Declaration of Independence. Subsequently, the first full-fledged pension program was developed in America, although it did not extend to the general population. It is interesting that Social Security has notable similarities.

Another such program was proposed in 1795 by Thomas Paine, a Revolutionary War figure. In Paine's last great pamphlet, *Agrarian Justice* (1795), he called for a national system of economic security for the new nation, which included protection against poverty in old age.

One of the first formal company pension plans was introduced in 1882 by the Alfred Dolge Company for industrial workers who built pianos and organs. Unfortunately, it was also one of the first plans to vanish as the company went out of business a few years later.

By 1900, there were only five companies in the U.S., including Dolge, that offered their employees (industrial workers) employer-sponsored pensions. As late as 1932, only about 15% of the U.S. labor force had any kind of employment-related pension plan. Sadly enough, because pensions were granted or withheld at the employer's discretion, most of these workers never actually received their retirement pensions. In reality, only about 5% of retired individuals were receiving pensions in 1932.

A surge of legislation was passed in the years immediately preceding passage of the Social Security Act, which led to thirty states having some type of old-age pension program by 1935. However, these pension programs were ineffective and inadequate. Only about 3% of the elderly were actually covered under these state plans, with the average beneficiary receiving only about sixty-five cents a day.

On January 17, 1935, President Franklin D. Roosevelt asked Congress for social security legislation. That same day, Representative David Lewis of Maryland and Senator Robert Wagner of New York introduced bills intended to reflect the views of that administration. Their bills encountered much opposition from those who sought exemption from payroll taxes for employers who adopted government-approved pension plans as well as those who considered such legislation a governmental invasion of the private sector.

However, a few months later, the bill was passed by Congress, and on August 14, President Roosevelt signed into law our federal insurance program (the Social Security Act of 1935). The initial Social Security tax rate (which began January 1937) was 2.0%, shared equally between the employee and the employer, of the first $3,000 of the employee's earnings. Three years later (1940), the rate increased to 3%. By 1943 the rate had increased to 4% and by 1946 had climbed to 5%. Beginning January 1949, the rate was 6% shared equally between the employee and the employer up to a maximum of $3,000 per year.

The original Social Security Act included the first program for national unemployment compensation, the Aid to Dependent Children program, and aid to the states for other health and welfare programs. State and local government employees were excluded from Social Security coverage under the original statute because there was a constitutional question regarding the federal government's authority to tax state and local governments. Certain individuals and groups were included at various times following the original statute.

According to the 1935 statute, retirement benefits were paid only to primary workers over the age of 65. Farm workers, anyone employed by an employer with fewer than ten employees, self-employed individuals, and railroad workers were excluded from receiving benefits. Although these limitations were initially proposed to exclude those for whom it would be difficult to oversee compliance, these groups comprised about half of the U.S. civilian labor force at that time.

In 1936, the year after Social Security was signed into law, a pamphlet published by the federal government offered the following promise: "Beginning in 1949, twelve years from now, you and your employer will each pay three cents on each dollar you earn, up to $3,000 a year. That is the most you will ever pay." The first red flag might have been the error in this simple addition—twelve years from 1936 would have been 1948, *not* 1949. Regardless of the year, 6% of employee earnings up to a $3000 cap was supposed to have been the maximum for Social Security taxes.

The first payroll taxes were collected, and the first lump sum death benefits were paid to 53,236 beneficiaries in 1937.

In 1939, the age restrictions were eliminated.

Ida May Fuller of Brattleboro, Vermont, was the recipient of the first monthly retirement payment, which was issued on January 31, 1940. This first check was for $24.22.

Ida Mae Fuller, recipient of the first Social Security retirement check, 1/31/1940. This first check was for $24.22.

In 1941, President Roosevelt attempted to clarify why Social Security was based on payroll contributions when he exclaimed,

"We put those payroll contributions there so as to give the contributors a legal, moral, and political right to collect their pensions and their unemployment benefits.

With those taxes in there, no damn politician can ever scrap my social security program."

Since, by definition, a contribution is freely given, it's ironic that President Roosevelt chose to refer to workers as contributors when they, in fact, had no choice but to pay the imposed tax.

In 1950 farm and domestic workers and non-farm self-employed individuals, but not professional groups, were covered, as were federal civilian employees who were not already covered by a retirement program.

U.S. citizens employed outside the United States by U.S. employers were included, as well as the Virgin Islands and Puerto Rico. The individual states had the option of including state and local government employees who were not covered under a retirement system. Nonprofit organizations could elect coverage for their employees, except ministers.

In 1954 the Self-Employment Contributions Act was enacted, making self-employed individuals, including professionals (except lawyers, dentists, doctors, and other medical groups) and self-employed farmers or home-workers responsible for the employer's as well as the employee's portion of the tax. Self-employed individuals are still required to pay the employee's as well as the employer's portion. However, they are allowed to deduct half of the self-employment tax. Ministers had the option of electing coverage while local and state government employees (except policemen and firemen) were automatically included.

In 1956, the Social Security tax was raised to 8.0%, disability benefits were added, and women were allowed to retire at age 62 with reduced benefits (70%). In addition, all professionals who were self-employed (except doctors) and members of the uniformed services were covered, as were policemen and firemen in certain designated states.

In 1961, the tax rate was increased to 12.0% (shared equally between the employee and the employer), and men were allowed to retire at age 62.

In 1965, Medicare was added, and self-employed doctors, interns, and all tips were covered.

In 1967, ministers (except those who claimed exemption on grounds of conscience or religious principles) and firemen in all states were included who were not already under a retirement system.

In 1972, members of religious orders subject to a vow of poverty were included. Another huge red flag flared in 1972 when yet another mathematical error was made. This mistake was significantly greater than not being able to add two figures. This mistake turned out to be gargantuan in size, span, and scope. In the 1972 amendments to Social Security, Congress increased benefits 20% and endeavored to index benefits to inflation so that benefits would increase automatically and the real value of benefits wouldn't decrease. However, benefits doubled the rate of inflation. During the 1970s, the Unites States experienced double-digit inflation rates, which led to increases in Social Security retirement benefits that could not be sustained financially.

Attempting to fix this double-indexing mistake, in 1977, President Jimmy Carter signed legislation that was approved by Congress and confidently proclaimed, "Now this legislation will guarantee that from 1980 to the year 2030, the Social Security funds will be sound." This has certainly turned out not to be the case. The signature ink had barely dried before the financial status of Social Security had declined once again.

In 1975, COLAs (the automatic annual cost-of-living

adjustments, which did not require legislation) began. During President Carter's administration, immigrants who had never paid into the system became eligible for SSI (Supplemental Security Income) benefits when they reached 65 years of age.

The system was in crisis by 1982. Projections at that time suggested that the Social Security Trust Fund would run out of money the following year (1983), and there would not be funds to pay benefits. A commission was thus created to address the new crisis, and Alan Greenspan (who had not yet been named Chairman of the Federal Reserve) was appointed as chairman of this commission. Concerns included the long-term impact of baby boomers on the Social Security system.

The Greenspan commission made several recommendations, and President Ronald Regan signed into law the 1983 Amendments to Social Security, which included a) increasing the rate of payroll tax, b) increasing the age for full retirement benefits, c) increasing the potentially taxable amount of Social Security benefits up to 50%, and d) including all employees of nonprofit organizations, as well as state, local, and federal civilian employees hired after 1983, including members of Congress, the president, vice president, federal judges, all other executive level political appointees who entered federal service after 1983, and all incumbent senators and representatives regardless of when they entered Congress. The Greenspan commission also confidently projected that the Social Security system would be solvent for the entirety of its seventy-five-year forecast period—until 2058.

Thus, in 1984, all federal employees were required to pay Social Security payroll taxes. However, federal employees have VPAs (Voluntary Personal Accounts) in addition to Social Security because federal government employees recognized the benefits of voluntary personal accounts. Thus, federal employees have the option of investing a portion of their income in a

TSP (Thrift Savings Plan), which typically offers a conservative mix of stocks and bonds.

In 1990, it became mandatory that state and local government employees who were not covered under a retirement plan be included.

In summary, Social Security is funded through payroll employment taxes specified under the Federal Insurance Contributions Act (FICA). All individuals who work in employment covered by Social Security are subject to the FICA payroll tax. This is not, nor has it ever been, voluntary. As previously discussed, there are a few exceptions to mandatory participation. Individuals who work for some state or local governments may still have the option of choosing whether their employment will be covered. In 2007, approximately 165 million Americans (96% of all workers) were covered under Social Security.

Social Security retirement payouts have continued to increase and have followed this path with figures quoted in nominal dollars not adjusted for inflation: in 1950, payouts totaled $961 million, 1960 = $11.2 billion, 1970 = $31.9 billion, 1980 = $120.5 billion, 1990 = $247.8 billion, 2000 = $445 billion, 2007 = $586 billion, and in 2008, payouts are expected to reach the astronomical total of 608 billion dollars.

The Social Security tax is now more than double the amount President Roosevelt promised the maximum would ever be. The promise was that the most employees and employers would ever pay would be three cents on each dollar earned, up to $3,000 a year. The present rate is 12.4%—6.2% for employees and 6.2% for employers. The $3,000 cap, or maximum income level, he promised, is now $102,000! The maximum level (Social Security Wage Base) is based on average national wages and goes up each year accordingly. Typically, the Social Security Wage Base increases at a faster rate than the CPI-U

(Consumer Price Index). Today, 75% of taxpayers pay more in FICA taxes than they do in income taxes.

As a result of the accelerated rate of tax increases, the Social Security system began to accumulate a large, but short run, excess in funds. These funds were intended to cover the projected retirement demands of the baby boomers.

Congress invested the excess funds into non-marketable, special series U.S. government bonds held by the Social Security Trust Fund. During President Johnson's administration and under the unified federal budget, excess funds were used to offset the total fiscal debt, making it look much smaller than it actually was. However, bonds currently held in the Social Security Trust Fund are not included in the U.S. national debt calculation.

FICA does not apply to investment income. The FICA tax has no personal exemption or standard deduction and is considered a *regressive* tax. By definition, a *regressive* tax rate *decreases* as the amount to which it applies *increases*. FICA tax is actually a *flat percentage* tax with a cap.

FICA tax is not deductible. It never has been, and there was never any promise that it would be. However, since 1993, up to 85% of Social Security benefits are considered taxable income if the taxpayer's total income exceeds certain limits. At lower income levels, only 50% of Social Security benefits are taxed.

Perhaps the most unsettling realization for many people is the fact that although we have paid Social Security taxes for most of our adult lives, none of us have any "right" to Social Security benefits. The fact that individuals have no "rights" to Social Security benefits based on taxes they've paid in was made clear in the Supreme Court ruling in *Fleming v. Nestor (1960)*. The president and Congress are free to change, reduce, or eliminate Social Security benefits at their discretion.

Social Security taxes are delegated to several trust funds.

However, the two main trust funds are: 1) The Federal Old-Age and Survivors Insurance Trust Fund (OASI), which was established January 1, 1940, and from which retirement benefits are paid to eligible retirees, as well as to their eligible dependents or survivors, and 2) The Federal Disability Insurance Trust Fund (DI), which was established August 1, 1956, and from which benefits are paid to individuals who are determined unable to work due to physical or mental conditions, as well as to their eligible dependents. Both funds are separate accounts in the U. S. Treasury.

In addition to Social Security retirement, the Social Security program currently finances other large programs such as Medicare, Medicaid, Unemployment Insurance, SCHIP (State Children's Health Insurance Program), Temporary Assistance to Needy Families, and SSI (Supplemental Security Income), as well as many other smaller programs. Only about 21% of the Social Security program is actually for the 50 million Social Security participants, while 20.5% is for the 45 million Medicare beneficiaries and 22.5% is for the 57 million Medicaid recipients. The remaining 36% is appropriated for other smaller programs.

Reformation of Social Security has been a major political issue for nearly forty years and spans the presidencies of Gerald Ford, Jimmy Carter, Ronald Reagan, George H. W. Bush, Bill Clinton, and George W. Bush. Questions regarding solvency have ranged from immediate crisis to projected future deficits. In the early 1980s, Social Security became known as the "Third Rail of American Politics," and touching it meant political death. Subsequently, any amendments to Social Security were deemed to take place in odd numbered years (not election years) because Social Security reform meant increases in taxes and/or reductions in benefits.

The Social Security Administration offered this press release on April 23, 2007: "The projected point at which tax revenues will fall below program costs comes in 2017. The projected point at which the Trust Funds will be exhausted comes in 2041." So in less than nine years, there will be more going out of the Social Security fund than will be coming in, and in about thirty years, the fund will be depleted if immediate steps are not taken. This translates into great concern as to whether there will be sufficient funds to pay Social Security benefits to the tens of thousands of boomers who will be retiring every week.

Other reports paint an even bleaker picture of the state of affairs for the entire Social Security Program.

> For example, in the "*Summary of the* 2007 *Annual Reports*" of the Federal Social Security Administration, it was revealed that, "Medicare's Hospital Insurance (HI) Trust Fund is already expected to pay out more in hospital benefits this year than it receives in taxes and other dedicated revenues. The growing annual deficits in both programs are projected to exhaust the HI reserves in 2019 and Social Security reserves in 2041."

This reiterated the notion that the entire Social Security reserve would be exhausted by 2041—the same projection that was offered in 2006 and earlier in 2007.

> The conclusive paragraph to this report was signed by the trustees of the Social Security Administration and reads:

> "The financial difficulties facing Social Security and Medicare pose enormous, but not insurmountable, challenges. The sooner these challenges are addressed, the more varied and less disruptive their solutions can be. We urge the public to engage in informed discussion and policymakers to think creatively about the changing needs and preferences of working and retired Americans. Such a national conversation and timely political action are essential to ensure that Social Security and Medicare continue to play a critical role

in the lives of all Americans." This report may be viewed online at: www.ssa.gov/OACT/TRSUM/trsummary.html.

Perhaps I'm missing something here, but in light of the information given in this report, it seems we need more than a "national conversation." I am, once again, not comforted by having this dire situation *confirmed by the powers that be* without any suggestions as to how this runaway train might be stopped, other than for the public to *discuss* and policymakers to *think* about our "changing needs and preferences." I can only speak for myself, but my *preference* doesn't require much *thinking*. My *preference* is to be assured that I will receive the Social Security retirement and Medicare benefits I was led to believe would be there when I retire.

Social Security is the ultimate pyramid scheme. The excess money left after paying benefits was supposed to have been placed into a trust fund. However, the government has been borrowing this money, using it for other programs, and depositing IOUs (referred to as bonds) instead. The U.S. Treasury loaned the money to the Department of Agriculture and the Pentagon, as well as other federal programs, including education and the environment, to help pay their bills. Unfortunately, this money has been *spent*.

Many believe the Social Security Trust Funds are mere entries on a budget sheet. In fact, as already mentioned, Social Security funds are shown as a separate account in the federal budget and thus considered "off-budget."

Others also attest to the fact that the federal government uses the Social Security trust fund to disguise the tremendous deficit of the federal budget. It is reported that about half of the Social Security Trust Fund consists of those worthless IOUs, while the other half is technically an accounting entry attributing interest to the "bonds." The federal government is no longer collecting enough payroll taxes to pay Medicare benefits and does not have the funds to pay the borrowed money back.

It is also interesting to note that between 2017 and 2041, the government will have to come up with an additional 8 *trillion dollars* just to continue paying promised benefits. That part of the financial crisis begins in about eight years.

The U.S. Social Security program is the single greatest expense "on" or "off" the federal budget. It is the largest government program in the world—larger than the entire budget of most countries. The U.S. government spends more on Social Security than on our national defense, even during times of war. For the fiscal year of 2008, $608 billion was budgeted for Social Security (not including Medicare, Medicaid, SCHIP, and other programs paid with FICA funds). This represents a 34% increase for Social Security in just the last four years. Yet, only $481.4 billion was budgeted for national defense.

Currently, 50 million Americans receive Social Security retirement benefits. By 2030, there will be twice as many Americans 65 and older as there are today. This will quickly take Social Security retirement benefits to well over a trillion dollars a year. What's even scarier is the projection that Medicare payouts will be five times greater than the demands of Social Security retirement benefits.

This means that there will also not be funding for many federal programs, including those for defense, education, and the environment, which have relied on monies borrowed from the Social Security Trust Fund. $394.5 billion was budgeted for Medicare in 2007. However, actual payouts totaled $426 billion. President Bush's proposed budget for 2008 requests an increase of $28 billion for a total of 454 billion dollars.

Nearly twelve years ago, in *My Turn,* I wrote how my anxiety increased as I read the newspaper or watched the six o'clock news, following members of Congress and representatives as they argued and became angry over the national problem of how to care for our elderly citizens. Proposals have included limiting benefits, delaying the retirement age, raising taxes, and limiting spending. Yet more than a decade later, these same arguments continue with no resolution. I realized then I didn't have the luxury of waiting until the president and Congress decided how much money they would budget for elder care. The needs of my folks had to be met, and I had to figure out how. Once again, I don't have the luxury of waiting until the president and Congress figure out how they'll pay for elder care—for my care. I will have to figure it out along with millions who are in this same boat with me.

It appears the government will perhaps have to employ a number of options in order to pay back the trust fund. One option might be to *decrease outputs.* This could include a) raising the age requirement for full benefits, which is 66 for those born between 1943 and 1954 and increases until the age for full retirement benefits reaches 67 for those born in 1960 or later (see chart at the end of this section), b) imposing a "wealth factor," which would limit full benefits based on gross taxable income, c) reducing benefit payouts—the average monthly benefit for 2008 was $1079 with a maximum benefit of $2185 a month (Refer to the chart at the end of this section.), d) imposing entitlement annuities that are based on need, and/or e) carefully scrutinizing Medicare payouts.

Another option might be to *increase inputs.* This could include a) seeking loans from foreign markets, b) raising the FICA tax rate, which in 2008 is 15.3% (12.4% for Social Security and 2.9% for Medicare)—half paid by the employer (7.65%) and half paid by the employee (7.65%) with self-employed individuals responsible for the entire 15.3%, c) selling bonds, d) changing the Social Security tax to a *progressive* rather than a flat tax, which is erroneously referred to as a *regressive* tax, e) raising the Social Security gross compensation tax cap, which in 2008 is $102,000, and/or f) eliminating the compensation cap entirely.

There are many ways problems associated with the deficits

in Social Security might be resolved. However, at the root of operational change lies the necessity for a fundamental change in attitudes and expectations.

As stated earlier, the trustees of the Social Security Administration left us with this statement in their final report: "We urge the public to engage in informed discussion and policymakers to think creatively about the changing needs and preferences of working and retired Americans." I have done as they have asked. I have "engaged in informed discussions" with lots of folks, and without exception, opinions are voiced with great emotion. I have also "thought creatively" about this and offer the following thoughts and questions.

It is apparent the Social Security tax is in fact that—a *tax,* not a *contribution.* Why doesn't the language reflect what it is, and why don't we call it what it is?

It is also a *flat percentage* tax, not a *regressive* tax. There's nothing regressive about it; we all pay the same flat percentage rate. Again, why doesn't the language reflect what it is, and why don't we call it what it is?

Since it is and always has been a *tax,* how could some groups/individuals be allowed the option of not paying it, especially the very members of Congress that imposed it? For nearly fifty years in the history of Social Security, neither the president, vice president, nor members of Congress were required to pay this *tax.* It makes little sense to me to have individuals writing and deciding laws that do not pertain to them.

How could it have been Constitutional for certain individuals/groups not to pay an imposed tax or be excluded from coverage?

If it was such a great program, why would members of Congress have opted out?

It seems preposterous to me that the president and Congress are free to change, reduce, or eliminate Social Security benefits at their discretion.

How will decisions about "fixing" the problems of Social Security be made? What kinds of input will there be, and from whom?

I propose we open these decisions to political process, as opposed to allowing the trustees to make these very serious decisions. History speaks for itself regarding the extremely poor judgment and irrational decisions made by presidents and members of Congress. In fact, I believe every U.S. citizen should be allowed to vote on possible resolutions. After all, our Constitution begins with "We the people..." not "We the Congress..." or "We the trustees..."

I, along with every person I have talked with about this grave subject, have little confidence in our government's ability to "fix" this problem. Members of Congress have been trying to "fix it" for the past forty years, and every decision they've made has not only created more problems but has created problems that are even more serious.

I've recently learned that a lot of folks didn't know they only have to pay Social Security Tax (6.2%) on the first $102,000 they earn in 2008, regardless of how much they make. The reason they don't know this is because mainstream America doesn't earn $102,000 a year! In 2007, the average worker made less than $40,000 a year, while the average income for those 65 and older was less than $25,000. Salaries for members of Congress were $169,000, with the Speaker of the House making $217,400.

What is much more disturbing is that the top Major League Baseball players were paid an average of $20 million a year, the top National Football League players averaged $20 million, and the top National Basketball Association players averaged $20 million. The top ten endorsement athletes averaged $28 million, with Tiger Woods leading the field, earning $100 million in 2007. Top actors average $20 million per film, with percentages of gross receipts adding another $50 million to $160 million. For example, Keanu Reeves was paid a total of $185 million for *The Matrix Reloaded* and *The Matrix Revolutions*. Plus, Wall Street's bonuses were a record $38 *billion* in 2007. All of them paid only 6.2% Social Security Tax (12.4% if self-employed, which is probably the case with Tiger Woods and others under contract) on just $97,500—the income cap for 2007.

Since FICA is only paid on wages and not on earnings on investments, the billions of dollars paid in interest income and dividends, etc. are not subject to Social Security or Medicare taxes. As of 2008, there was no income limit for Medicare Tax. Every employee was required to pay 1.45% (2.9% for those self-employed) on all earnings.

While there is certainly room for debate over the notion of eliminating the Social Security wage limit, many believe, as I do, that this would be much fairer. If the annual income cap were to be eliminated, everyone would pay 6.2%/12.4% (or whatever the going rate is) on *total* annual earnings. Thus, instead of Tiger Woods paying $12,090 (12.4% since he is self-employed) in Social Security Tax, in 2007, he would have paid $12.4 million.

The total for all the MLB players would have contributed about $300 million in additional Social Security taxes, perhaps another $250 million for the top fifty actors, $200 million for the NFL, $200 million for the NBA, and another $1.24 million for every $20 million contract/salary. There are thousands of those. Plus, Wall Street bonuses would contribute another $2.35 *billion*. The math is simple. Billions of dollars could easily be collected in Social Security revenues each year by simply eliminating the income cap.

Although I am definitely not in the same league as the NFL players or Tiger Woods, I am blessed to be included in the group that would be required to pay more in Social Security Taxes on total earnings should the cap be removed, and I am more than willing to pay my fair share.

On the other side of this coin, it is only fair that payouts be computed using a flat percentage of the amount a person has paid in *without* a maximum benefit cap. Those who have paid substantially more in Social Security taxes should draw more in benefits when they reach retirement age. Yes, those who have paid in huge amounts would receive huge monthly benefit checks, but that's fair because Social Security retirement benefits are based on the amount of Social Security taxes paid in by the individual.

To impose a "wealth factor" or remove the maximum income cap without removing the maximum benefit cap would reduce the Social Security system to that of another welfare program. It would also "punish" individuals for working hard, which is the opposite of the principles on which our country was founded.

Some think that removing the maximum income and benefit caps would just postpone the problem, and when these young athletes and actors reach retirement age, the problems of Social Security would once again have to be dealt with. This would not be the case, provided these additional funds are *invested* and not *spent*. Surely the "powers that be" must have learned something over the past seventy years.

Others argue that removing the income cap would open the floodgates for tax evasion with individuals "hiding" taxable income. There is less likelihood of this if the maximum benefit cap is also removed and individuals know they will be entitled to greater benefits when they retire. There will always be dishonest people and those who don't want to pay their fair share. However, the Social Security tax is not easily evaded because it is a flat percentage that must be paid before other deductions are allowed.

As I also stated earlier, we must do more than simply engage in a "national conversation." It is my opinion that our thoughts, opinions, and suggestions have no effect unless they are voiced to elected federal officials who are in positions to implement change.

This problem is best resolved sooner than later. I strongly urge each of you to think about possible solutions to the Social Security deficit problem, talk with others, and make your voices heard. Write to your senators and representatives. If you belong to AARP, contact them. It is one of the largest organizations for people 50 years of age and older in the U.S., with a membership of more than forty million. It also has one of the most powerful lobbying groups in the country.

I am enclosing a sample letter at the end of this book in the section *Additional Information*.

We *can* affect change, and we *must*. We have our children's and grandchildren's futures to protect. After all, we didn't learn how to protest together in the 1960s for nothing!

Retirement Age for Full Social Security Benefits

$2,185 a month is the maximum full benefit if you retire in 2008.
Source: Social Security Administration

Year of Birth	Age for Full Benefits
Prior to 1943	65
1943–54	66
1955	66 plus 2 months
1956	66 plus 4 months
1957	66 plus 6 months
1958	66 plus 8 months
1959	66 plus 10 months
1960 and later	67

Early Retirement and Percent of Full Benefits

(Reductions are permanent.)
Source: Social Security Administration

Years Prior to Full Benefit Age	% Of Full Benefit Amount
0	100.0%
1	93.3%
2	86.7%
3	80.0%
4	75.0%
5	70.0%

Delayed Retirement and Percent of Full Benefits

(Increases are permanent.)
Percentages are calculated for individuals born in 1943 or later.
Source: Social Security Administration

Years After Full Benefit Age	% Of Full Benefit Amount
1	108%
2	116%
3	124%
4	132%
5	140%

Age 70 is the mandatory age for receiving Social Security benefits.

Although you may delay Social Security benefits, you may

want to apply for Medicare when you turn 65 to avoid higher premiums.

2008 Budget for Social Security's Major Programs

Source: Bush Budget—2008

Program	Participants	Amount
Social Security	50 Million	$608 Billion
Medicare	45 Million	$454 Billion
Medicaid and SCHIP	65 Million	$211 Billion

SILVER TSUNAMI EXPECTED TO HIT WITH A VENGEANCE!

Wherever we look upon this earth, the opportunities
take shape within the problems.
(Nelson A. Rockfeller)

Continuing the domino effect, a multiplicity of problems will
be created as boomers vacate their positions. There simply are
not enough younger workers to fill the millions of vacated slots.
Within just the next two years, by the end of 2010, about half
(more than 50% of supervisory and over 40% of non-supervi-
sory positions) of the full-time federal civil service workers,
including postal workers, will be eligible to retire. According
to the U. S. Department of Labor, there will be over 930,000
new construction job openings within the next five years. It
is also estimated that by 2011, our country will be short over
100,000 pharmacists at a time when the demand for them will
be at an all time high.

There's already a shortage of long-term care workers in
the US, and many long-term care facilities are presently struggling with the increased demand for workers. That situation
will become significantly more problematic within the next
few years. We are the generation that changed virtually everything, and we are definitely changing expectations regarding
health care services. Boomers will insist on more and better

health care options than have been delivered in the past. Yet, the health care industry seems to be making few strides toward getting prepared for the upcoming *Boomer* crisis. However, there is a four-year initiative called "Better Jobs Better Care" that is currently researching solutions to this fast moving tidal wave.

We were the first generation expected to exceed the earnings of our parents, and now we may well be the first generation to be worse off in retirement than the previous generation. The reality is that most baby boomers will have to work for years after they retire. Many will never realize their anticipated life of leisure. Instead, they will, out of necessity, work longer than any generation heretofore. Many boomers will likely realize retirement is not an option for them when they reach retirement age. Eight out of ten boomers believe they will have to continue working after they retire from their present jobs and are preparing themselves for a second career.

Although we have earned, on average, 53% more than our parents at similar ages, it seems boomers have lived for the present and not saved enough for their retirement. Only the top 20% of boomers appear to have a secure retirement that offers them financial independence. Sadly enough, the average baby boomer's net worth is only about $145,000. Given present low returns on investments, this nest egg will not sustain them for very long. Many have already had a wake-up call reminding them Social Security is, in fact, the "supplement" it was intended to be, and in all likelihood, they will never receive their full benefits. It's estimated that by 2010, Social Security will only be able to payout approximately 75% of earned benefits to retirees. Even those who thought they had planned well and have good pensions will still have to work, at least part-time, to pay for food, gas, and medications.

The double-edged sword is that our life span has significantly and steadily increased, while the cost of health care has also significantly and steadily increased. In the early 1960s, life expectancy for males was only 69. Let's suppose a man worked until he was 62 and lived until age 69. He would have only seven years in retirement.

According to the IRS life-expectancy table, those who begin taking retirement distributions in 2008 at age 62 will live another 22.7 years, taking them to almost 85. Presently, a man who lives to see his 65th birthday has a one in two chance he'll live beyond 85, and a one in four chance he'll live to see his 92nd birthday. This data supports the notion of raising the age requirement for full Social Security retirement benefits that was previously discussed.

On average, females are expected to live two or three years longer than their male counterparts. Plus, a married couple who reaches 65 has a one in two chance that one or the other will live beyond 92 and a one in four chance one of them will live to be 97 years old. Thus, centenarians are rapidly on the increase. That's the good news. The not-so-good news is that the majority of boomers will spend four, maybe five, times as long in retirement as the generation before them. The all-too-personal question remains: "Are there enough eggs in your nest to last as long as you do?"

For some, inheritances will play an important role in their retirement. The largest exchange of wealth in the history of our nation will take place as baby boomers' parents bequeath their life savings to their children. Between 1990 and 2030, approximately $9 trillion will be inherited by boomers. Without careful planning, the majority of this will go for taxes, leaving boomers not nearly as secure as they had thought. A good example is the estate of Joe Robbie, who founded the Miami Dolphins football team in 1966. His estate was estimated at $72 million when he died in 1990. By 1994, the Miami Dolphins had to be sold in order to pay $47 million in estate taxes.

Even if you anticipate inheriting only a few thousand dollars, the time to ensure half or more of it does not go to Uncle Sam is before your parents die, not afterward. Part of the confusion is that the allowable amount of exemption for estate tax keeps changing from one year to the next. This gives rise to discussion as to how your parents' nest egg might be passed on to you unbroken, as well as how your nest egg might pass to your heirs in one piece.

The two primary questions are, "How might unnecessary taxes be avoided?" and "How can probate be avoided?" One of the best ways both of these might be accomplished is through a *Living Trust with a Pour-Over Will.* A Pour-Over Will tells the courts that assets not transferred into the trust for any reason were intended to be placed into the trust. However, items in the Pour-Over Will are still subject to probate. I highly recommend individuals talk with an estate planner to determine what's best for their particular situation.

ARE THERE ENOUGH
EGGS IN YOUR NEST?

RETIREMENT

Retirement, we understand, is great if you are busy,
rich, and healthy. But then, under those conditions,
work is great too.
(Bill Vaughn)

Most boomers are concerned about their retirement, given the
present state of Social Security. Plus, many company pension
plans, as well as personal investments, are subject to a volatile market, which renders retirement income uncertain and
unpredictable. Since baby boomers are retiring earlier and living longer, many are unsure whether their nest eggs will be
sufficient to see them through to the end. To determine this to
one's best ability, there are important questions that must be
answered, such as:

1. What is your current net worth?
2. How much do you presently have in savings and investments earmarked for retirement? How much do you think
   you'll have by the time you stop working?
3. How is this money taxed?
4. How much annual income will you need to retire in the
   manner you realistically expect to?

5. How much of your annual income do you expect to be provided by Social Security and pension benefits?
6. How much do you plan on inheriting?
7. How many years are there before you plan to retire without working?
8. Approximately how many years do you anticipate spending in retirement?
9. Do you have a Long-Term Care insurance policy?
10. How many years will your Long-Term Care policy pay, and how much will it pay per month?
11. Do you have adequate medical insurance coverage, or will you depend solely on Medicare?
12. Do you have prescription drug coverage that will pick up where Medicare Part D leaves off?
13. How much life insurance do you currently have?
14. How will your spouse be provided for in the event you die first and the two of you have depended on each other's retirement income?
15. Have you planned your estate so as to avoid unnecessary taxes and probate?

Now that you've closely examined your nest, let's consider ways your own eggs might be protected from cracking and hopefully grow sufficiently to sustain you throughout your retirement years. Unless your nest eggs are growing and multiplying, you may outlive them and become a financial burden on your family, or at best not be able to enjoy your golden years as you had hoped to.

Federal and state taxes play a huge role in whether your retirement eggs expand or shrivel to nothing. Unfortunately, taxes paid on interest income are often viewed as normal rather than as the all too real fox in the hen house stealing as many eggs as possible. In fact, many people think fees and commissions are the number one cost considerations for investments, when in reality taxes far exceed even the highest fees. Most folks also believe taxes will only increase. Unfortunately, that is probably a safe bet.

For example, let's assume you are earning 5% APY (annual percentage yield) on an investment of $100,000. You will earn $5,000 on that $100,000 over a twelve-month period. This $5,000 in earnings will be subject to federal and state income taxes unless you had it invested in an after tax/tax free (AT/TF) vehicle. For the sake of illustration, let's assume you are in a 25% federal tax bracket. You will owe $1,250 in taxes on that $5,000, leaving you with only $3,750 in earnings. Let's also assume you have a low state income tax of only 5%. You will owe an additional $250 in state taxes, leaving $3,500. Money paid in the form of taxes is money you will never see again. Let's further assume inflation is low—about 2.5%. That lowers your purchasing power by another $87.50, leaving you with only $3,412.50 growth on your $100,000. The prognosis for survival of your egg looks even bleaker if it's invested in stocks or volatile markets, which offer no guarantees in times of greater inflation rates and/or lower interest rates.

There are also many other factors that shrink your nest egg. It is quite common for Medicare and other insurance co-pays for doctor visits and prescription medications to easily run at $400.00 a month ($4,800 a year) after the deductibles are met. Should that come into play, your nest would be minus one egg worth about $1,387.50. You would then have to start dipping into your principal amount and would actually be worse off than you were at the beginning of the year.

Continuing this example, let's assume that instead of paying $1,500 each year in federal and state income taxes, you invested that amount in a tax-deferred account at a 5% rate of return over ten years. The money you sent to Uncle Sam would total $19,810. Even if your federal tax bracket remained at 25% at the time of withdrawal, rendering $4,952.50 due in owed federal taxes, and your state income tax remained at 5%, resulting in $990.50 in state taxes for a total of $5,943, you would still have $13,867 for your own benefit. Money prematurely paid in taxes is not only a cost but is also a lost opportunity to put your money to work for you. This example is illustrated in the following chart.

Investment Fund Accumulation Illustration

$1,500 Sent Annually to Uncle Sam
Invested in a 5% Tax Deferred Account

Year	Annual Payment	Net Annual Interest	Fund Balance
1	$1,500	$75	$1,575
2	$1,500	$154	$3,229
3	$1,500	$236	$4,965
4	$1,500	$323	$6,788
5	$1,500	$414	$8,703
6	$1,500	$510	$10,713
7	$1,500	$611	$12,824
8	$1,500	$716	$15,040
9	$1,500	$837	$17,367
10	$1,500	$943	$19,810

It is vitally important individuals take time to carefully plan their investments so they are not putting their retirement savings at risk or paying unnecessary or premature taxes. In attempts to avoid probate, some people choose to put their adult child's or children's name(s) on their account(s). They presume since their estate will be left to their child or children, they can avoid unnecessary expenses. Sometimes even careless attorneys suggest doing this. However, this is *not* a good idea. By doing so, you set yourself up for possible liquidation of your assets.

For example, should the adult child named on your account(s) divorce, injure someone in an automobile accident, file bankruptcy, or get sued for any reason, your assets become vulnerable and are subject to filed claims. There are much safer ways to avoid probate and unnecessary taxes. These will be discussed in the next section.

The following questions are commonly asked by boomers who are trying to digest the alphabet soup served by financial planners.

1. What are defined contribution plans?

Defined contribution plans are retirement plans in which the amount contributed is *defined* by the employer or the employee. IRAs, 401ks, SEPs, and Simple IRAs, as well as profit sharing and money purchase plans, are all defined contribution plans. Such plans qualify for a tax advantage and are referred to as "qualified" plans.

2. What is a 401k?

A 401k is a qualified individual retirement plan established by employers. Employees may make contributions on a post-tax and/or pre-tax basis. Contributions are usually automatically deducted from employees' paychecks. Employers typically match employee contributions with a pre-determined percentage, which can be as high as 100%. Employees decide where and how contributions will be invested. A profit-sharing feature may also be offered to employees. Earnings grow on a tax-deferred basis.

3. What is an IRA?

An IRA is an Individual Retirement Account that anyone can establish as long as they have earned income. IRAs are qualified accounts that offer tax advantages for retirement savings, including reduced or deferred taxes. IRAs may be plans provided by employers, like 401ks, with higher contribution limits for their employees or plans provided by individuals for themselves. There are several types of IRAs.

Some are funded after taxes are paid on the monies intended for the account, while some are funded with monies that are deposited before taxes are paid, allowing taxes to be deferred. For some, the interest earned on deposits is taxed at the end of each year, while others allow taxes on interest income to be deferred. Yet others allow interest income to be completely tax-free. Consequently, it is in one's best interest to invest in retirement savings accounts, which allow individuals to pay the least amount of taxes on earnings. All IRAs have limitations and restrictions. However, the IRA with the greatest tax advantages is a *Roth*.

The *Roth IRA*, named for Senator William Roth, is an after tax/tax free (AT/TF) investment. Therefore, contributions made to a Roth are made after taxes have been paid on assets intended to fund the Roth. Growth within a Roth, as well as distributions, are tax free, provided the funds have been held in the account for a minimum of five years and the investor is at least 59.5 years of age. Roth contributions are limited to investors who make less than a certain income per year. However, there are no income limitations for rollover funds from a Traditional IRA or from a 401k account to a Roth IRA account. Given Roth IRAs have the greatest tax advantages, individuals who qualify would be wise to contribute the maximum allowable amount each year into this type of retirement savings account.

The *Roth 401k* is a relatively new retirement plan that combines the most advantageous tax features of the Traditional 401k and the Roth IRA. This option is also appropriate for individuals who are self-employed as sole proprietors (not incorporated).

President Bush signed this into law on August 15, 2006, making it retroactive to January 1, 2006. Since then, employers have been allowed to modify their 401k plans to allow employees to select a Roth IRA for all or part of their retirement contributions. This new law also allows the same provisions for 403(b) retirement plans.

There are significant differences between a Traditional 401k and a Roth 401k:

- Traditional 401k contributions are funded with pre-tax dollars (income that is not taxed in the current year), thus, the contribution is tax deductible. Taxes are deferred and taxed at the time of distribution as ordinary income.
- Roth contributions are funded with after-tax dollars (income that is taxed in the current year as ordinary income).
- Traditional 401k earnings are tax-deferred and taxed at the time of distribution as ordinary income.
- Roth earnings are *tax-free* as long as distributions are not taken within the first five years after the Roth was established and the individual is at least 59.5 years of age. There are some exceptions to this rule.
- Traditional IRAs have income limitations.
- Roth 401ks have no income limitations.
- Traditional IRA contributions are limited to $5,000 for participants 49 or younger and $6,000 for those 50 and older for 2008.
- Roth 401k contributions can be as much as $15,500 for participants 49 or younger. Participants 50 and older are allowed an additional $5,000, for a total allowable amount of $20,500. That is, provided no other traditional 401k contributions were made for the current tax year.

An individual's combined contribution to a Traditional 401k, a Roth 401k, or to both cannot exceed $15,500 (49 and younger), or $20,500 (50 and older) for 2008.

- The employer's matching funds are not included in the individual's deferral cap of either $15,500 (49 and younger) or $20,500 (50 and older).
- The employer's matched contributions to an employee's 401k account are funded with pre-tax dollars on the traditional 401k side of the plan. Taxes are deferred, and the employee does not pay tax on the employer's contributions until the time of distribution, at which time it is taxed as ordinary income.
- The employer's maximum contribution, which is $25,500 in 2008, is the traditional 401k part of this Roth 401k combination.
- The employer's contributions are considered part of the maximum limit, which is $46,000 for individuals 50 and older and $41,000 for those 49 and younger in 2008.

What this means for individuals who are self-employed as sole proprietors is:

- You are allowed to contribute up to the allowable amount of either $15,500 or $20,500 as the *employee*. This contribution is funded with after-tax dollars.
- Earnings on contributions are tax-free.
- You are also allowed to contribute the matched limit up to a total combined contribution of $46,000 as the *employer*.
- The amount contributed by you as the *employer* of yourself (as the *employee*) is tax deductible as a business expense.

For example, let's assume you are self-employed, 49 or younger, and you contribute $15,500 (AT/TF), the maximum allowable amount, into a Roth 401k as the employee. You could then contribute $25,500 (PT/TD), the maximum allowable amount for employers, as the employer of yourself. The total contribution would then be $41,000. The $25,500 you contributed as the employer is tax deductible as a business expense.

Now, let's assume you are self-employed, 50 or older, and

you contribute $20,500 (AT/TF), the maximum allowable amount, into a Roth 401k as the employee. You could then contribute $25,500 (PT/TD), the maximum allowable amount for employers, as the employer of yourself. The total contribution would then be $46,000, which is the total combined allowable limit. Again, the $25,500 you contributed as the employer is tax deductible as a business expense.

The Roth 401k retirement account can also be managed through an annuity. Many of the larger insurance companies offer riders, which provide a guaranteed minimum income benefit (GMIB). Plus, some offer up front bonuses on deposits.

Adopting Roth 401k retirement plans has been relatively slow, primarily due to a lack of awareness. However, some of the large firms, including General Motors, Johnson & Johnson, JP Morgan, Chase, IBM, Chevron Corporation, FedEx, and Morgan Stanley, are now offering their employees Roth 401k retirement plans.

The Roth 401k was originally scheduled to sunset, or no longer be available, after December 31, 2010. However, it has been extended as part of the Pension Protection Act of 2006. Unlike Roth IRAs, participants of Roth 401ks must begin taking distributions at 70.5 years of age.

A *Simple IRA* is referred to as an IRA but is actually treated differently. A Simple IRA is an employee pension plan that allows the employee and the employer to make tax-deductible contributions. The portion contributed by the employee is deducted from her/his taxable income, and the portion contributed by the employer is deducted as an allowable business expense. This means the pension is funded with assets for which taxes have not yet been paid. Withdrawals will be taxed as ordinary income at the time of withdrawal.

A *Traditional IRA* is a pre-tax/tax deferred investment. Contributions are funded with monies for which taxes have not yet been paid. Thus, contributions are tax-deductible.

Contributions, as well as earnings, are tax deferred each year and taxed at the time of distribution at ordinary income rates. Allowable contributions for 2008 are $5,000 for participants below 50 years of age and $6,000 for those 50 and older.

A *Simplified Employee Pension Plan (SEP) IRA* is a pre-tax/tax deferred investment. It is intended for self-employed individuals and small business owners who do not have a pension fund in the company's name. Just as with a Traditional IRA, contributions are funded with monies for which taxes have not yet been paid. Thus, contributions are tax-deductible. Contributions, as well as earnings, are tax deferred each year and taxed at the time of distribution as ordinary income. SEPs have higher contribution limits than Traditional IRAs. In 2008, tax-deductible allowable contributions for SEPs are limited to 25% of the participant's compensation, with a cap of $46,000. This is the highest limit allowed by law.

A *Self-Directed IRA* requires a qualified custodian or trustee to hold account assets on behalf of the account owner. Qualified holders must make investments and investment decisions on behalf of the retirement plan according to IRS regulations, which are far too complex to be discussed here. Individuals interested in a Self-Directed IRA should consult a financial advisor.

An *Educational IRA* is also a qualified plan designed to help individuals with higher education expenses. Contributions of up to $2,000 per child under the age of 18 may be made each year, provided the child is enrolled in school. Allowable amounts for contributions are based on the annual income of the investor and are subject to change. Distributions that are used for higher education are usually tax-free.

The *College Education* 529 *plan* is a state-run college savings plan that allows parents to contribute as little as $25 a month and as much as they can afford to invest, without restrictions, up to a lifetime cap, which ranges between $100,000 and

$270,000, depending on the individual state. Money invested in these accounts may be used at any school for all qualified expenses incurred in paying for higher education, including tuition, books, and room and board. Annual tax advantages include certain benefits from the IRS, as well as state tax advantages in some states.

Typically, after meeting certain IRS criteria, most retirement plans are allowed to accept funds from an IRA, and most retirement plans may be rolled into an IRA. However, non-governmental 457 plans cannot. Withdrawals made from an IRA, a 401k, or an annuity are subject to a 10% federal tax penalty if taken before the individual is at least 59.5 years of age.

4. What is an annuity?

Annuities have recently become quite popular. In 2007 alone, annuity sales exceeded $200 billion. However, this concept of saving is not new. It can be traced back to Roman times with contracts that were called *annua* (Latin for annual stipends). During the emperor's time, Roman citizens would exchange a one-time payment made to the annua for lifetime payments, which were to be made annually.

Then, during the 17th century, European governments created a *tontine* as a means of raising revenues to fund their wars with other countries. Governments sold shares to their citizens and promised to repay them over an extensive period of time. One of the first group annuities was started by the United Kingdom as a way to finance its many wars with France and was called the State Tontine of 1693.

However, it was not until 1759 that the first group annuity was created in America. A company in Pennsylvania formed the first annuity retirement plan for Presbyterian ministers. They could make contributions to this fund in exchange for lifetime payments for them and their families.

Americans could not buy annuities outside of a group until

1912, when the Pennsylvania Company for Insurance on Lives and Granting Annuities offered annuities to the general public. Although annuities continued to grow steadily, it was not until the 1930s, during the midst of the Great Depression, that annuities really started to catch on in the U.S. During that time, insurance companies were seen as considerably more stable than banking institutions and better able to make the payouts promised by annuities.

The *New Deal Program* introduced by Franklin D. Roosevelt encouraged Americans to save for their retirement. About this same time, corporate pension plans started developing group annuities. One of the reasons annuities were attractive then, as they are now, is partially due to their tax-deferred status. However, tax-deferral is not the only reason why annuities have become so popular. Other important features of annuities are: a) they do not require medical exams, b) they typically have maturity dates between 5–7 years, and c) they can normally be opened by simply filling out a basic annuity contract and submitting it with the opening funds.

The initial contracts for annuities were simple. They guaranteed a return on principal with a fixed rate of return. When it was time for the annuity to make payouts, individuals could choose to receive payments over a set number of years or as a fixed income for life.

Annuities are tax-deferred and a great way to supplement pensions and other retirement savings. Tax-deferred annuities allow individuals to defer income for use at a later time and pay no taxes on the growth (investment gains) until distributions are made.

In summary, an annuity is a secure, flexible, financial investment offered through insurance companies that can guarantee income for the rest of your life and even provide income for your spouse or any other person you may designate after you are gone. This protects individuals from the possibility of out-living their assets.

Distributions may be made as single lump-sum payments, as a series of payments taken over a defined period of time, or calculated to last a lifetime. Distributions can also be custom-ized to begin as soon as the first premium payment is made or deferred for a number of years after the contract is established. Annuity owners also have the choice of receiving regular fixed interest rates in a *fixed* annuity or allowing their investment to grow in a *variable* annuity, where gains vary according to separate accounts. Plus, there is typically the benefit of life insurance as part of an annuity.

Annuities can be set up to accommodate *qualified* (tax-exempt or tax-deferred) funds, as well as *non-qualified* (money which does not qualify for a tax advantage) funds. Funds may be invested over time or in one payment. There is a tax penalty if qualified funds are distributed before 59.5 years of age.

Most annuities have fewer restrictions than those of con-ventional retirement plans and are designed to help individu-als reach their long-term financial goals. Under current tax laws, annuities are allowed to grow tax-deferred because they are issued by insurance companies. All annuities grow tax-deferred during the accumulation phase.

However, do not confuse *tax-deferred* investments with *tax-free* investments, such as municipal bonds, which normally do not incur income taxes on gains. Annuities are taxed on gains but not until those gains are distributed from the annu-ity. There are literally hundreds of annuities to choose from, and many are designed for specific retirement goals.

Annuity contracts may have higher fees than some invest-ments. However, certain fees ensure protection of the princi-pal and earnings against declining markets as well and in the event of a premature death of the participant. Fees associated with particular riders may also provide a guaranteed minimum income benefit. As previously demonstrated, the cost savings secondary to deferring taxes far exceed the cost of fees more than a hundredfold.

Commissions are paid by the insurance companies and not out of participant's deposits. Therefore, 100% of the money goes to work for the participant immediately. Millions of investors, especially those with retirement in mind, are able to use annuities to their advantage.

According to the Life Insurance and Market Research Association (LIMRA International Inc.), an independent service that tracks the insurance industry, the growth in sales of fixed and variable annuities has followed this track: $98.5 billion in 1995, $155 billion in 1999 (with the majority of this growth in variable annuities), and 2008 sales are estimated at over $200 billion, making them more popular than ever. The most common types of annuities are fixed, variable, index, and immediate.

Fixed annuities offer stability and assurance because they offer fixed interest rates that are set by the insurance company for up to ten years. Owners always know exactly how much their money is earning and when interest will be credited. Some companies initially offer bonuses for initial investments or higher interest rates to attract buyers. However, most companies offer fixed interest rates set by the company, which remain constant throughout the life of the contract, or change annually. In addition to interest rates, maturity periods and death benefits are other options to consider when purchasing a fixed annuity. Fixed annuities offer a fixed income guaranteed for a certain period of time, for life, or a combination of both, although they are not regulated by the Securities and Exchange Commission (SEC).

The first *variable annuity* was created in the U.S. in 1952. Interest paid on variable annuities was calculated on the performance of individual accounts within the annuity. Owners could actually choose the type of accounts they wanted and typically received a modest guarantee in exchange for the greater risk they assumed. As annuities evolved, more features were added. These features included shorter maturity periods, guaranteed death benefits, bonus rates, and checkbook access to funds. Plus, some companies guarantee the value of the annuity will not decrease below the initial premium. This is accomplished with *riders* to the policy, which are provided at an additional cost.

Although there is risk with this investment, variable annuities, unlike fixed annuities, are regulated by the SEC. Individuals may also transfer funds from one investment option to another within a variable annuity without being taxed. However, when the money is taken out of a variable annuity, earnings are taxed as ordinary income rather than as capital gains, which could be lower. Consequently, the tax-deferral benefits of a variable annuity outweigh the costs only if held as a long-term investment. Variable annuities are intended to help individuals meet their retirement and other long-range goals.

Variable accounts have accelerated the popularity of annuities, primarily due to the increased popularity of mutual funds over the past twenty years. There are now about twice as many mutual funds as there are stocks. Sub-accounts within the annuity allow for investments in equities inside the annuity. Investment options are typically equity accounts, such as mutual funds, that invest in money market instruments, stocks, bonds, or some combination of these. Modern variable annuities are offered by many of the most respected money managers and financial advisors in the industry. Individuals still have the option of deciding how their money will be invested in the separate accounts within the variable annuity. In addition, many insurance companies provide a death benefit that will never be lower than the initial amount invested in the annuity, less any withdrawals made prior to death.

Should you find a different annuity with a broader selection of investment choices, a better interest rate, better payout options, or a greater death benefit, you are allowed to exchange one annuity contract for a different one without paying tax on investment gains. This is referred to as a 1035 *exchange* and is authorized under section 1035 of the U.S. tax code. You could be required to pay surrender penalties on your old annuity. However, most companies offer enhanced rates or bonuses to compensate for possible surrender penalties. You could also incur additional fees if withdrawals are made prior to maturity dates. A new surrender charge period typically begins with the new annuity. Always ask how much an exchange will cost you. *A 1035 exchange is not recommended unless the new contract has lower fees.*

The Guaranteed Minimum Income Benefit (GMIB) does precisely what the name implies. It guarantees minimum annual payments, regardless of how the annuity performs. One of the greatest fears for many retirees is that they will outlive their income. Consequently, many investors find that the lifetime stream of income offered by the GMIB brings them a wonderful sense of peace. Having peace of mind is a major reason why many investors prefer this type of variable annuity rather than standard mutual funds. This provision can be purchased as a rider on some variable annuities but is not offered by all major insurance companies. Contracts vary, so you would be wise to shop.

A *bonus* annuity usually offers a 3–6.5% up front bonus with a nine-year surrender period. The *standard-type* annuity usually offers no bonus and a seven-year decreasing surrender period, while the *L-Share* annuity offers no bonuses but only has a three to four year surrender period. The *no-surrender charge* annuity requires no fee to get in and no fee to get out, with no bonus.

Participants are typically allowed to exercise this GMIB

provision after the tenth year, although some companies may require you to annuitize the entire contract at that time. However, some contracts allow provisions to be exercised before the tenth year and for partial annuitizations.

Payout options vary. Participants typically are allowed to choose between variable payments that are based on market performance or fixed payments that remain the same throughout the payout period. Most contracts allow you to receive payments for a time between five and twenty years or to receive payments for the remainder of your life, your spouse's life, or any combination of the two. One product that is particularly attractive and that is becoming quite popular allows participants to annuitize on a variable basis and receive the upside of the market, while still guaranteeing a minimum benefit payment no matter how the market performs. This ensures payments will keep up with inflation.

Another popular and attractive variable annuity is the *Guaranteed Retirement Income Benefit (GRIB)*. This is a *living benefit annuity*. Some of the most popular GRIBs guarantee a net return (in 2008) between 4%-7% after all fees are paid or the greatest value is attained on each anniversary during the surrender period, whichever is greater.

The percentage typically depends on the age of the participant—the older individuals are, the greater the percentage. For example, participants between 55 to 65 years of age might get 4%, those between 65 to 75 years old might get 5%, and those between 75 and 85 years old might get 6%, while participants 85 and older might get 7%.

Some companies offer up front bonuses, and most have a surrender charge or penalty for early withdrawal. They may also charge a slightly higher annual fee in exchange for this living guarantee. GRIB rider contracts vary significantly depending on the insurance company and the various products, so ask lots of questions and shop before you make your choice.

Indexed annuities are fixed annuities that provide benefits or earn interest based on links to an external equity index. These types of annuities are designed to mirror the performance of the stock markets, such as the NASDAQ, DOW, S&P 500, or European Indexes. Interest is calculated and credited using a formula based on changes in the index to which the annuity is linked. Indexed annuities may be deferred or immediate. The value of the index is typically tied to a stock or other equity reference, which is not predictable and varies from day to day. However, it is easy to track their performance month-to-month and point-to-point because yearly average market figures are readily available.

Immediate annuities have no accumulation phase and thus begin paying in regular increments the moment the contract is purchased.

With an *ordinary annuity,* also called an *annuity-immediate,* payments are made at the end of each monthly, quarterly, or annual period.

5. What is estate tax?

The estate tax is part of the *Unified Gift and Estate Tax* system in the United States. Estate tax is imposed when property is transferred either by a will or according to state law if the estate is left intestate (without a will) after an individual's death. Life insurance benefits and other financial instruments that are "payable at death" are included in the "gross tax" imposed by the federal government. The "unified gift tax" is a tax imposed on transfers of property while an individual is still living and prevents individuals from avoiding estate taxes by transferring property just before they die. Many states also impose an estate or inheritance tax in addition to the federal estate tax. Estate tax is also referred to as "death tax." There is no federal estate tax on estates with a total taxable value of $2,000,000 or less. Once this credit exemption is met, the federal estate tax is a flat 45% of taxable assets. Assets left to a spouse or a charitable organization may be exempt.

6. What is the difference between a will and a trust?

A will is a common document that allows an individual (the testator) to establish her/his intentions as to how she/he wants her/his estate to be dealt with after her/his death. The assets of an estate, whether left in a will or a trust, are typically referred to as "property," which is legally understood to be personal possessions such as furs, jewelry, clothes, automobiles, boats, recreational vehicles, homes, cash, certificates of deposit, annuities, bonds, stocks, life insurance, monies owed (collections), interests in businesses, royalties, and/or commercial, personal, or rental real estate.

People often use wills as the last means of expressing their deepest feelings for their loved ones. An executor, or personal representative, is normally appointed in the will to carry out the wishes of the testator. Wills are also intended to simplify the transition for survivors by transferring assets quickly, avoiding unnecessary taxes, and providing peace of mind for the testator. Assets are normally distributed as single, individual gifts. Despite the numerous advantages of wills, however, only about 30% of Americans have valid wills.

When individuals die without a valid will, they leave their estate *intestate*. If the husband and wife both die without a valid will and leave minor children, the state will decide who will be their guardian. Close family members could end up fighting court battles over the children, or, what could be even worse, the kids might end up with strangers raising them.

When assets are left, *intestate* survivors are often faced with a heavy tax burden in addition to a difficult, lengthy, and expensive legal course of action. Estates left *intestate* are subject to decisions made by a probate court. The court will decide how the estate is to be divided after death expenses and unpaid debts are paid. Although probate courts are required to follow legal guidelines, state intestacy laws only recognize relatives. Therefore, charitable organizations and close friends intended to be beneficiaries will not receive any benefits from estates left *intestate*. Unfortunately, assets may go to individuals who would never have been chosen by the testator to receive benefits. If the court cannot find any living relatives, assets from the estate are typically awarded to the state or local government. For obvious reasons, it is by far better to leave a will specifying who you would want to care for your minor children, as well as how you want your assets to be distributed, rather than subject your survivors and property to government-mandated court decisions.

It is also important to keep in mind that even though there is a will that clearly specifies how an estate is to be distributed, it will still be subject to probate, which will cost the estate a certain percentage and could tie up the inheritance for months or years, as well as being subject to taxes where appropriate.

Valid wills remain in force until they are superseded by a subsequent valid will or completely revoked. Changes are typically allowed by an amendment, referred to as a *codicil,* without having to rewrite the will entirely. Once a will is submitted to a probate court, it becomes a matter of public record, just as all the other documents associated with probate, including the deceased person's debts as well as assets. The terms of a *living* trust, however, are not a matter of public record.

Simple wills are most commonly used for simple estates and normally outline the individual's preference as to distribution of her/his assets in a straightforward manner.

A *joint will* is actually one document intended to shield two people—normally a husband and wife. Joint wills are considered unwise for estates greater than $675,000 and are often considered a huge mistake in estates of a far lesser value.

A *pour-over will* allows individuals to leave some or all of their assets in a trust established prior to their death. It also tells the courts that assets that were not transferred into the trust prior to the person's death were intended to be included in the trust.

Individuals who feel the need to have one or more trusts to handle various assets in their estate may choose a *testamentary trust will.*

In most states, wills must be written and preferably outlined in a pre-printed document, or at least typed. However, about twenty states allow wills to be in the testator's own handwriting. A *holographic will* is handwritten by the testator and may or may not have been witnessed.

An *oral will,* which is also referred to as a *nuncupative will,* is only communicated verbally. Very few states recognize oral wills.

Trusts are documents intended to help individuals manage their estates while they are still living, as well as ensure their intentions are in place in the event they should die. A trust allows individuals to manage assets by transferring and distributing specific assets and obligations to different people. Trusts also allow individuals to specify particular circumstances for receipt of benefits, as well as spread distribution of benefits over a period of time instead of as single gifts. Trusts allow individuals to accomplish goals after their deaths. Therefore, many individuals prefer to have trusts instead of wills. However, a pour-over will should be included in the trust as part of the estate plan. There are several types of wills, while trusts fall into only two major categories. The two broad classifications of trusts are *testamentary trusts,* and *living trusts.*

Testamentary trusts allow for assets to be transferred into the trust only after the grantor dies. For example, a single parent might include a testamentary trust in her/his will assigning her/his assets to a trustee who has been appointed the responsibility of managing these assets for the benefit of minor children. Since a testamentary trust is not automatically created

SANDRA W. HAYMON, Ph.D.

upon the death of the individual but normally specified as a provision of the will, the assets allotted to a testamentary trust are required to go through probate prior to commencement of the trust.

Living trusts, also referred to as *Inter Vivos* trusts, are initiated while the grantor is still living and may be planned to continue after her/his death. Living trusts are intended to help individuals avoid probate, which could tie up the estate for months and consume about 5% of the estate in court costs and attorney fees. Assets transferred into a living trust before the grantor's death typically do not go through probate because it is the grantor who dies, not the trust. Therefore, any and all assets transferred to a revocable trust are no longer part of the grantor's estate and subsequently not subject to probate.

A living trust does not protect one's assets from creditors. Typically, after the grantor's death, all assets, including those held in a living trust, are subject to lawful debts and creditors who have won lawsuits against the grantor. Even the grantor's home, which is held in a living trust and intended to be given to surviving children, could be ordered sold in order to pay debts up to the value of the home.

The person (trustee) appointed to handle the trust after the death of the grantor simply transfers ownership from the living trust to the specified beneficiaries named in the trust. Typically, this takes only a few weeks, and there are no court costs or attorney fees. After all of the property in the living trust has been transferred to the beneficiaries, the living trust ceases to exist. Other benefits of a living trust are that a) they significantly reduce estate taxes for large estates, and b) they can provide for long-term property management.

7. What are the differences between revocable and irrevocable trusts?

Living trusts may be *revocable* or *irrevocable.* The terms of a revocable living trust may be changed or revoked by the grantor at any time after the trust is initiated. A revocable living trust is normally used as a supplement to a will. It often names a specific person to manage the grantor's affairs should he or she become incapacitated and usually specifies that it is to become irrevocable at the death of the grantor. However, the grantor of an irrevocable living trust permanently surrenders his or her right to make changes after the trust commences.

Ideally, a revocable living trust would be enhanced by a *pour-over will*, which specifies that all assets not already transferred to the living trust would be transferred to the trust at the grantor's death.

8. What is a charitable trust?

Individuals who want to give large sums to charities may elect a charitable trust, which offers them several substantial tax breaks in addition to helping out their favorite charities. However, if an individual only wants to donate small charitable amounts, a charitable trust probably isn't advisable.

Charitable trusts are irrevocable. Consequently, once you have formed it and it commences, you cannot regain legal control of the assets placed in the trust. Allowable charities must be approved by the Internal Revenue Service (IRS), with tax-exempt status.

A charitable remainder trust is the most common type of charitable trust. Those who donate to a charitable remainder trust are typically allowed to write off the value of their gift over a five-year period. In addition, at the end of the specified payment period or the individual's death, trust property goes to the charity outright and is not considered part of the estate. Consequently, it is not subject to federal estate tax. This would only be advantageous to large estates.

A charitable trust also allows individuals to avoid paying capital gains tax by allowing assets, which have significantly increased in value, to be converted into cash without paying tax on the profits. Non-income-producing assets in a charitable trust are typically sold, and the proceeds are used to purchase assets that produce income. However, charities are not required to pay capital gains tax. Consequently, the proceeds stay in the trust and are not subject to capital gains tax.

In addition to receiving huge tax breaks, individuals who set up a charitable remainder trust normally structure it so that they will receive regular payments from the trust. They may opt for a fixed annuity so they will receive the same amount of income from the trust each year, even if the trust investments perform at a rate lower than expected. Individuals may request annual payouts for as much as they want. However, greater payouts naturally result in a lesser amount allowed for income tax deduction. Plus, payments that are set too high might start to tap into the principal amount and perhaps exhaust the trust before the payment term is over, leaving nothing for the charity. Most charities are unlikely to accept a donation in the form of a charitable trust if it is possible the payout schedule will outlast the assets.

Annual payments may also be set up as a percentage of the value of the trust each year, to be reappraised annually. For example, the charitable trust could stipulate that the donor receive 10% of the value of the trust each year. Since payments are dispersed as a percentage rather than a fixed dollar amount, if the value of the assets in the trust increases, annual payments to the donor would increase proportionately. Under current IRS code, individuals must receive a minimum of 5% of the value of the trust annually.

9. What is an Irrevocable Life Insurance Trust (ILIT)?

Another way some individuals are able to avoid paying estate tax is by establishing an Irrevocable Life Insurance Trust (ILIT). An ILIT is established to purchase life insurance intended to pay estate taxes so assets won't have to be sold in order to pay taxes owed to the IRS. Typically, death benefits paid from the insurance policy to the ILIT are excluded from the insured's estate. An ILIT can also be prepared so benefits passed to the surviving spouse will also be excluded from her/his estate. This trust is irrevocable and cannot be changed in any way once it is established.

10. What is Long-Term Care Insurance (LTCI)?

Long-Term Care Insurance helps pay for many services required by individuals who have chronic illnesses or disabilities that are not normally covered by ordinary health insurance policies, including Medicare. Most long-term care insurance policies typically pay for a) home-health care providers to assist with activities of daily living (ADLs), including eating, bathing, dressing, meal preparation, and light housekeeping, b) residential assisted living services, including a private room or small apartment, meals, assistance with ADLs, health monitoring, and dispersing medications, c) visiting nurses, d) nursing home care, and e) adult day care or other community services. Customarily, the only eligibility requirement is that the individual is unable to perform two or more ADLs.

The best time to buy long-term care insurance is perhaps during middle age, when premiums are lower. Industry experts content that age 59 is the ideal age for purchasing long-term care insurance. The older you are, the higher the premiums will be. Also, the younger individuals are, the more likely they are to be insurable.

Most long-term care policies have restrictions on age and health status, yet many people don't think about long-term care until their health begins to fail. By then, it could be too late to make this purchase, as there are many diagnoses that render people ineligible for long-term care insurance.

Healthy individuals who wait until they are in their 70s or

80s to think about long-term health care may discover they are too high a risk, due to their age, for an insurer to cover them. Even if they do qualify, the premiums would probably be cost-prohibitive.

Long-term care is very expensive. One's life savings can evaporate within a few months due to expenses incurred in long-term care services. Having long-term care insurance is perhaps one of the best ways individuals can ensure they do not outlive their savings, especially given most people will need to stretch their retirement savings through twenty or more years while continuing to pay the soaring costs of health care. Long-term care insurance helps individuals protect their assets, in addition to minimizing their dependence on other family members and friends. *Long-term care insurance also allows individuals to decide what services they want to receive and where they want to receive them.*

However, premiums for long-term care insurance are also expensive. In 2008, healthy individuals who waited until they were 65 years old could expect to pay between $2,000 and $3,000 in annual premiums for long-term care insurance, with premiums adjusted for inflation. There are a couple of important considerations when purchasing long-term care (LTC) insurance: 1) Can you afford to pay the premiums without lowering your standard of living? And 2) Will you be able to afford the premiums should your present income decline?

There are several considerations when choosing appropriate coverage. Individuals may choose from a smorgasbord of coverage options, including a) nursing home care only, b) home care only, c) a combination of coverage options, including assisted living and adult day care, in addition to skilled nursing and home care, and d) policies that will pay for a family member or friend to take care of the individual in her/his own home.

Another consideration is the amount of coverage the policy will pay as a daily or monthly benefit. If the cost of care is more than the allowable daily or monthly benefit, individuals will be required to pay the balance out of pocket or by some other means.

The benefit period is the length of time the policy will pay benefits. Benefit periods could span from two to six years or for the remainder of the person's life.

There is also an elimination, or waiting period, typically from zero to one hundred days, which requires individuals to pay all of their long-term care expenses out of pocket before the policy begins to pay benefits. Naturally, the longer the elimination period, the lower the premiums will be.

It is also important to choose a policy that has inflation protection. Given the soaring costs of health care, purchasing a policy without inflation protection will probably mean you will have a policy that doesn't cover many of your expenses by the time you need the benefits. The two main types of inflation protection are 1) automatic coverage increases, which will hopefully keep up with inflation, and 2) the right to add coverage at a later date to the existing policy.

Inflation riders usually consist of either: a) a simple percentage rate, which is set by the company and allowed for each year, b) a percentage rate that is compounded annually but tied to the Consumer Price Index (CPI), which is set by the Federal Government, or c) a percentage rate that is set by the company and compounded annually. Although premiums are a bit higher for riders that have a compounded rate (which is not tied to the CPI), this is usually a much better deal in the long run.

Policies with a *non-forfeiture benefit* continue paying benefits, even if you stop paying premiums. However, this feature typically adds 10%-100% to the initial premium.

Other important considerations are to make sure the policy: a) clearly explains how eligibility will be determined and when you will be eligible for coverage, b) does not require a hospital stay before benefits begin, c) is renewed as long as you pay the premiums, d) allows you to stop paying premiums once you begin receiving benefits, e) has only one lifetime deductible, f) covers pre-existing conditions disclosed at the time the policy was written, g) allows you to downgrade coverage should you no longer be able to afford the initial premiums, h) provides coverage for dementia, i) offers a minimum of one year of home-health care coverage, and j) provides skilled nursing care. Although there is a *free look* clause that allows individuals to cancel an insurance policy within a certain number of days after they've signed and paid for it, it is important to ensure the policy allows you to cancel it for any reason within thirty days of purchase and to also receive a refund.

Since long-term care insurance policies come in all shapes and sizes, it is important to shop companies, as well as policies, and compare them prior to making a decision. Do not pay an agent with cash. Always write the check payable to the insurance company and note what it is for on the check. As soon as you get your policy, review it to ensure you have the coverage you thought you were paying for.

The *Federal Long-Term Care Insurance Policy (FLTCIP)* offers long-term care insurance for individuals associated with our federal government, including active and retired members of the uniformed services and federal and postal employees, as well as their qualified relatives. About 20 million people are eligible to apply for federal long-term care insurance.

A DRESS REHEARSAL
BEFORE YOU RETIRE

Yesterday is experience. Tomorrow is hope. Today is
getting from one to the other as best we can.
(John M. Henry)

With so many options to consider and so many choices (over
8,000 mutual funds alone), it is little wonder many cope by
trying to avoid the subject of retirement altogether. However,
postponing decisions pertaining to this most important life
event could be financially costly and could actually create a
greater level of stress later. Financial experts suggest most individuals could benefit from a sort of *dress rehearsal,* which needs
to start at least five years prior to her/his actual retirement
date and preferably ten years prior to the time she/he plans to
stop working. Unfortunately, many boomers have waited too
long, and now it's too late. The offspring of boomers would be
wise to begin seriously planning for their retirement today.

One of the first and perhaps the most important step individuals might take to reduce stress and prepare for retirement
is to focus on paying off all existing debt and avoid making any
future purchases for which they cannot pay cash. This requires
maturity, discipline, commitment, and delaying gratification.
However, the peace of mind and self-satisfaction of being

debt-free far exceed any momentary pleasure obtained from self-indulgence and immediate gratification.

Having outstanding balances is an incredibly bad idea for anyone, and especially for retired individuals. If you haven't already done so, make a list of outstanding balances, monthly payment amounts, and rates of interest. My initial advice would be to concentrate on paying off the balance with the highest rate of interest first. Then, take that monthly payment and apply it to the balance with the next highest interest rate, and so on, until you are debt-free.

However, most folks who find themselves with numerous debt payments seem better able to pay off the debt with the smallest balance first, then take that monthly payment and apply it to the next smallest balance until that one is paid off, and so on and so forth. It seems the gratification in seeing a debt paid off and having one less monthly payment is enough reward to keep individuals and families committed to their goal of breaking out of the bondage of debt so that they may enjoy the peace of not owing anyone for anything.

If you have committed the cardinal sin of incurring credit card debt, you would be wise to cut up any and all credit cards in your possession or that you have access to. Carry-over balances on credit cards are blatant evidence that you lack personal discipline and obviously don't understand the intent of credit cards. When you pay the entire balance each month, you allow the credit card to work for you. A credit card not only offers convenience, it might also add to your portfolio by contributing points for airline tickets, hotels, or cash-back percentages. However, if you presently carry over balances or have done so in the past, you would perhaps be better off simply paying cash for all your purchases and expenditures.

Credit card balances are also a red flag that you are obviously living beyond your means and perpetuating your debt situation by foolishly paying exorbitant interest rates. It has been suggested that even Howard Hughes, much less those of us with considerably less net worth and income, could not have afforded credit card debt.

The number one stressor for individuals and in marriages is financial problems created by debt—primarily credit card debt. There is great wisdom in an old saying: "If you can't afford to pay for it, you can't afford it."

According to Dave Ramsey, in days past a BMW or Mercedes Benz was the status symbol many worked for. However, according to him, the new status symbol is that of being debt-free. There are radio and TV shows, such as Dave Ramsey's, that not only challenge folks to "eat rice and beans and beans and rice" until they are debt-free, but also teaches them how to achieve this elevated status. Being debt-free means paying off everything, including one's house. I highly recommend Dave Ramsey's book, *The Total Money Makeover,* and his debt-free program, *Financial Peace University.* More information about Dave Ramsey may be found at www.daveramsey.com. It seems it's taken an entire generation for us to come full circle and realize what our parents seemed to have known intuitively— that true satisfaction and success come from living within one's means, avoiding debt, and saving for a rainy day.

Research suggests individuals who save at least 10% of their income actually have a higher standard of living than folks who do not save. Ideally, individuals would pay themselves first and then live on the other 90% of their income. It is also interesting to note that individuals who adhere to the Christian belief of paying 10% of their income in tithes, in addition to saving 10%, have an even higher standard of living on 80% of their income and report their money seems to go further than those who live on 100% or more of their income.

Beginning at least five years prior to retiring, develop a retirement budget based on projections of your anticipated level of income, as well as your projected expenditures once you are no longer working. Create a list of all income sources and amounts. Determine what the monthly income will be from your pension plan, Social Security, personal savings, investments, inheritances, rental income, reverse mortgage, and/or other sources of income.

You will also need to list all possible expenditures, including normal living expenses such as rent/mortgage, food, clothing, utilities, landline and cell phones, Internet and cable/dish services, as well as premiums for health, automobile, home, dental, life, and long-term care insurance. You need to include anticipated out-of-pocket expenses for insurance deductibles, co-pays, and medicines. Be sure you budget for auto expenses, including regular servicing, tires, and a realistic amount to cover unexpected expenses, home repairs, and maintenance.

Don't forget to include budgeted amounts for vacations, as well as birthdays, graduations, weddings, anniversaries, and baby gifts, as well as added expenses incurred during Thanksgiving, Christmas, Hanukah, Valentine's Day, Easter, and other celebrated holidays. Over the course of a year, gifts and holidays translate into hundreds or thousands of extra dollars, which can wreak havoc on a budget that has not allowed for these expenditures.

Try to anticipate medium and large purchases or moves and include an educated forecast of those expenses—amounts as well as probable dates these will be incurred. Another future expense that you and your spouse might want to take care of would be to purchase a pre-paid funeral and burial package, which could include burial plots and grave markers or cremation expenses. This not only locks in the purchase amount at current prices, it also provides an opportunity to make these decisions at a time when you might be better able to think more sensibly rather than waiting until one passes away forcing the other to make choices under emotional duress.

It might help to observe your spending habits closely to

discover unnecessary spending by keeping track of every cent you spend for at least two months. Get receipts for every purchase, no matter how small or seemingly insignificant—even a pack of gum—and toss those receipts into a box to be tallied at the end of each month and included in your budget. Many are surprised at the amount of money they spend frivolously that could more wisely be spent on legitimate retirement expenditures.

Make a commitment to live within your retirement budget for at least five years, preferably ten. This should provide a fairly realistic view as to whether your retirement plans are feasible. It could also offer an opportunity for you to make adjustments and corrections while you have the means to do so.

Annuities purchased through insurance companies are a good way of ensuring you will have a steady stream of income throughout your retirement life. As previously discussed, there are several different types of annuities.

Should you find that you need additional income, you might consider a reverse mortgage on your home. Although reverse mortgages are becoming a lot more popular now than when I suggested this as a potential source of steady income twelve years ago, many believe this should, perhaps, be a last resort after a critical analysis of all other options has been explored. The upshot of reverse mortgages is if your home is paid for or you have a large amount of equity in it, you could have the lending institution convert your home equity into a monthly stream of income for you. However, you need to clearly understand the conditions and limitations of the reverse mortgage, have no intentions of selling or bequeathing your home, and ensure the income generated by a reverse mortgage will not interfere with government assistance that you might be receiving.

Long-term care insurance may be one of the best ways of protecting your nest eggs. In addition to long-term care, many

LTC policies offer temporary care, which may be necessary following an accident, surgery, stroke, or other medical situation where persons may need assisted or skilled care for only a short period of time. Some policies now offer refunds of all or a percentage of the monthly premiums in the event coverage is not utilized. Long-term care policies were discussed in greater detail in a previous chapter.

At least six months to a year before you plan to retire, it is a good idea to find out if your health insurance coverage will change when you are no longer an employee of that company. If so, how will it change? Will you have the same coverage should you move out of the insurance company's coverage area, or will you need to change to a different company? If you are required to change, are pre-existing illnesses, disorders, and conditions covered, or is there a waiting period? What happens should you have an accident or become ill while traveling outside the United States? How does your present health insurance fit with Medicare coverage? Will you need a supplemental policy? Given the accelerated rate of rising health care costs, having sufficient medical coverage is of the utmost importance, and the time to ensure you will be covered is prior to retiring. Additional information about Medicare and other programs is provided in the chapter titled *Assistance Programs.*

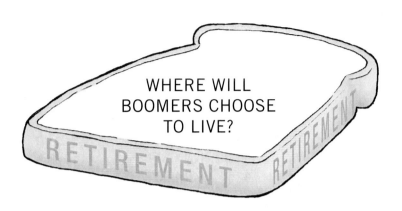

WHERE WILL
BOOMERS CHOOSE
TO LIVE?

RETIREMENT   RETIREMENT

There is a time to let things happen and a time to
make things happen.
(Hugh Prather, Notes on Love and Courage)

As would be expected, the need for soccer fields is on the decline, while the demand for golf courses is soaring. So where and how will boomers live when they retire? This question calls for even more choices and decisions.

Many will have their home mortgages paid off, and this alone will afford them additional options they otherwise would not have. Some will choose to move to warmer climates so they will no longer have to shovel snow and risk broken hips due to falls on ice. Others will be snow birds—choosing to keep their homes up north for the summers and buying or renting a smaller home or condo in warmer climates for the winters. One consideration is the differential prices of homes between regions. It's best to check out cost of living indexes in addition to the prices of homes. Garden spots are expensive.

Some couples will have to work through compromises due to differences of opinions about where and how they will live out their retirement years. This may require thinking outside the box in order to find the optimum situation where both partners feel they're in their ideal environment. After all, many have worked their entire adult lives just so they could live their last years exactly as they dreamed.

Most individuals who live in mainstream America will continue to live in their present homes, especially if their homes are paid for. They will want to enjoy the freedom from mortgage payments as well as the comfortable familiarity that their old neighborhood and community afford. Many will likely find moving, even to a smaller home, to be cost prohibitive or at least not cost effective, and doing so could actually lower their standard of living.

However, millions of boomers are ready to scale down and want a different lifestyle. They no longer need nor want big houses and large yards. They don't want to spend their time taking care of houses, lawns, and other material possessions they've spent their lives accumulating. Many feel they've paid their dues by raising kids and volunteering in addition to working in responsible careers the past thirty-five to forty years. Some now feel it's their *turn* to live their lives playing tennis, golfing, hiking, and traveling without unnecessary stress and responsibility.

To accommodate this demand, retirement communities are popping up all over the country, as well as many exotic places outside the United States. Del Webb, the first pioneer in this area, was featured on the cover of Time magazine after opening Sun City, Arizona, on January 1, 1960, and more than 100,000 people toured his community during the three-day grand opening. Webb had expected only about 10,000 visitors. Since then, Webb has built similar retirement communities in sixteen states.

Many communities offer a variety of retirement living venues, from single-family homes to townhouses and condominiums without the responsibility of lawn care. These active adult communities normally require single residents to be at least 50 or 55 years of age. In the case of a couple, at least one has to meet the age requirement. Children and grandchildren are encouraged to visit but not allowed to live there on a full-time basis. These communities typically resemble fine resorts, offering numerous golf courses, indoor and outdoor pools, hot tubs, saunas, exercise rooms, biking and hiking trails, tennis courts, movie theaters, bowling, restaurants (with fine dining), and community centers with planned activities and classes as well as cultural events. Many residents find they have need for only one automobile since golf carts are the usual mode of transportation within the community.

Others boomers will prefer greater flexibility and choose to live in RV (recreational vehicle) retirement communities, which may offer many of the same amenities, such as golf courses, pools, etc. In addition to being less expensive, RV retirement is ideal for those who want to see the country (perhaps visiting relatives and friends along the way), hike, or bike a variety of trails, play hundreds of different golf courses, or just be able to pick up and go when the urge hits them.

Non-traditional retirement communities are now springing up. A new and different concept is The Academy Village, near Tucson, Arizona, which offers individuals a new way of aging—lifelong learning. At the center of the village is the Arizona Senior Academy, a non-profit organization founded by Dr. Henry Koffler, President Emeritus of the University of Arizona.

Members are offered a smorgasbord of ongoing learning opportunities. Last year, the Senior Academy sponsored over one hundred events and continues to add to the menu. Selections include five and ten-week courses, presentations, mini-programs, seminars, and panel discussions on such topics as music theory, geology, astronomy, watercolors, yoga, poetry, book reviews, healthcare, gardening, piano recitals, and opportunities to learn other languages.

In addition to continuing one's own learning, members are

given opportunities to give back to the larger community by sharing their talents, experience, and expertise in mentoring students, serving as science fair judges, offering school and civic presentations, or perhaps sponsoring young musicians, among many other opportunities.

The best place to retire depends on individual interests, priorities, and level of retirement income. For some, the criteria used will be weather and landscape, proximity to airports, sporting events, golf courses, and/or cultural events. Others will be more focused on costs and proximity to grandchildren and other family members. Many will make decisions about their own retirement based on their level of involvement in caring for aging parents or other elderly loved ones. Others may be required to move into their parents' home or move their parents in to their homes not only to take care of them, but to combine incomes so that they may all live more comfortably at a higher standard of living.

Presently, 33% of baby boomers are already helping their families out financially. Nine out of ten boomers report they have helped their adult children out financially, and 29% attribute helping their adult children financially to the demise of their own savings. Consequently, this severely limits their choices of where and how they will live out their retirement years.

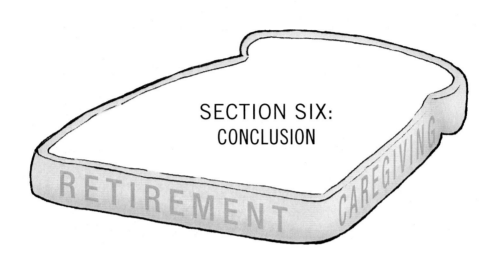

SECTION SIX:
CONCLUSION

RETIREMENT   CAREGIVING

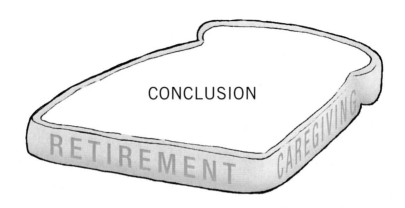

CONCLUSION

Forgiveness simply means we give up our need to
judge the other person.
(Sandra W. Haymon)

Caring for aging loved ones could be a wonderful opportunity for us to learn more about them, more about ourselves, and more about humanity in general. We have a choice. We may choose to experience this process as difficult, stressful, and unpleasant. We may also choose to experience it as positive, meaningful, and as adding value to our lives.

As I look back on those years when I took care of my mother and stepfather, as Charles Dickens might say, "It was the best of times; it was the worst of times..." However, having the opportunity to provide care for them was truly a rewarding, learning experience in my own growth process. It enabled me to examine my personal values, as well as come to terms with my own mortality.

I want to emphasize that saying good-bye and bringing closure is not only different for each of us but is different for us each time it occurs, depending on the nature of the relationship and on where we are in our own growth process. I have merely shared my experiences in saying good-bye to my father, stepfather, friend, and mother to illustrate this point.

Each of these occurrences has afforded me remarkable opportunities to explore, distill, and evaluate my truths. Hopefully, the lessons I've learned from saying good-bye to loved ones will enable me to better tend to and cherish those I still have with me.

One truth I've learned is that relationships actually don't end just because individuals are no longer physically present. Those relationships only change in material ways. I've found that my relationships with many of my deceased loved ones have actually grown deeper and more meaningful, especially as I have forgiven and have been reassured of my own forgiveness. I also find that, much like my client, Sarah, I enjoy their "dream visits" and look forward to those special times.

I believe that just as we grow and learn together in reciprocal relationships with those who are still living, so it is with those who are no longer physically present. I have been both surprised and encouraged by the lessons I've learned about relationships just while writing this book. I've often felt the presence of my deceased loved ones while I was writing—helping me to clarify my thoughts and solidifying my notion that our relationships continue.

Others folks have shared similar beliefs with me. Some say they visit their loved one's grave "just to chat" or "to talk about serious matters." Others say an article of clothing worn by their deceased loved ones is the median they use to feel closer to them. A friend recently said he sits in his deceased father's recliner every night just to feel close to him. The chair is old, worn, and broken. He said that he even has to place something underneath the footrest to hold it up, but he will not part with it or even consider having it reupholstered. Hearing of that kind of love makes my heart swell.

A dear client, Beth, whom I have worked with for years, continued to struggle, until recently, about making the decision to take her mother off life support. Although it had happened several years ago and her mother had been brain dead for quite some time, with absolutely no hope of recovery, Beth continued being tormented. She would sit in my office and cry pitifully from the emotional pain she could not get free of.

We spent many sessions exploring Beth's beliefs about relationships not only continuing in the afterlife but having begun long before mortal birth. Then one day something occurred to me. I suggested to Beth that since she believed she and her mother had enjoyed a loving relationship prior to mortality, that possibly she and her mother had made promises to one another a long time ago. Perhaps her mother had promised to help Beth get *into* her body (by giving birth to her), and Beth had promised her mother to help her get *out of* hers (by terminating the life support). Beth sat staring at me without even blinking for what seemed like a very long time. I watched as a transformation took place. The energy in her aura became clear and bright. Beth began to look much lighter. Her face relaxed, and the lines left by the tides of stress and pain softened. Her eyes smiled.

Finally, she spoke in a voice that sounded like velvet feels. "That's true," she said. "I remember that now." Beth was finally at peace about that agonizing decision made all those years ago.

I have also learned that the older I get, the more flexible I need to be. While processing our retirement, my husband and I made the decision that as soon as this manuscript was finished we would put our house, with the big yard and swimming pool, on the market and move to an adult retirement community. We decided others could have the joy of maintaining lawns and pools while we enjoyed golf courses and hiking trails.

Although we had purchased the "For Sale" sign, we had not decided exactly where we were going to move; thus, putting our home on the market was a long stretch for me because

I like to think I can see the end from the beginning. However, I decided to take the leap of faith. I would step into the darkness and keep walking until the light was on once again, and I could see more clearly what the next step was to be.

However, just six days after I sent this manuscript to the editor, I was afforded the opportunity to take yet another *turn* at caregiving. My sister Nita called me to say that she had made the decision to stop dialysis and allow her death to take a natural course. She had been on dialysis three times a week for more than four years, and she was tired. I told her I would immediately fly to California and stay with her until the end.

We arranged for Hospice care and had her transported from the hospital to her home for the first time in nearly three months. We also hired in-home caregivers to be with her around the clock. My sister and I had four and a half wonderful days together. She was happy to be in her home once again and to be able to eat anything she wanted. I prepared her favorite foods, which she thoroughly enjoyed, and we spent time talking between her naps. Hospice had explained that as the toxins accumulated in her system, her blood would not be able to carry oxygen and she would sleep more and more. Then, she would just go to sleep and not be able to wake up.

Although my sister was a good person, I had not known her to be either spiritual or religious, and she had shown no interest in talking about such matters. So, I was quite surprised when she said: "Sandy, when I get to the pearly gates, what do I tell them so I can get in?"

Her eyes were closed, so I leaned close to her ear and said, "You'll just give them the password. And the password is *love.*"

That was our last exchange. She drifted off to sleep for the last time, and about three hours later she was gone.

The Hospice nurse, the sitter, and the Hospice team leader were all there with me. My best friend, Patty, who lived only about a fifteen-minute drive from Nita's house, had stayed with us most of the night and had been gone less than an hour when I called her with the news that Nita had passed away. Although it was in the wee hours of the morning, she drove back and waited with me until the hearse came to pick Nita up. My sister had donated her body to Stanford University and had made all the arrangements in advance. I only had to make one phone call.

Nita drove a gold Cadillac for years, and she absolutely loved that car. I supposed it was in keeping with the *Law of Attraction*, but the most amazing event occurred. The vehicle my sister took her last ride in was none other than a gold Cadillac hearse! Patty and I concurred we had never seen a gold Cadillac hearse before and could only smile as we discussed the reality that we do, in fact, attract to us that which is important to us.

Fortunately I had the opportunity to include my most recent experiences and thoughts before I had to send this manuscript to the publisher for the final time. Since Nita had appointed me Trustee of her Living Trust, I had to remain in California several weeks to take care of her affairs. My two other sisters and my husband flew out to help me clean out her house and get it ready to sale.

Needless to say, my husband and I had to put our plans to move on hold. However, the weeks following my sister's death afforded me an opportunity to continue processing my ideas about retirement. I decided to look up the word "retirement" in a couple of dictionaries. As I read the definitions, I realized descriptors such as "to withdraw," "to go into seclusion," "to remove from active service," etc. did not fit with my notion of retirement. I have no intentions to "withdraw into seclusion away from active service."

I also decided to talk with fellow baby boomers about what retirement means to them. Without exception, we all agreed that the years labeled *retirement* for us will not mean we quit being active and productive. For us, retirement will simply mean we are active and productive in different ways. During the first years of our retirement, many of us plan to continue doing paid work that will, perhaps, be significantly different from the work we've spent the past thirty to forty years performing. We also concurred we will do more unpaid work—volunteering and giving back to our communities and families. We will have more time to do more of what we want to do and on our own timetables.

Most of the peers I talked with have ongoing plans and goals for the future. Some plan to take educational courses just because they are interested in the subjects. Some plan to finish degrees that they put on hold in order to raise their children. Some plan to start small businesses, while others plan to learn new hobbies, such as how to golf or to play a musical instrument. However, most agree they will spend more time in the present. Perhaps, more time reading, gardening, hiking, playing golf, listening to music, and/or visiting with friends and family members.

As for me, I still want it all. I want to take more classes, write more books, play more golf, hike more, and travel with my husband more. I want to do lots of volunteer work and maintain political involvement. I want to have lunch with my friends, run another marathon, and climb Mt. Kilimanjaro. A few years ago my husband and I flew from Katmandu, Nepal, to Lukla and climbed to Mt. Everest base camp. Now, my goal is to summit Mt. Kilimanjaro. What else can I say other than I am truly a baby boomer in every respect and count it a blessing to have been born into such an amazing generation of people at the most incredible and wonderful time in the history of the world. We are the great producers, and we will continue to be productive.

In closing, I would like to talk about the value of staying

in touch with your own inner voice. Sometimes, even in the face of much information to the contrary, our own heartfelt, internal voice tells us to do just the opposite of what others and even our own brain tell us to do.

You may have to clear out the *shoulds*, but I encourage you to pay close attention to promptings that come from a place deep within your soul, especially where individual, personal matters are concerned. All too often we are inundated with so much information that we seem paralyzed regarding what to do. Unfortunately, we may then start looking outside ourselves for answers and maybe even for someone else to make our decisions for us.

One of the ways I identify when I'm in this position is to note my confusion. Sometimes I think, *Oh, well, maybe I'll go to the left, or maybe I'll go to the right. Maybe I'll go forward, maybe I'll back up. I don't really know what I'm doing.* Perhaps you've heard the old saying, "I just stand there turning around in circles because I don't know which way to go." When I feel that confused, it's helpful for me to find a place where I can be still—a place that is quiet. Then I listen to my own inner voice. I block out all the chatter from outside then look and listen within.

We all have this wonderful gift of being inner-directed—an internal mechanism that will guide us if we'll just take the time to pay attention to it. When we listen to and adhere to that still, small voice within us, the choices we make will be in our highest good. If they're in our highest good, they're also in the highest good of everything in the universe, and the universe will rush to support those choices. So trust the voice that speaks from the deepest recesses of your soul, even when everything outside of you is screaming the opposite.

There is a lot more that I *don't* know about all of this than there is that I *do* know. What I *am* sure of is that answers to all our questions are there for us when we're ready to receive them, and we will perhaps realize the solutions were contained within the problems all along.

Finally, my wish for you is that this book has stimulated thoughts and questions about your life, how you are blessed to participate in the caregiving of loved ones, and the opportunities at hand to lead a rewarding and meaningful life today and in the future, even if it is called *retirement*. Always remember, the password is *love!*

* * * * * * * *

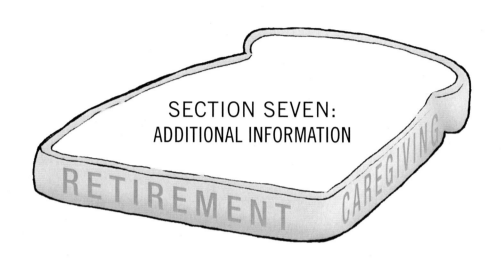

SECTION SEVEN:
ADDITIONAL INFORMATION

RESOURCES

GLOSSARY

SAMPLE LETTER
REGARDING SOCIAL SECURITY

RESOURCES

The following addresses, phone numbers, and Web sites are subject to change. All efforts were made to ensure accuracy at the time of publication.

Abuse

National Center on Elder Abuse
c/o Center for Community Research and Services
University of Delaware, 297 Graham Hall
Newark, DE 19716
Phone: 302–831–3525 Web site: www.ncea.aoa.gov

Adult Day Care Services

National Adult Day Services Association Inc.
2519 Connecticut Ave. NW
Washington, DC 20008
Phone: 800–558–5301
Fax: 202–783–2255
Web site: www.nadsa.org

Nursing Home Information Service—
National Council of Senior Citizens
1331 F Street NW
Washington, DC 20004
Phone: 202–347–8800 Extension 340

Afro-American Elder Services

National Caucus and Center on Black Aged Inc.
1220 L Street NW, Suite 800
Washington, DC 20005
Phone: 202–637–8400
Fax: 202–347–0895

Alaskan Natives Elder Services

National Indian Council on Aging
6400 Uptown Blvd. NE City Center, Suite 510W
Albuquerque, NM 87110
Phone: 505–888–3302

National Resource Center on Native American Aging
(NRCNAA)
Center for Rural Health
University of North Dakota
School of Medicine and Health Sciences, Room 4535
501 North Columbia Road Mail Stop 9037
Grand Forks, ND 58202–9037
Phone: 800–896–7628 or (701) 777–6780
Fax: 701–777–6779
Web site: http://ruralhealth.und.edu

Alcohol and Substance Abuse

Alcoholics Anonymous
A.A. World Services Inc.
P.O. Box 459
New York City, NY 10163
Phone: 212–870–3400
Web site: www.alcoholics-anonymous.org

Al-Anon Family Groups
P. O. Box 862, Midtown Station
New York City, NY 10018
Phone: 888–4AL-ANON or 888–425–2666
Web site: www.al-anon.alateen.org

Al-Anon Family Group Headquarters Inc.
Al-Anon Family Group Headquarters (Canada) Inc.
1600 Corporate Landing Parkway

Virginia Beach, VA 23454–5617
Phone: 757–563–1600
Fax: 757–563–1655

National Clearinghouse for Alcohol and Drug Information
P.O. Box 2345
Rockville, MD 20847
Phone: 800–729–6686

SAMHSA's National Clearinghouse for Alcohol and
Drug Information
P.O. Box 2345
Rockville, MD 20847–2345
Phone: 800–729–6686
Web site: http://ncadi.samhsa.gov

National Council on Alcoholism and Drug Dependence
Inc.
244 East 58th Street, 4th Floor
New York City, NY 10022
Phone: 212–269–7797
Web site: www.ncadd.org

American Indian Elder Services

National Association of Area Agencies on Aging
1730 Rhode Island Avenue NW, Suite 1200
Washington, DC 20036
Phone: 202–872–0888
Web site: www.n4a.org

National Indian Council on Aging
6400 Uptown Blvd. NE
City Center, Suite 510W
Albuquerque, NM 87110
Phone: 505–888–3302
Web site: www.nicoa.org

National Indian Council On Aging Inc.
10501 Montgomery Blvd. NE, Suite 210
Albuquerque, NM 87111
Phone: 505–292–2001

Asian/Pacific Elder Services

National Asian Pacific Center on Aging
1511 Third Ave., Suite 914
Seattle, WA 98101
Phone: 800–33-NAPCA
Fax: 206–624–1023
Web site: NAPCA.org

Caregiver Services and Care Managers

American Association of Retired Persons
601 East St. NW
Washington, DC 20049
Phone: 800-OUR-AARP
Web site: http://www.aarp.org

Adult Help USA
HELP Central
5 Hanover Square, 17th Floor
New York City, NY 10004
Phone: 800–311–7999
Fax: 212–400–7005
Web site: www.helpusa.org

Aging Network Services
Topaz House
4400 East-West Highway, Suite 907
Bethesda, MD 20814
Phone: 301–657–4329
Web site: www.agingnets.com

American Self-Help Clearinghouse
St. Clare's Riverside Medical Center
25 Pocono Rd.
Denville, NJ 07834
Phone: 973–326–6789
Web site: www.selfhelpgroups.org

American Society on Aging
833 Market Street; Suite 511
San Francisco, CA 94103
Phone: 415–974–9600
Web site: www.asaging.org

Caregivers Program
Administration on Aging
Washington, DC 20201
Phone: 202–619–0724
Web site: www.aoa.gov

Children of Aging Parents
P.O. Box 167
Richboro, PA 18954
Phone: 800–227–7294
Web site: www.caps4caregivers.org

Sage Eldercare
290 Broad Street
Summit, NJ 07901
Phone: 908–273–5550
www.sageeldercare.org

Disabilities and Handicaps

Adaptive Environments
180–200 Portland Street, Suite 1
Boston, MA 02114
Phone: 617–695–1225

Fax: 617–482–8099
Web site: www.AdaptiveEnvironments.org

American Association of Retired Persons
601 East Street NW
Washington, DC 20049
Phone: 888–687–2277
Web site: www.aarp.org

The Center for Universal Design, College of Design
North Carolina State University
Campus Box 8613
Raleigh, NC 27695–8613
Phone: 919–515–3082
Fax: 919–515–8951
Web site: http://design.ncsu.edu/cud/index.htm

Direct Link for the Disabled Hotline
P.O. Box 1036
Solvang, CA 93464
Phone: 805–688–1603 or 805–688–5285

National Rehabilitation Information
Center and ABLEDATA
8201 Corporate Drive, Suite 600
Landover, MD 20785
Phone: 800–346–2742
Fax: 301–459–4263
Web site: www.naric.com

Paralyzed Veterans of America
801 Eighteenth Street NW
Washington, DC 20006–3517
Phone: 800–424–8200 or 800–555–9140
Web site: www.pva.org

Driving

Department of Highway Safety
Consult your local phone directory

AAA Foundation for Traffic Safety
607 14th Street NW, Suite 201
Washington, DC 20005
Phone: 202–638–5944
Fax: 202–638–5943
Web site: www.aaafoundation.org

National Safety Council
1121 Spring Lake Drive
Itasca, IL 60143–3201
Phone: 630–285–1121
Fax: 630–285–1315
Web site: www.nsc.org

Financial

American Institute of Certified Public Accountants
1211 Avenue of the Americas
New York City, NY 10036–8775
Phone: 212–596–6200
Web site: www.aicpa.org

American Safe Deposit Association
P.O. Box 519
Franklin, IN 46131
Phone: 317–738–4432
Fax: 317–738–5267
Web site: www.tasda.com

Campaign for Home Energy Assistance
1615 L Street NW, Suite 520
Washington, DC 20036
Phone: 202–429–8855
Fax: 202–429–8857
Web site: www.liheap.org

Certified Financial Planners
1425 K Street NW, Suite 500
Washington, DC 20005
Phone: 800–487–1497
Fax: 202–379–2299
Web site: www.cfp.net

Elderly Homeowner Rehabilitation Program
Consult your local phone book

Federal National Mortgage Association
(FNMA/Fannie Mae)
3900 Wisconsin Avenue NW
Washington, DC 20016–2892
Phone: 202–752–7000
Web site: www.fanniemae.com

Financial Industry Regulatory Authority
1735 K St. NW
Washington, DC 20006
Phone: 301–590–6500
Web site: www.finra.org

Financial Planning Association
4100 East Mississippi Ave., Suite 400
Denver, CO 80246–3053
Phone: 800–322–4237
Fax: 303–759–0749
Web site: www.fpanet.org

Financial Planning Association
5775 Glenridge Dr. NE, Suite B-300
Atlanta, GA 30328–5364
Phone: 800–945-IAFP (800–945–4237)
Web site: www.plannersearch.org

Home Energy Assistance Program
Local agencies may offer this assistance
Home Ownership Subsidy Program
Consult your local Department of Housing
and Urban Development
Phone: 202–708–1112
TTY: 202–708–1455
Web site: www.hud.gov

Institute of Certified Financial Planners
7600 East Eastman Ave., Suite 301
Denver, CO 80231–4397
Phone: 800–282–7526 or 1–303–751–7600
Web site: www.fpanet.org
Internal Revenue Service
Phone: 800–829–1040
Web site: www.irs.gov

National Association of Personal Financial Advisors
3250 North Arlington Heights Road, Suite 109
Arlington Heights, IL 60004
Phone: 800–366–2732
Fax: 847–483–5415
Web site: www.napfa.org

National Center for Home Equity Conversion
360 North Robert #403
St. Paul, MN 55101
Phone: 651–222–6775
Fax: 651–222–6797
Web site: www.reversemortgage.org

National Endowment for Financial Education
5299 DTC Blvd., Suite 1300
Greenwood Village, CO 80111
Phone: 303–741–6333
Fax: 303–220–0838
Web site: www.nefe.org

National Foundation for Credit Counseling
801 Roeder Road, Suite 900
Silver Spring, MD 20910
Phone: 301–589–5600
Web site: www.nfcc.org

Pension Rights Center
1350 Connecticut Avenue NW, Suite 206
Washington, DC 20036–1739
Phone: 202–296–3776
Fax: 202–833–2472
Web site: www.pensionrights.org

Reverse Mortgages
Contact your local bank or other lending institutions

Section Eight Housing or Rental Assistance Program
Consult your local Deptartment Of Housing
and Urban Development

Securities Exchange Commission
100 F Street NE
Washington, DC 20549
Phone: 202–942–8088
Web site: www.sec.gov

Social Security Administration, Office of Public Inquiries
Windsor Park Building
6401 Security Blvd.
Baltimore, MD 21235

Phone: 800–772–1213
TTY: 800–325–0778
Web site: www.ssa.gov

Society of Financial Service Professionals Headquarters
17 Campus Blvd., Suite 201
Newtown Square, PA 19073–3230
Phone: 610–526–2500
Fax: 610–527–1499
Web site: www.financialpro.org

Fraud

Fraud Hotline, Office of Inspector General
Department of Health and Human Services
Attn: HOTLINE
P.O. Box 23489
Washington, DC 20026
Phone: 800–447–8477
Fax: 800–223–8164
Web site: www.oig.hhs.gov/hotline.html

Social Security Fraud Hotline
P.O. Box 17768
Baltimore, MD 21235
Phone: 800–269–0271
TTY: 866–501–2101
Fax: 410–597–0118
Web site: www.ssa.gov/oig/hotline

Medicare Hotline
Centers for Medicare & Medicaid Services
7500 Security Boulevard
Baltimore, MD 21244–1850
Phone: 800–633–4227
TTY: 877–486–2048
Web site: www.medicare.gov/CallCenter.asp

Ombudsman Council
Consult your local phone book under State Agencies

General Information

American Red Cross National Headquarters
2025 East Street NW
Washington, DC 20006
Phone: 800–733–2767
Web site: www.redcross.org

Catholic Charities USA
1731 King Street
Alexandria, VA 22314
Phone: 703–549–1390
Fax: 703–549–1656Web site: www.catholiccharitiesusa.org

Compassion & Choices
P.O. Box 101810
Denver, CO 80250–1810
Phone: 800–247–7421
Fax: 303–639–1224
Web site: www.compassionandchoices.org

Community Resources
Consult your local place of worship

Council of Better Business Bureaus
4200 Wilson Blvd, Suite 800
Arlington, VA 22203–1838
Phone: 703–276–0100
Fax: 703–525–8277
Web site: http://welcome.bbb.org

Federal Citizen Information Center
Department WWW
Pueblo, CO 81009

Phone: 888–878–3256
Fax: 719–948–9724
Web site: www.pueblo.gsa.gov

Elder Abuse
Phone: 800–962–2873
Elder Helpline and Elder Options
Phone: 800–262–2243

Eldercare Locator
The U.S. Department of Health and Human Services
200 Independence Ave. SW
Washington, DC 20201
Phone: 800–677–1116
TTY: 800–677–1116
Web site: www.eldercare.gov

Elder Support Network
Association of Jewish Family & Children
620 Cranbury Road, Suite 102
East Brunswick, NJ 08816–5419
Phone: 800–634–7346
Fax: 732–432–7127
Web site: www.jirs.org/jirs/jirs0018ak.html

Federal Emergency Management Agency
500 C Street SW
Washington, DC 20472
Phone: 800–621–3362
TTY: 800–462–7585
Fax: 800–827–8112; Web site: www.fema.gov

Food Stamp Program
Department of Social Security
Phone: 800–772–1213
Web site: www.fns.usda.gov/fsp

Hemlock Society USA
Compassion & Choices
P.O. Box 101810
Denver, CO 80250–1810
Phone: 800–247–7421
Fax: 303–639–1224
Web site: www.compassionandchoices.org/hemlock

Kelly Assisted Living
Phone: 800–866–0860 Extension 5880
Web site: www.rescarehome.com

ResCare HomeCare–National Office
9901 Linn Station Road
Louisville, KY 40223–3808
Phone: 800–866–0860 Extension 5880
Web site: www.rescarehomecare.com

Local Elder Care Services
Contact your local elder care agency

National Center on Elder Abuse
c/o Center for Community Research and Services
University of Delaware
297 Graham Hall
Newark, DE 19716
Phone: 800–677–1116
Fax: 302–831–4225
Web site: www.ncea.aoa.gov

National Hospice and Palliative Care Hotline
200 Varick Street
New York City, NY 10014–0148
Phone: 800–989-WILL (800–989–9455) or 212–366–5540
Web site: www.caringinfo.org

New Ways to Work
103 Morris Street, Suite A
Sebastopol, CA 95472
Phone: 707–824–4000
Fax: 707–824–4410
Web site: www.newwaystowork.org

New Your State Partnership for Long-Term Care
New York State Department of Health
1 Commerce Plaza, Room 826
Albany, NY 12210
Phone: 888–697–7582
Web site: www.nyspltc.org

Older Americans Act
Consult your local elder care agency

Senior Citizens Centers
Contact your local senior citizens center

Shepherd's Centers of America
One West Armour Blvd., Suite 201
Kansas City, MO 64111–2087
Phone: 800–547–7073
Fax: 816–960–1083
Web site: www.shepherdcenters.org

Social Security Administration, Office of Public Inquiries
Windsor Park Building
6401 Security Blvd.
Baltimore, MD 21235
Phone: 800–772–1213
TTY: 800–325–0778
Web site: www.ssa.gov

Supplemental Security Income
Social Security Administration
Office of Public Inquiries
Windsor Park Building
6401 Security Blvd.
Baltimore, MD 21235
Phone: 800–772–1213
TTY: 800–325–0778
Web site: www.socialsecurity.gov/ssi/

Stamps By Mail
United States Post Office
Phone: 800–782–6724
Web site: www.usps.com

United Seniors Health Cooperative
409 Third Street SW, Suite 200
Washington, DC 20024
Phone: 202–479–6973

Visiting Nurse Associations of America
900 19th Street NW, Suite 200
Washington, DC 20006
Phone: 202–384–1420
Fax: 202–384–1444
Web site: www.vnaa.org

Volunteers of America Inc.
1660 Duke St.
Alexandria, VA 22314
Phone: 800–899–0089
Fax: 703–341–7000
Web site: www.voa.org

Well Spouse Association
63 West Main Street, Suite H
Freehold, NJ 07728

Phone: 800–838–0879
Fax: 732–577–8644
Web site: www.wellspouse.org

Widowed Persons Service
AARP
601 East Street NW
Washington, DC 20049
Phone: 202–434–2260
Web site: www.aarp.org

Grief and Bereavement

The Center for Loss and Life Transition
3735 Broken Bow Road
Fort Collins, CO 80526
Phone: 970–226–6050
Fax: 800–922–6051
Web site: www.centerforloss.com

Caring Connection
1700 Diagonal Road, Suite 625
Alexandria, VA 22314
Phone: 800–658–8898
Web site: www.caringinf.org

Compassion & Choices
P.O. Box 101810
Denver, CO 80250–1810
Phone: 800–247–7421
Fax: 303–639–1224
Web site: www.compassionandchoices.org

The Compassionate Friends Inc.
P.O. Box 3696
Oak Brook, IL 60522–3696
Phone: 877–969–0010

Fax: 630–990–0246
Web site: www.compassionatefriends.org

Funeral Consumers Alliance
33 Patchen Road
South Burlington, VT 05403
Phone: 800–765–0107
Web site: www.funerals.org

Grief Recovery Institute
P.O. Box 6061–382
Sherman Oaks, CA 91413
Phone: 818–907–9600
Fax: 818–907–9329
Web site: www.grief-recovery.com

National Catholic Ministry to the Bereaved
P.O. Box 16353
St. Louis, MO 63125–0353
Phone: 314–638–2638
Fax: 314–638–2639
Web site: www.griefwork.org

National Funeral Directors Association
13625 Bishop's Drive
Brookfield, WI 53005–6607
Phone: 800–228–6332 or 262–789–1880
Fax: 262–789–6977
Web site: www.nfda.org

National Funeral Directors' Service Consumer Arbitration Program
13625 Bishop's Drive
Brookfield, WI 53005–6607
Phone: 800–228–6332 or 262–789–1880
Fax: 262–789–6977
Web site: www.nfda.org

National Office of Consumer Funeral Alliance
Phone: 800–765–0107
Web site: www.funerals.org

National Right to Life Committee
512 10th St. NW
Washington, DC 20004
Phone: 202–626–8800
Web site: www.nrlc.org

Hearing/Speech Impaired

American Academy of Otolaryngology
—Head and Neck Surgery
One Prince Street
Alexandria, VA 22314–3357
Phone: 703–836–4444
Web site: www.entnet.org

American Hearing Research Foundation
8 South Michigan Avenue, Suite #814
Chicago, IL 60603–4539
Phone: 312–726–9670
Fax: 312–726–9695
Web site: www.american-hearing.org

American Speech-Language Hearing Association
2200 Research Boulevard
Rockville, MD 20850–3289
Phone: 800–638–8255
TTY: 301–296–5650
Fax: 301–296–8580
Web site: www.asha.org

American Tinnitus Association
P.O. Box 5
Portland, OR 97207–0005

Phone: 800–634–8978 or 503–248–9985
Fax: 503–248–0024
Web site: www.ata.org

Association of Late-Deafened Adults
8038 MacIntosh Lane
Rockford, IL 61107
Phone: 866–402–2532
Web site: www.alda.org

AT&T Accessible Communication Product Center
14250 Clayton Road
Town & Country, MO 63017
Phone: 800–222–3111

Better Hearing Institute—Hearing Helpline
1444 I Street NW, Suite 700
Washington, DC 20005
Phone: 202–449–1100
Fax: 202–216–9646
Web site: www.betterhearing.org

Hearing Aid Helpline
International Hearing Society
16880 Middlebelt Rd., Suite 4
Livonia, MI 48154
Phone: 800–521–5247 or 734–522–2900
Fax: 734–522–0200

Hearing Loss Association of America
7910 Woodmont Avenue, Suite 1200
Bethesda, MD 20814
Phone: 301–657–2248
Fax: 301–913–9413
Web site: www.shhh.org

Hear Now—The Starkey Hearing Foundation
Administrative Offices
1245 South Main Street, Suite 200
Grapevine, TX 76051
Phone: 866–354–3254
Fax: 817–442–8653
Web site: www.sotheworldmayhear.org

Modern Talking Picture SVC Inc.
5000 Park St. N
St. Petersburg, FL 33709
Phone: 800–237–6213

National Aphasia Association
350 Seventh Avenue, Suite 902
New York City, NY 10001
Phone: 800–922–4622
Web site: www.aphasia.org

National Association of the Deaf
8630 Fenton Street, Suite 820
Silver Spring, MD 20910–3819
Phone: 301–587–1788
TTY: 301–587–1789
Fax: 301–587–1791
Web site: www.nad.org

National Institute on Deafness and
Other Communication Disorders
31 Center Drive, MSC 2320
Bethesda, MD 20892–2320
Phone: 800–241–1044
TTY: 800–241–1055
Fax: 301–402–0018

Self-Help for Hard of Hearing People
Hearing Loss Association of America
7910 Woodmont Avenue, Suite 1200
Bethesda, MD 20814
Phone: 301–657–2248
TTY: 301–913–9413
Web site: www.shhh.org

Hispanic Services

Asociación Nacional Pro Personas Mayores
National Association for Hispanic Elderly
234 East Colorado Boulevard, Suite 300
Pasadena, CA 91101
Phone: 626–564–1988
Web site: www.anppm.org

National Hispanic Council on Aging
734 15st St. NW, Suite 1050
Washington, DC 20005
Phone: 202–347–9733
Fax: 202–347–9735
Web site: www.nhcoa.org

Home Care

American Association for Continuity of Care
P.O. Box 532
Dunedin, FL 34697
Phone: 800–816–1575
Fax: 727–738–8099
Web site: www.continuityofcare.com

National Association for Home Care
228 Seventh Street SE
Washington, DC 20003
Phone: 202–547–7424

Fax: 202–547–3540
Web site: www.nahc.org

Visiting Nurse Associations of America
900 19th St. NW, Suite 200
Washington, DC 20006
Phone: 202–384–1420
Fax: 202–384–1444
Web site: www.vnaa.org

Hospice

Family Resource Service
1400 Union Meeting Rd., Suite 102
Blue Bell, PA 19422
Phone: 800–847–5437

All Family Resources
P.O. Box 5338
Novato, CA 94948–5338
Phone: 415–209–0502
Web site: www.familymanagement.com/aging-index.html

Foundation for Hospice and Homecare
513 C Street NE, Stanton Park
Washington, DC 20002
Phone: 202–547–6586
Web site: www.naric.com

National Association for Home Care
228 Seventh Street SE
Washington, DC 20003
Phone: 202–547–7424
Fax: 202–547–3540
Web site: www.nahc.org

Hospice Association of America
228 Seventh Street SE
Washington, DC 20003
Phone: 202–546–4759
Fax: 202–547–9559
Web site: www.nahc.org

Hospice Education Institute
P.O. Box 98
Machiasport, ME 04655–0098
Phone: 207–255–8800
Fax: 207–255–8008
Web site: www.hospiceworld.org

National Hospice & Palliative Care Organization
1700 Diagonal Road, Suite 625
Alexandria, VA 22314
Phone: 703–837–1500
Fax: 703–837–1233
Web site: www.nhpco.org

Incontinence

American Foundation for Urologic Disease
1000 Corporate Boulevard
Linthicum, MD 21090
Phone: 866–746–4282 or 410–689–3700
Fax: 410–689–3800
Web site: http://afud.org/AUAFoundation/auafhome.asp

National Association for Continence
P.O. Box 1019
Charleston, SC 29402–1019
Phone: 800-BLADDER (800–252–3337)
Web site: www.nafc.org

National Association For Incontinence
P.O. Box 1019
Charleston, SC 29402–1019
Phone: 800–252–3337
Fax: 843–377–0905
Web site: www.nafc.org

International Foundation for Func-
tional Gastrointestinal Disorders Inc.
P.O. Box 170864
Milwaukee, WI 53217–8076
Phone: 888–964–2001 or 414–964–1799
Fax: 414–964–7176
Web site: www.iffgd.org

National Kidney and Urologic Diseases Information
Clearinghouse
3 Information Way
Bethesda, MD 20892–3580
Phone: 800–891–5390
Fax: 703–738–4929
Web site: http://kidney.niddk.nih.gov

Simon Foundation for Incontinence
P.O. Box 815
Wilmette, IL 60091
Phone: 800–237–4666
Fax: 847–864–9758
Web site: www.simonfoundation.org

Insurance: Health and Long-Term Care (Supplemental)

Center for Medicare Advocacy
P.O. Box 350
Willimantic, CT 06226
Phone: 860–456–7790

Fax: 860–456–2614
Web site: www.medicareadvocacy.org

Connecticut Partnership for Long-Term
Care, Office of Policy and Management
450 Capitol Avenue
Hartford, CT 06106–1379
Phone: 800–286–2214 or 860–418–6200

Indiana Long-Term Care Program
Indiana Department of Insurance
311 W. Washington Street, Suite 300
Indianapolis, IN 46204
Phone: 866–234–4582
Web site: www.longtermcareinsurance.in.gov

Group Health Incorporated
441 Ninth Avenue
New York, NY 10001–1681
Phone: 212–615–0000
Web site: www.ghi.com

Group Health Plans
Web site: www.grouphealthplans.com

America's Health Insurance Plans
601 Pennsylvania Avenue NW
South Building, Suite 500
Washington, DC 20004
Phone: 202–778–3200
Fax: 202–331–7487
Web site: www.hiaa.org

America's Health Insurance Plans
601 Pennsylvania Avenue NW
South Building, Suite 500
Washington, DC 20004

Phone: 202–778–3200
Fax: 202–331–7487
Web site: www.hiaa.org

Health Insurance Counseling and Advocacy Program
Contact your State Insurance Division of Consumer Affairs or State Office on Aging
These numbers are normally listed under
State or *Government* listings

Health Management Organization
Contact your state insurance counselor or
Health Care Financing Administration
U.S. Department Of Health and Human Services
200 Independence Ave. SW
Washington, DC 20201
Phone: 800–772–1213

Medicare Hotline
The U.S. Department of Health and Human Services
200 Independence Avenue SW
Washington, DC 20201
Phone: 800–633–4227
Web site: www.medicare.gov

National Association of Claims Assistance Professionals
5329 South Main Street
Downers Grove, IL 60515
Phone: 800–660–0665

National Association of Insurance Commissioners
2301 McGee Street, Suite 800
Kansas City, MO 64108–2662
Phone: 816–842–3600
Fax: 816–783–8175
Web site: www.naic.org

National Consumers League
1701 K Street NW, Suite 1200
Washington, DC 20006
Phone: 202–835–3323
Fax: 202–835–0747
Web site: www.nclnet.org

Federal Emergency Management Agency
500 C Street SW
Washington, DC 20472
Phone: 888–379–9531
TTY: 800–427–5593
Fax: 202–646–2818
Web site: www.floodsmart.gov

National Health Information Center
P.O. Box 1133
Washington, DC 20013–1133
Phone: 800–336–4797 or 301–565–4167
Fax: 301–984–4256
Web site: www.health.gov/NHIC/

National Insurance Consumers Helpline
1001 Pennsylvania Avenue NW
Washington, DC 20004
Phone: 800–942–4242

United Seniors Health Cooperative
Web site: www.unitedseniorshealth.org

Legal

American Bar Association
Service Center
321 North Clark Street
Chicago, IL 60610
Phone: 800–285–2221 or 312–988–5522
Web site: www.abanet.org

Commission on Legal Problems of the
Elderly—American Bar Association
740 15th Street NW
Washington, DC 20005–1019
Phone: 202–662–1000
Web site: www.abanet.org/aging

Health Care Financing Administration
Department of Health and Human Services
200 Independence Avenue SW
Washington, DC 20201
Phone: 410–786–3000
Web site: www.hhs.gov

Centers for Medicare & Medicaid Services
7500 Security Blvd.
Baltimore, MD 21244
Phone: 800–633–4227
TTY: 877–486–2048
Web site: www.cms.hhs.gov

Internal Revenue Service
Phone: 800–829–1040
TDD: 800–829–4059
Web site: www.irs.gov

Legal Counsel for the Elderly—American
Association of Retired Persons

601 E Street NW
Washington, DC 20049
Phone: 202–434–2120 or 202–434–2170
Web site: www.aarp.org/states/dc/dc-lce

National Academy of Elder Law Attorneys Inc.
1604 North Country Club Road
Tucson, AZ 85716

Phone: 520–881–4005
Fax: 520–325–7925
Web site: www.naela.org

National Clearing House for Legal Services Inc.
50 East Washington Street, Suite 500
Chicago, IL 60602
Phone: 312–263–3830
Fax: 312–263–3846
Web site: www.povertylaw.org

National Organization of Social Security
Claimants Representatives
560 Sylvan Ave
Englewood Cliffs, NJ 07632
Phone: 800–431–2804
Fax: 201–567–1542
Web site: www.nosscr.org

National Senior Citizens Law Center
1101 14th Street NW, Suite 400
Washington, DC 20005
Phone: 202–289–6976
Fax: 202–289–7224
Web site: www.nsclc.org

NOLO Press
950 Parker Street
Berkeley, CA 94710–2524
Phone: 800–728–3555
Fax: 800–645–0895
Web site: www.nolo.com

Social Security Administration
Office of Public Inquiries
Windsor Park Building
6401 Security Blvd.

Baltimore, MD 21235
Phone: 800–772–1213
TTY: 800–325–0778
Web site: www.ssa.gov

Living Arrangements and Housing

Aging Network Services, LLC
Topaz House
4400 East-West Highway, Suite 907
Bethesda, MD 20814
Phone: 301–657–4329
Fax: 301–657–3250
Web site: www.agingnets.com

American Association of Homes
and Services for the Aging
2519 Connecticut Avenue NW
Washington, DC 20008–1520
Phone: 202–783–2242
Fax: 202–783–2255
Web site: www.2aahsa.org

American Health Care Association
1201 L Street NW
Washington, DC 20005
Phone: 202–842–4444
Fax: 202–842–3860
Web site: www.ahcancal.org

Assisted Living Facilities Association of America
11200 Waples Mill Road, Suite 150
Fairfax, VA 22030
Phone: 703–691–8100
Fax: 703–691–8106
Web site: www.alfa.org

Assisted Living Federation of America
1650 King Street, Suite 602
Alexandria, VA 22314–2747
Phone: 703–894–1805
Fax: 703–894–1831
Web site: www.alfa.org

California Advocates for Nursing Home Reform
650 Harrison Street, 2nd Floor
San Francisco, CA 94107
Phone: 800–474–1116 or 415–974–5171
Web site: www.canhr.org

CARF International
4891 E. Grant Road
Tucson, AZ 85712
Phone: 888–281–6531 or 520–325–1044
Fax: 520–318–1129
Web site: www.carf.org

Concerned Relatives of Nursing Home Patients
P.O. Box 18820
Cleveland Heights, OH 44118–8820
Phone: 216–321–0403

Council of Better Business Bureaus
4200 Wilson Blvd, Suite 800
Arlington, VA 22203–1838
Phone: 703–276–0100
Fax: 703–525–8277
Web site: www.bbb.org

Local Elder Care Services
Contact your local elder care agency

National Citizens Coalition for Nursing Home Reform
1828 L Street NW, Suite 801
Washington, DC 20036
Phone: 202–332–2275
Fax: 202–332–2949
Web site: www.nccnhr.org

National Association of Area Agencies on Aging
1730 Rhode Island Ave NW, Suite 1200
Washington, DC 20036
Phone: 202–872–0888
Fax: 202–872–0057
Web site: www.n4a.org

National Association for Home Care
228 Seventh Street SE
Washington, DC 20003
Phone: 202–547–7424
Fax: 202–547–3540
Web site: www.nahc.org

National Association of Professional
Geriatric Care Managers
1604 N. Country Club Road
Tucson, AZ 85716
Phone: 520–881–8008
Fax: 520–325–7925
Web site: www.caremanager.org

National Association of Social Workers
750 First Street NE, Suite 700
Washington, DC 20002–4241
Phone: 202–408–8600
Web site: www.naswdc.org

National Citizens' Coalition for Nursing Home Reform
1828 L Street NW, Suite 801
Washington, DC 20036
Phone: 202–332–2275
Fax: 202–332–2949
Web site: www.nccnhr.org

National Council on the Aging
1901 L Street NW, 4th Floor
Washington, DC 20036
Phone: 202–479–1200
Web site: www.ncoa.org

National Council of Senior Citizens
8403 Colesville Road, Suite 1200
Silver Spring, MD 20910–3314
Phone: 301–578–8800
Fax: 301–578–8999

National Family Caregivers Association
10400 Connecticut Avenue, Suite 500
Kensington, MD 20895–3944
Phone: 800–896–3650 or 301–942–6430
Fax: 301–942–2302
Web site: www.nfcacares.org

National Institute on Aging Information Center
Building 31, Room 5C27
31 Center Drive, MSC 2292
Bethesda, MD 20892
Phone: 301–496–1752
TTY: 800–222–4225
Fax: 301–496–1072
Web site: www.nia.nih.gov

National Shared Housing Resource Center
364 South Railroad Avenue
San Mateo, CA 94401
Phone: 650–348–6660
Fax: 650–348–0284
Web site: www.nationalsharedhousing.org

Nursing Home Information Service—
National Council of Senior Citizens
1–1331 F Street NW
Washington, DC 20004
Phone: 202–347–8800 Extension 340/341
Web site: www.angelfire.com/tn/NursingHome/

ResCare HomeCare—National Office
9901 Linn Station Road
Louisville, KY 40223–3808
Phone: 800–866–0860 ext 5880
Web site: www.rescarehomecare.com

Meals and Nutrition

Food Stamp Program
Consult your local phone directory or call
Social Security at the number below
Phone: 800–772–1213
Web site: www.fns.usda.gov/fsp

Meals on Wheels Association of America
203 South Union Street
Alexandria, VA 22314
Phone: 703–548–5558
Fax: 703–548–8024
Web site: www.mowaa.org

National Safety Council
1121 Spring Lake Drive
Itasca, IL 60143–3201
Phone: 630–285–1121
Fax: 630–285–1315
Web site: www.nsc.org

Nutrition Hotline—American Dietetic Association
120 South Riverside Plaza, Suite 2000
Chicago, IL 60606–6995
Phone: 800–877–1600
Web site: www.eatright.org

Medical

Alzheimer's and other Dementias

Alzheimer's Association
225 North Michigan Avenue, Floor 17
Chicago, IL 60601–7633
Phone: 800–272–3900
TDD: 866–403–3073
Fax: 866–699–1246
Web site: www.alz.org

Alzheimer's Disease, Education, and Referral Center
National Institute on Aging
Building 31, Room 5C27
31 Center Drive, MSC 2292
Bethesda, MD 20892
Phone: 800–438–4380
Web site: www.nia.nih.gov/alzheimers

The American Occupational Therapy Association Inc.
4720 Montgomery Lane
P.O. Box 31220
Bethesda, MD 20824–1220

Phone: 301–652–2682
TDD: 800–377–8555
Fax: 301–652–7711
Web site: www.aota.org

Family Caregiver Alliance
180 Montgomery Street, Suite 100
San Franciso, CA 94104
Phone: 800–445–8106 or 415–434–3388
Web site: www.caregiver.org

Arthritis

Arthritis Foundation
P.O. Box 7669
Atlanta, GA 30357–0669
Phone: 800–283–7800
Web site: www.arthritis.org

National Arthritis and Musculoskeletal and Skin Diseases
1 AMS Circle
Bethesda, MD 20892–3675
Phone: 877–226–4267 or 301–495–4484
TTY: 301–565–2966
Fax: 301–718–6366
Web site: www.niams.nih.gov

National Osteoporosis Foundation
1232 22nd Street NW
Washington, DC 20037–1202
Phone: 800–231–4222 or 202–223–2226
Web site: www.nof.org

Cancer

American Cancer Society
250 Williams Street NW, Suite 600
Atlanta, GA 30303–1002

Phone: 800–227–2345
Web site: www.cancer.org

American Cancer Society Hotline
235 Montgomery Street, Suite 320
San Francisco, CA 94104
Phone: 800-ACS-2345 or 415–394–7100
Web site: www.cancer.org

R.A. Bloch Cancer Foundation
1 HandR Block Way
Kansas City, MO 64106
Phone: 800–433–0464
Web site: www.blochcancer.org

National Cancer Institute, NCI Public Inquiries Office
6116 Executive Boulevard, Room 3036A
Bethesda, MD 20892–8322
Phone: 800–422–6237
TTY: 800–332–8615
Web site: www.cancer.gov

National Coalition for Cancer Survivorship
1010 Wayne Avenue, Suite 770
Silver Spring, MD 20910
Phone: 301–650–9127
Fax: 301–565–9670
Web site: www.canceradvocacy.org

Dental

National Institute of Dental and Craniofacial Research
National Institutes of Health
1 Nohic Way
Bethesda, MD 20892–3500 Phone: 301–496–4261
Web site: www.nidcr.nih.gov

Diabetes

American Association of Diabetes Educators
200 West Madison Street, Suite 800
Chicago, IL 60606
Phone: 800–338–3633
Web site: www.diabeteseducator.org

American Diabetes Association
ATTN: National Call Center
1701 North Beauregard Street
Alexandria, VA 22311
Phone: 800–342–2383
Web site: www.diabetes.org

National Diabetes Information Clearinghouse
1 Information Way
Bethesda, MD 20892–3560
Phone: 800–860–8747Fax: 703–738–4929
Web site: http://diabetes.niddk.nih.gov/

Foot Disorders

American Podiatric Medical Association Inc.
9312 Old Georgetown Road
Bethesda, MD 20814–1621
Phone: 301–581–9200
Web site: www.apma.org

Heart

American Heart Association National Center
and Stroke Connection
7272 Greenville Avenue
Dallas, TX 75231
Phone: 800–242–8721 or 888–478–7653
Web site: www.americanheart.org

American Medical Association
515 North State Street
Chicago, IL 60610
Phone: 800–621–8335
Web site: www.ama-assn.org

American Physical Therapy Association
1111 North Fairfax Street
Alexandria, VA 22314–1488
Phone: 800–999–2782 or 703–684–2782
TDD: 703–683–6748
Fax: 703–684–7343
Web site: www.apta.org

National Heart, Lung, and Blood Institute
Information Center
P.O. Box 30105
Bethesda, MD 20824–0105
Phone: 301–592–8573
TTY: 240–629–3255
Fax: 240–629–3246
Web site: www.nhlbi.nih.gov

Huntington's Disease

Huntington's Disease Society of America
505 Eighth Avenue, Suite 902
New York City, NY 10018
Phone: 800–345–4372 or 212–242–1968
Fax: 212–239–3430
Web site: www.hdsa.org

Medicare and Medicaid

Concerned Relatives of Nursing Home Patients
P.O. Box 18820
Cleveland Heights, OH 44118–8820
Phone: 216–321–0403

National Citizens Coalition for Nursing Home Reform
1828 L Street NW, Suite 801
Washington, DC 20036
Phone: 202–332–2276
Fax: 202–332–2949
Web site: www.nccnhr.org

Connecticut Partnership for Long-Term Care
450 Capitol Avenue
Hartford, CT 06106–1379
Phone: 800–286–2214 or 860–418–6200

Health Care Financing Administration
The U.S. Department of Health and Human Services
200 Independence Avenue SW
Washington, DC 20201
Phone: 877–696–6775 or 202–619–0257
Web site: www.hhs.gov

Indiana Long-Term Care Program
Indiana Department of Insurance
714 West 53rd Street
Anderson, IN 46013
Phone: 866–234–4582
Web site: www.state.in.us/fssa/iltcp

Medicare Insurance Help Line
Social Security Administration, Office of Public Inquiries
Windsor Park Building
6401 Security Blvd.
Baltimore, MD 21235
Phone: 800–772–1213
TTY: 800–325–0778
Web site: www.ssa.gov

New York State Partnership for Long-Term Care
New York State Department of Health
NYS Partnership for Long Term Care
1 Commerce Plaza, Room 826
Albany, NY 12210
Phone: 518–473–8083
Web site: www.nyspltc.org

Social Security Administration
Office of Public Inquiries
Windsor Park Building
6401 Security Blvd.
Baltimore, MD 21235
Phone: 800–772–1213
TTY: 800–325–0778
Web site: www.ssa.gov

Medicines and Miscellaneous Health Issues

Council on Family Health
900 19th Street NW, Suite 700
Washington, DC 20006
Web site: www.OTCsafety.org

Family Caregiver Project
Bet Tzedek Legal Services
145 S. Fairfax Avenue, Suite 200
Los Angeles, CA 90036
Phone: 323–939–0506
Fax: 323–549–5880
Web site: www.bettzedek.org

National Digestive Diseases Information Clearinghouse
2 Information Way
Bethesda, MD 20892–3570
Phone: 800–891–5389

Fax: 703–738–4929
Web site: http://digestive.niddk.nih.gov

National Health Information Center
The U.S. Department of Health and Human Services
200 Independence Avenue SW
Washington, DC 20201
Phone: 877–696–6775 or 202–619–0257
Web site: www.health.gov/nhic/

National Institutes of Health
9000 Rockville Pike
Bethesda, MD 20892
Phone: 301–496–4000
TTY: 301–402–9612
Web site: www.nih.gov

National Organization for Rare Disorders
55 Kenosia Avenue
P.O. Box 1968
Danbury, CT 06813–1968
Phone: 800–999–6673 or 203–744–0100
TDD: 203–797–9590
Fax: 203–798–2291
Web site: www.rarediseases.org

National Osteoporosis Foundation
1232 22nd Street NW
Washington, DC 20037–1202
Phone: 800–231–4222 or 202–223–2226
Web site: www.nof.org

National Rural Health Association
301 E. Armour Blvd., Suite 420
Kansas City, MO 64111
Phone: 816–756–3140
Web site: www.nrharural.org

National Safety Council
1121 Spring Lake Drive
Itasca, IL 60143–3201
Phone: 630–285–1121
Fax: 630–285–1315
Web site: www.nsc.org

Office of Disease Prevention and Health Promotion
Office of Public Health and Science, Office of the Secretary
1101 Wootton Parkway, Suite LL100
Rockville, MD 20852
Phone: 240–453–8280
Fax: 240–453–8282
Web site: http://odphp.osophs.dhhs.gov

United Seniors Health Cooperative
409 Third Street SW, Suite 200
Washington, DC 20024
Phone: 202–479–6973

Mental Health: Psychological and Psychiatric Services

American Association for Marriage and Family Therapy
112 South Alfred Street
Alexandria, VA 22314–3061
Phone: 703–838–9808
Fax: 703–838–9805
Web site: www.aamft.org

American Psychiatric Association
1000 Wilson Blvd., Suite 1825
Arlington, VA 22209–3901
Phone: 703–907–7300
Web site: www.psych.org

American Psychological Association
750 First Street NE

Washington, DC 20002–4242
Phone: 800–374–2721 or 202–336–5500
TDD/TTY: 202–336–6123
Web site: www.apa.org

American Self-Help Group Clearinghouse
25 Pocono Road
Denville, NJ 07834
Phone: 973–326–6789
Web site: http://mentalhelp.net/selfh

Jean Posner, M.D. Neuro-Psychiatrist
6 Cradock Lane
Owings Mills, MD 21117
Phone: 410–363–6551

National Alliance for the Mentally Ill
Colonial Place Three
2107 Wilson Blvd., Suite 300
Arlington, VA 22201–3042
Phone: 800–950–6264 or 703–524–7600
Fax: 703–524–9094
Web site: www.nami.org

National Association of Social Workers
750 First Street NE, Suite 700
Washington, DC 20002–4241
Phone: 202–408–8600
Web site: www.socialworkers.org

International Foundation for Research
and Education on Depression
2017-D Renard Ct.
Annapolis, MD 21401
Phone: 410–268–0044
Fax: 443–782–0739
Web site: www.ifred.org

National Institute of Mental Health
Science Writing, Press, and Dissemination Branch
6001 Executive Boulevard, Room 8184, MSC 9663
Bethesda, MD 20892–9663
Phone: 866–615–6464 or 301–443–4513
TTY: 866–415–8051 or 301–443–8431
Fax: 301–443–4279
Web site: www.nimh.nih.gov

National Mental Health Association
Mental Health America
2000 N. Beauregard Street, 6th Floor
Alexandria, VA 22311
Phone: 800–969–6642 or 703–684–7722
TTY: 800–433–5959
Fax: 703–684–5968
Web site: www.nmha.org

National Self-Help Clearinghouse
365 5ᵗʰ Avenue, Suite 3300
New York City, NY 10016
Phone: 212–817–1822
Web site: www.selfhelpweb.org

Parkinson's Disease

American Parkinson Disease Association
135 Parkinson Avenue
Staten Island, NY 10305
Phone: 800–223–2732 or 718–981–8001
Fax: 718–981–4399
Web site: www.apdaparkinson.org

National Institute of Neurological Disorders and Stroke
NIH Neurological Institute
P.O. Box 5801
Bethesda, MD 20824

Phone: 800–352–9424 or 301–496–5751
TTY: 301–468–5981
Web site: www.ninds.nih.gov

National Parkinson Foundation Inc.
1501 NW 9th Avenue/Bob Hope Road
Miami, FL 33136–1494
Phone: 800–327–4545 or 305–243–6666
Fax: 305–243–5595
Web site: www.parkinson.org

Parkinson's Disease Foundation
1359 Broadway, Suite 1509
New York City, NY 10018
Phone: 800–457–6676 or 212–923–4700
Fax: 212–923–4778
Web site: www.pdf.org

Respiratory and Lung Diseases

The American Lung Association
61 Broadway, 6th Floor
New York City, NY 10006
Phone: 800–548–8252 or 212–315–8700
Web site: www.lungusa.org

Skin Disorders

American Academy of Dermatology
P.O. Box 4014
Schaumburg, IL 60618–4014
Phone: 866–503–7546
Fax: 847–240–1859
Web site: www.skincarephysicians.com

National Arthritis and Musculoskeletal and Skin Diseases
1 AMS Circle
Bethesda, MD 20892–3675
Phone: 877–226–4267 or 301–495–4484
TTY: 301–565–2966
Fax: 301–718–6366
Web site: http://www.niams.nih.gov

Stroke

American Heart Association National Center
and Stroke Connection
7272 Greenville Avenue
Dallas, TX 75231
Phone: 800–242–8721 or 888–478–7653
Web site: www.americanheart.org

American Physical Therapy Association
1111 North Fairfax Street
Alexandria, VA 22314–1488
Phone: 800–999–2782 or 703–684–2782
TDD: 703–683–6748
Fax: 703–684–7343
Web site: www.apta.org

American Speech-Language Hearing Association
10801 Rockville Pike
Rockville, MD 20852
Phone: 800–638–8255
Fax: 240–333–4705
Web site: www.asha.org

AHA Stroke Connection
(formerly The Courage Stroke Network)
American Heart Association
7272 Greenville Avenue

Dallas, TX 75231
Phone: 800–553–6321

Family Caregiver Alliance
180 Montgomery Street, Suite 1100
San Francisco, CA 94104
Phone: 800–445–8106 or 415–434–3388
Web site: www.caregiver.org

National Aphasia Association
350 Seventh Avenue, Suite 902
New York City, NY 10001
Phone: 800–922–4622
Web site: www.aphasia.org

National Institute of Neurological Disorders and Stroke
NIH Neurological Institute
P.O. Box 5801
Bethesda, MD 20824
Phone: 800–352–9424 or 301–496–5751
TTY: 301–468–5981
Web site: www.ninds.nih.gov

National Stroke Association
9707 E Easter Lane Building B
Centennial, CO 80112
Phone: 800–787–6537
Fax: 303–649–1328
Web site: www.stroke.org

Military-related Services

Blinded Veterans Association
477 H Street NW
Washington, DC 20001–2694
Phone: 202–371–8880
Fax: 202–371–8258
Web site: www.bva.org

Department of Defense
Office of Public Communication
Assistant Secretary of Defense for Public Affairs
1400 Defense Pentagon
Washington, DC 20310–1400
Phone: 703–428–0711
Web site: www.defenselink.mil

Paralyzed Veterans of America
801 Eighteenth Street NW
Washington, DC 20006–3517
Phone: 800–424–8200
TTY: 800–795–4327
Web site: www.pva.org

Department of Veterans Affairs
VA Benefits: 800–827–1000
Health Care Benefits: 877–222–8387
TDD: 800–829–4833
Web site: www.va.gov

Older Women's Issues

National Institute on Aging Information Center
Building 31, Room 5C27
31 Center Drive, MSC 2292
Bethesda, MD 20892
Phone: 301–496–1752
TTY: 800–222–4225
Fax: 301–496–1072
Web site: www.nia.nih.gov

Older Women's League
3300 N Fairfax Drive, Suite 218
Arlington, VA 22201
Phone: 800–825–3695 or 703–812–7990

Fax: 703–812–0687
Web site: www.owl-national.org

People's Medical Society
P.O. Box 868
Allentown, PA 18105–0868
Phone: 610–770–1670
Web site: www.peoplesmed.org

Physical Fitness for the Elderly

American Alliance for Health, Physical
Education, Recreation, and Dance
1900 Association Dr.
Reston, VA 20191–1598
Phone: 800–213–7193 or 703–476–3400
Web site: www.aahperd.org

American Physical Therapy Association
1111 North Fairfax Street
Alexandria, VA 22314–1488
Phone: 800–999–2782 or 703–684–2782
TDD: 703–683–6748
Fax: 703–684–7343
Web site: www.apta.org

Arthritis Foundation
P.O. Box 7669
Atlanta, GA 30357–0669
Phone: 800–283–7800
Web site: www.arthritis.org

President's Council on Physical Fitness and Sports
Department W
200 Independence Ave. SW, Room 738-H
Washington, DC 20201–0004
Phone: 202–690–9000

Fax: 202–690–5211
Web site: www.fitness.gov

Vision Impairment and Services for the Blind

American Council of the Blind
1155 15th Street NW, Suite 1004
Washington, DC 20005
Phone: 800–424–8666 or 202–467–5081
Fax: 202–467–5085
Web site: www.acb.org

American Foundation for the Blind
11 Penn Plaza, Suite 300
New York City, NY 10001
Phone: 800–232–5463 or 212–502–7600
Fax: 212–502–7777
Web site: www.afb.org

Association for Macular Diseases
210 East 64th Street, 8th Floor
New York City, NY 10021
Phone: 212–605–3719
Fax: 212–605–3795
Web site: www.macula.org

Blinded Veterans Association
477 H Street NW
Washington, DC 20001–2694
Phone: 202–371–8880
Fax: 202–371–8258
Web site: www.bva.org

Glaucoma Research Foundation
251 Post Street, Suite 600
San Francisco, CA 94108

Phone: 800–826–6693 or 415–986–3162
Fax: 415–986–3763Web site: www.glaucoma.org

Lighthouse International
The Sol and Lillian Goldman Building
111 East 59th Street
New York City, NY 10022–1202
Phone: 800–829–0500 or 212–821–9200
TTY: 212–821–9713
Fax: 212–821–9707
Web site: www.lighthouse.org

National Association for the Visually Handicapped
22 West 21st Street, 6th Floor
New York City, NY 10010
Phone: 212–889–3141 or 212–255–2804
Fax: 212–727–2931
Web site: www.navh.org

National Eye Care Project—Ameri-
can Academy of Ophthalmology
American Academy of Ophthalmology
P.O. Box 7424
San Francisco, CA 94120–7424
Phone: 800–222–3937 or 415–561–8500
Fax: 415–561–8533
Web site: www.aao.org

National Eye Institute Information Office
31 Center Drive, MSC 2510
Bethesda, MD 20892–2510
Phone: 301–496–5248
Web site: www.nei.nih.gov/index.asp

National Federation of the Blind
1800 Johnson Street
Baltimore, MD 21230
Phone: 410–659–9314
Fax: 410–685–5653
Web site: www.nfb.org

National Library Service for the Blind
and Physically Handicapped
Library of Congress
Washington, DC 20542
Phone: 888–657–7323 or 202–707–5100
Fax: 202–707–0712
Web site: www.loc.gov/nls/

Prevent Blindness America
211 West Wacker Drive, Suite 1700
Chicago, IL 60606
Phone: 800–331–2020
Web site: www.preventblindness.org

GLOSSARY

The following definitions are for educational
purposes only and not intended for legal
use. It is recommended that you contact an
attorney within the state for which you may
have specific legal questions or concerns.

1035 exchange: A provision under Section 1035 of the U.S. tax
code that allows funds, which have accrued in an annuity,
endowment, or life insurance policy, to be directly transferred to another annuity, endowment, or life insurance
policy of like kind without being taxed.

401k Plan: An individual retirement account defined by the
employer. Contributions are allowed on a post-tax and/or a
pre-tax/tax-deferred (PT/TD) basis. Neither contributions
nor earnings on contributions are taxed until withdrawn.
Contributions are normally deducted from employees' salaries by their employers before tax and directly deposited
into the plan. Employers typically match employee contributions with a pre-determined percentage, which may be
as much as 100%. Employees have a choice as to where and
how contributions will be invested.

AARP (American Association of Retired Persons): A nonprofit, non-
partisan, non-government organization (NGO). It is one
of the largest membership organizations and has one of
the most powerful lobbying groups for people 50 years of
age and older in the United States. AARP claimed nearly
40 million members in 2008, and membership is expected
to grow significantly as baby boomers age. AARP offers
a full range of benefits, services, and products, including
insurance and investment funds for members. Web site:
AARP.org.

ACLFs (Adult Care Living Facilities): Formally known as Adult Congregate Living Facilities and refers to facilities that provide residential assisted living.

ACLS (Advanced Cardiac Life Support): ACLS includes clinical interventions initiated in the treatment of cardiac arrest and/or other life threatening medical emergencies. Medical professionals certified in ACLS are required to have the ability to read and interpret electrocardiograms, administer defibrillation, understand emergency pharmacology, manage the patient's airway, and initiate IV access.

ADLs (Activities of Daily Living): ADLs include activities normally performed on a daily basis, such as feeding, toileting, bathing, dressing, and grooming. ADLs also include other routine activities, including cooking and meal preparation as well as leisure activities. Health-care providers typically assess an individual's ability to perform ADLs in order to determine what healthcare services the patient might need and whether she/he is safe living alone.

Advance Directives: Legal advance health-care directives that allow competent individuals to make medical choices in advance. Signed advance directives outline the individual's choices regarding certain medical treatments.

Advantage Plans (Medicare Advantage Plans): Healthcare coverage options that are part of the Medicare program. These plans typically provide all Medicare-covered health care. Certain plans also include prescription drug coverage. Medicare Advantage Plans include Preferred Provider Organizations (PPOs), Health Maintenance Organization (HMOs), Medicare Special Needs Plans (SNPs), and Private Fee-for-Service Plans. These plans typically offer extra benefits and lower co-payments than the Original Medicare Plan. However, choices in providers and hospitals many be limited to those who belong to that particular plan. Such plans are referred to as Medicare Part C.

Alcohol Specific Indicators: Assessment indicators, included in the *Red Flag Checklist* (Haymon, 1996), used to help evaluate an individual's level of functioning and ability to care for her/himself.

Alphabet Soup: A term coined by Dr. Sandra Haymon and first used in her book *My Turn: Caring for Aging Parents & Other Elderly Loved Ones (1996)* to describe the barrage of acronyms common to medical and legal professionals but unfamiliar to most people.

ALS (Artificial Life Support): Medical systems that use technology to support or replace a vital function of the body that has been critically damaged. Such medical techniques include but are not limited to mechanical ventilators, mechanical feeding, artificial pacemakers, internal defibrillators, and dialysis machines. Life-support systems are intended to prolong life.

Alzheimer's Disease: Also known as *Dementia Alzheimer's Type (*DAT). Alzheimer's disease is a type of dementia (brain disorder) that is progressive and gradually diminishes the patient's memory, as well as her/his abilities to perform activities of daily living. Symptoms include confusion (difficulty organizing and expressing thoughts), forgetfulness (short-term and eventually long-term memory loss), and behavioral and personality changes. There is no cure for Alzheimer's disease. However, there are medications that help treat symptoms. Approximately 5 million people in the U.S. were reported to have DAT in 2007.

America's Silver Tsunami: A label used to describe the 78 million baby boomers who began turning 62 years old January 1,

2008. Approximately 10,000 boomers will turn 62 every day for the next two decades.

Annuity: A secure, flexible, financial investment offered through insurance companies that guarantees income for life and provides income for a spouse or any other designated person after the death of the owner. There is typically the benefit of life insurance as part of an annuity. Annuities may be set up to accommodate *qualified,* as well as *nonqualified,* funds. Funds may be invested over time or as a single payment. There is a tax penalty if qualified funds are distributed before 59.5 years of age. Annuities grow tax-deferred during the accumulation phase.

Artificial Feeding: The act of providing nutrition through intravenous catheters, nasogastric, or gastrostomy tubes.

Artificial Intravenous Hydration: A method of artificially hydrating a person who is unable to swallow normally, suffering from severe dehydration, unconsciousness, recovering from surgery, or vomiting persistently. Fluids are administered through a vein.

Artificial Respiration: The act of artificially providing air for a person who is not breathing on her/his own but whose heart is still beating. The exchange of gases in the body is accomplished by pulmonary ventilation, external and internal respiration.

Asset: Personal items that have a monetary value (houses, vehicles, furs, jewelry, paintings, etc.) as well as financial investments (certificates of deposit, savings, stocks, bonds, IRAs, etc.).

AT/TX: Acronym for after-tax/taxable status of investments. Contributions made to AT/TX investments are made with funds after taxes have been paid. Earnings on these contributions are taxed as ordinary income during the tax year earnings were accrued.

Baby Boomers: A label assigned to individuals born between 1946 and 1964. In 2008 there were approximately 78 million baby boomers still alive.

Caregiver Syndrome: A constellation of symptoms, which might include constant fatigue, irritability, agitation, insomnia, forgetfulness, gastro-intestinal disturbance, headaches, and feelings of anger, resentment, and guilt secondary to constantly caring for another person with a chronic illness and/or dementia. In severe cases, the caregiver may develop high blood pressure, diabetes, and other life-threatening illnesses.

Case Law (decisional law): Judge-made law rather than law enacted by a legislature, thus it is a type of non-statutory law. Case law interprets prior case law, statutes, and other legal authority, as well as functions, by applying precedent law. It is derived from judicial decisions and is sometimes referred to as common law and as black letter law.

CFA (Chartered Financial Analyst): Financial analysts who have met education and work experience requirements and who have passed three exams covering financial, accounting, security analysis, portfolio management, and economics, as well as strict standards of conduct and ethics. This international professional designation is a requirement for analysts in the fields of financial and investment banking, financial analysis of stocks, bonds, and assets, and investment management.

Charitable Remainder Trust: The most common type of charitable trust. Those who donate to a charitable remainder trust are typically allowed to write off the value of their gift over a five-year period. At the end of the specified payment period or after the individual's death, trust property is given to the charity outright and is not considered part of the estate. Consequently, it is not subject to federal estate tax.

Charitable Trust: A type of trust that allows individuals to give large sums of money to charities. This type trust offers several substantial tax breaks in addition to allowing individuals to help their favorite charities. Charitable trusts are irrevocable. Allowable charities must be approved by the Internal Revenue Service (IRS) with tax-exempt status.

CMMS and CMS (Centers for Medicare and Medicaid Services): CMMS was formerly known as the Health Care Financing Administration (HCFA). This federal agency is responsible for administering Medicare, Medicaid, SCHIP (State Children's Health Insurance), HIPAA (Health Insurance Portability and Accountability Act), CLIA (Clinical Laboratory Improvement Amendments), and other health-related programs. Web site: www.cms.hhs.gov/

CNPs (Certified Nurse Practitioners): Registered nurses who typically have completed a master's degree or received other advanced nursing education. They diagnose and manage complex medical conditions in addition to common diagnoses. Nurse practitioners provide a full range of health care services and often fill the gaps created by a lack of medical doctors, especially in rural areas.

College Education 529 plans: State-run college savings plans that allow parents to contribute as much as they can afford to invest, without restrictions, up to a lifetime cap, which ranges between $100,000 and $270,000 depending on the individual state. Money invested in these accounts may be used at any school for qualified expenses incurred in paying for higher education, including tuition, books, and room and board. Annual tax advantages include certain benefits from the IRS, as well as state tax advantages in some states.

Comfort Measures Only: A method of health-care where the goal of medical treatment is to keep the person comfortable and to help prepare her/him for a natural and dignified death. It is often understood there is no cure and no means of stabilization. This is the goal of hospice programs.

Cost Basis: The initial cost of an investment.

CPA (Certified Public Accountant): Accountants who have met education and experience requirements for the particular state in which they are seeking certification and who have also passed the Uniform Certified Public Accountant Examination. Public accountants are *not* the same as certified public accountants.

CPR (Cardiopulmonary Resuscitation): An emergency medical procedure for victims of cardiac or respiratory arrest. CPR consists of chest compressions and lung ventilation. CPR is typically continued in the presence of advanced life support (ACLF) until the patient regains a heartbeat or is declared dead.

Critical Red Flags (Haymon, 1996): A list of critical indicators for potential neglect and/or harm to self or others. These assessment indicators are included in the *Red Flag Checklist* (Haymon, 1996) and used to help evaluate an individual's level of functioning, ability to care for her/himself, and propensity for harming her/himself or others.

Custodial care: Room and board in a nursing home or other long-term care facility where assistance with activities of daily living (ADLs) is required. Custodial care is not covered by Medicare, but Medicaid provides reimbursement for those who qualify.

DAT (Dementia Alzheimer's Type): See Alzheimer's Disease

Defined contribution plans: Defined contribution plans are retirement plans where the amount contributed is defined by the employer or the employee. IRAs, 401ks, SEPs, and Simple IRAs, as well as profit sharing and money purchase plans, are all defined contribution plans. Such plans qualify for a tax advantage and are referred to as "qualified" plans.

DI (Federal Disability Insurance Trust): One of the two primary trust funds created by the U. S. government for Social Security on August 1, 1956, and from which benefits are paid to individuals who are determined unable to work due to physical or mental conditions, as well as to their eligible dependents. This is a separate account in the U. S. Treasury.

DMV (Department of Motor Vehicles): State agencies that issue vehicle registrations and drivers' licenses.

DNAR, DNR, DNRO: Acronyms for a legal medical advance directive that prohibits cardiopulmonary resuscitation (CPR). Individuals who would rather not go through the trauma and the risk of CPR must have a *Do Not Resuscitate (DNR)* order placed in their medical records. Sometimes this order is referred to as No Code and No CPR, as well as DNRO (Do Not Resuscitate Order) and DNAR (Do Not Attempt Resuscitation).

DNH (Do Not Hospitalize Order): A legal medical advance directive intended to protect individuals from automatically being hospitalized without first carefully considering their state of health.

DNI (Do Not Intubate Order): A legal medical advance directive that prohibits the use of intubation (mechanical ventilation).

DNT (Do Not Transfer Document): A legal advance directive prohibiting the transfer of the individual from her/his resident care facility to a hospital.

DPOA (Durable Power of Attorney): A legal document that allows a competent person to assign power to another competent person to act as her/his agent. A DPOA specifies exactly what powers the individual is giving to her/his agent. Power may include consent to make medical, therapeutic, and surgical decisions, as well as which drugs may or may not be administered. The agent might also be able to transfer property, borrow money for, or even manage the person's bank accounts. The agent holding Durable Power of Attorney may have numerous specific or general powers.

DPOAHc (Durable Power of Attorney for Healthcare): A legal medical advance directive that allows individuals to name another person as their advocate (agent) to carry out medical choices they've made in advance. A DPOAHc typically limits the agent to decisions related only to healthcare. Decisions include therapeutic and surgical decisions, as well as which drugs may or may not be administered.

DRG (Diagnosis-Related Group Decision): DRGs are classifications of specific conditions. Medicare Part A typically pays a flat fee for each classification unless there are extenuating circumstances.

Drug Benefit Program: Medicare Part D—prescription drug coverage.

EAPs (Employee Assistance Programs): Programs offered by many employers designed to help employees handle personal problems adversely impacting their job performance and/or their physical, mental, or emotional well-being, such as emotional distress, work or family relationship issues, personal or family health concerns, major life events (births, deaths, accidents, concerns about aging parents), financial or legal concerns, and/or substance abuse.

Educational IRAs: Qualified investment plans that are designed to help individuals with high education expenses. Contributions of up to $2,000 per child under the age of 18 may be made each year, provided the child is enrolled in school. Allowable amounts for contributions are based on the annual income of the investor and are subject to change. Distributions that are used for higher education are usually tax-free.

Emergency Medical Information Kit (Haymon, 1996*):* A plastic envelope that contains commonly used medical advance directives. It has a magnet on the back so it may readily be displayed on a refrigerator door to help paramedics easily find personal advance directives should they be called to a person's home for a life-threatening emergency. This was first published in *My Turn: Caring for Aging Parents & Other Elderly Loved Ones* (Haymon, 1996) and may be ordered online at: www.babyboomerssandwich.com.

Endotracheal Tube: One method of mechanical ventilation. An endotracheal tube is passed through the mouth, the larynx, and vocal cords into the trachea. A bulb is then inflated near the distal tip of the tube to help secure it in place and to also protect the person's airway from secretions, blood, and/or vomit.

ESOP (Employee Stock Ownership Plan): Investment and retirement plans whereby a company makes contributions and pays benefits with its own stock rather than with cash funds.

Estate Plans: Documents such as trusts and wills that establish how assets are to be distributed after the death of the testator.

Estate Tax (Inheritance or Death Tax): The estate tax is part of the *Unified Gift and Estate Tax* system. Estate tax is imposed when property is transferred either by a will or according to state law if the estate is left intestate (without a will) after an individual's death. There is no federal estate tax on estates with a total taxable value of $2,000,000 or less (2008). Once this credit exemption has been met, the federal estate tax is a flat 45% of taxable assets. Assets left to a spouse or a charitable organization may be exempt. Many states also impose an estate or inheritance tax in addition to the federal estate tax.

Family Leave Act (FLA): A United States labor law enacted February 5, 1993, that allows individuals to take unpaid leave from their jobs due to situational issues that prohibit them from performing their jobs, such as personal health conditions, time off to care for a new child, whether by birth, adoption, or fostering, and/or issues related to caring for sick or elderly family members. The FLA allows individuals to take time off without having to worry about losing their jobs. Employees are guaranteed to have a job when they return, provided certain criterion is met.

FDIC (Federal Deposit Insurance Corporation): An agency of the U.S. Government, created by the Glass-Steagall Act (1933), that provides insurance on cash deposits as well as certificates of deposit in member financial institutions.

Federal Disability Insurance Trust (DI): See DI

Federal Old Age and Survivors Insurance Trust Fund (OASI): See OASI

FLTCIP (Federal Long-Term Care Insurance Policy): Long-term care insurance for individuals associated with the U.S. federal government, including active and retired members of the uniformed services and federal and postal employees, as well as their qualified relatives.

Feelings Checklist: A checklist of over one hundred feeling words reported as common among caregivers. This checklist was first published in *My Turn: Caring for Aging Parents & Other Elderly Loved Ones* (Haymon, 1996) and is included in *Baby Boomers—Sandwiched Between Retirement and Caregiving* (Haymon, 2009).

Fixed annuity: A secure, flexible, financial investment offered through insurance companies that guarantees income for life and provides income for a spouse or any other designated person after the death of the investor. This protects individuals from the possibility of outliving their assets. There is typically the benefit of life insurance as part of a fixed annuity.

Flower children: A label assigned to the baby boom generation in the 1960s.

Food Stamp Program: The Food Stamp Program is designed to guarantee an adequate diet to individuals who are living on low incomes. Food stamps are issued free of charge, and age is not a factor. People don't necessarily have to be destitute to get food stamps.

G-tube (Gastrostomy tube): A method of artificial hydration and nutrition, where a tube is surgically inserted into the stomach wall. Fluids can either be poured or pumped in mechanically.

GMIB (Guaranteed Minimum Income Benefit): A rider policy on a variable annuity offered by some insurance companies that guarantees minimum annual payments regardless of how the annuity performs. It also offers a lifetime stream of income.

GRIB (Guaranteed Retirement Income Benefit): A rider policy on a variable, living benefit annuity offered by some insurance companies. GRIBs guarantee a net return (in 2008) of 4%-7% after all fees are paid or the greatest value is attained on each anniversary during the surrender period, whichever is greater.

Guardian: Someone who has been appointed to handle the affairs of an individual who has been determined incompetent to handle her/his own affairs. Guardians may be given full power to make all decisions for the individual, power over just the person (emergency medical or healthcare decisions), power over the person's property, or any combination of these. Though most states provide for the same types of guardianship, there are specific laws pertaining to these provisions, and filing must be done by an attorney.

Guardianship: Legal status awarded to an appointed guardian to handle the affairs of an individual determined to be incompetent to handle her/his own affairs.

HealthCare Decisions Act: Some states refer to this as a *Natural Death Act,* which provides for living will declarations. In most states, this document must be prepared while the person is competent, and the person's signature must be witnessed.

Healthcare Proxy: A competent person judicially appointed to make healthcare decisions for an individual who is unable to make her/his own medical decisions. Healthcare proxies are appointed only if the individual does not have competent relatives to act on her/his behalf and has not named a healthcare surrogate or has perhaps named a surrogate who for some reason can't act on behalf of the individual. This most often occurs for persons who live in a long-term care facility. Many state laws require healthcare proxies be appointed from a priority list.

Healthcare Surrogate: A competent individual appointed by another competent individual to make medical decisions should she/he become incompetent or incapable of making her/his own informed decisions. Normally, a document must be in writing and signed by two witnesses. In many states, only one witness may be the spouse or a blood relative. Customarily, the named surrogate may not be one of the witnesses.

Heroic Measures: An intervention, treatment, or course of therapy that potentially has high risk of causing additional damage to an individual's health. Heroic measures are considered a last resort attempt to save a person's life, eyesight, or limbs. These measures might include but are not limited to cardiopulmonary resuscitation, oral or nasal intubation, cricothyroidotomy, emergency trauma surgery such as amputation, or giving certain medicines at high enough dosages to possibly cause serious side effects or death.

Hippies: A label assigned to the baby boomer generation in the 1960s.

HMOs (Health Maintenance Organizations): Managed care plans that provide basic Medicare coverage in addition to all other benefits needed to fill the gaps in Medicare. Additional coverage beyond basic Medicare, monthly premiums, amount of co-pays, and decisions as to whether a claim will be paid are all controlled by the HMOs, not by Medicare. The basic premise of HMOs is that members agree to receive care only from a specified list of doctors, hospitals, and health care providers in order to get reduced healthcare costs. Specified health care providers are referred to as a network.

Holographic will: A will that is handwritten by the testator and may or may not have been witnessed. Approximately twenty states allow such wills.

Hospice: Hospice care is an approach to health care that focuses on preserving the dignity and quality of life of terminally ill patients. It specifies a general philosophy of care rather than a particular place or facility. Hospice care offers a holistic approach and treats the whole person rather than just treating the illness or disease. The primary goal is to keep patients as comfortable as possible.

ICPs (Institutional Care Programs): A Medicaid program offered by some states and covered under spousal impoverishment policies. ICPs help individuals pay for nursing home care and provide assistance to the wife or husband who remains in the community while their spouse resides in a care facility. Since every state has its own Medicaid programs, individuals need to inquire about assistance within the state where eligibility is being sought. Beyond the worlds of Medicare and Medicaid, there are other state assistance programs for the elderly. Many of those pay for services not covered by Medicare Parts A, B, or D, or by Medicaid.

ILIT (Irrevocable Life Insurance Trust): An ILIT is established to purchase life insurance intended to pay estate taxes so assets won't have to be sold in order to pay taxes owed to the IRS. Typically, death benefits paid from the insurance policy to the ILIT are excluded from the insured's estate. An ILIT can also be prepared so benefits passed to the surviving spouse will also be excluded from her/his estate. This trust is irrevocable and cannot be changed in any way once it is established.

Immediate annuities: A type of annuity that has no accumulation phase and thus begins paying in regular increments the moment you purchase the contract.

Indexed annuities: Fixed annuities (insurance contracts) that provide benefits or earn interest based on links to an external equity index. These types of annuities are designed to mirror the performance of the stock markets, such as the NASDAQ, DOW, S&P 500, or European Indexes. Interest is calculated and credited using a formula based on changes in the index to which the annuity is linked. Indexed annuities may be deferred or immediate. The value of the index is typically tied to a stock or other equity reference, which is not predictable and varies from day to day.

Intestate: When individuals die without a valid will, they leave their estate *intestate.* If the husband and wife both die without a valid will and leave minor children, the state will decide who will be their guardian. When assets are left *intestate,* survivors are often faced with a heavy tax burden in addition to a difficult, lengthy, and expensive legal course of action. Estates left *intestate* are subject to decisions made by a probate court.

Intubation: The medical term intubation is most often used in reference to tracheal intubation (TI) but may also refer to endoscopic procedures. The purpose of intubation is to provide mechanical ventilation.

IRA: Individual retirement accounts that offer tax advantages for retirement savings, including reduced or deferred taxes. These accounts are referred to as "Qualified" accounts because they qualify for a tax-advantage. IRAs may be plans provided by employers for their employees or plans that are provided by individuals for themselves. There are several types of IRAs. The IRA with the greatest tax advantages is a Roth IRA.

Irrevocable Living Trust: A type of trust where the grantor permanently surrenders her/his right to make changes after the trust commences.

IRS (Internal Revenue Service): A bureau of the Department of the Treasury within the U.S. federal government that is responsible for enforcing revenue laws and collecting taxes.

IV (Intravenous Hydration): A method of artificial hydration and nutrition that enables patients to receive nutrition and medicines through a needle inserted into a vein.

Joint Will: A one document will intended to shield two people—normally a husband and wife. Joint wills are considered unwise for estates greater than $675,000 and are often considered a huge mistake in estates of a far lesser value.

Keogh plans (HR10 plans): Retirement plans named for U.S. Representative Eugene James Keogh created for self-employed individuals. Keogh plans are *not* IRAs. The difference between employer-sponsored plans and Keogh plans is the deductible limit. The net income under Keogh plans is adjusted to remove the double FICA tax paid by self-employed individuals.

Last Will and Testament: A legal document that allows an individual (the testator) to establish her/his intentions as to how she/he wants her/his estate to be dealt with after her/his death. The assets of an estate are typically referred to as *property,* which is legally understood to be personal possessions, such as furs, jewelry, clothes, automobiles, boats, recreational vehicles, homes, cash, certificates of deposit, annuities, bonds, stocks, life insurance, monies owed (collections), interests in businesses, royalties, and/or commercial, personal, or rental real estate. The testament part of the will dictates how the property will be disposed.

Limited Power of Attorney: A legal document typically given by investors to financial investment managers or institutions, allowing them to trade funds within the account but not transfer funds out of the account.

LIMRA (Life Insurance and Market Research Association): An independent service that tracks the insurance industry, now known as LIMRA International Inc.

Living Trust: A type of trust also referred to as an *Inter Vivos* trust. Living trusts are initiated while the grantor is still living and may be planned to continue after her/his death. Living trusts are intended to help individuals avoid probate, which could tie up the estate for months and consume about 5% of the estate in court costs and attorney fees. Assets transferred into a living trust before the grantor's death do not go through probate because it is the grantor who dies, not the trust. Therefore, all assets transferred to a revocable trust are no longer part of the grantor's estate and subsequently not subject to probate.

Living Will and Living Will Declaration: A type of legal, medical advance directive that allows individuals to state what they do and do not want regarding certain medical choices. Their wishes are stated in writing prior to becoming too ill or injured to direct their care. The primary purpose of living wills is to prohibit the use of artificial life support.

LTCI (Long-Term Care Insurance): Insurance that provides for long-term care, whether in the individual's home, an assisted living facility, or nursing home.

MA (Medicare Advantage Plan): See Advantage Plans

Medicaid: A joint state and federal program provided through Title XIX of the Social Security Act and signed into law July 30, 1965, the same day Medicare was enacted. Medicaid was created to provide health care for low-income individuals of all ages, including children and seniors who have no medical insurance or poor health insurance. Individuals who qualify for Medicaid have incomes at or below the poverty level. Therefore, Medicaid requires only a minimal cost-sharing contribution from those who qualify.

Medicaid for the Medically Needy: State programs designed for people whose income is too high for them to qualify for regular Medicaid but too low to be able to pay additional medical bills. The assistance provided by these programs is based on a month-to-month need for help to pay medical bills.

Medical Saving Accounts: There are two basic Medicare Medical Savings Account Plans: 1) a Medicare Advantage health plan, which normally has a high deductible, and 2) a Medical Savings Account into which Medicare deposits money to be used to pay costs until the deductible is met. Any money left in this account rolls over to the next year.

Medicare: Medicare is our nation's health insurance program, which was signed into law July 30, 1965 and is available to individuals 65 and older, whether they can afford healthcare insurance or not.

Medicare Advantage Plans: See Advantage Plans

Medicare Managed Care Plans (HMOs, PPOs, POSs): See Advantage Plans

Medicare Part A: Part A provides hospital insurance coverage. All individuals 65 or older qualify for premium free Medicare Part A if they are getting Social Security or Railroad Retirement. Even those who are not getting Social Security or Railroad Retirement but have worked long enough to qualify for those benefits could still be eligible.

Medicare Part B: Part B is optional medical insurance, which was part of the Original Medicare Program. Typically, anyone 65 or older may enroll in Medicare Part B by paying a monthly premium, a yearly deductible, and a co-payment of 20% of the Medicare-approved amount for all services covered by Part B. Members are also responsible for all unapproved charges.

Medicare Part C: Medicare Advantage (MA) plans provide coordinated care plans that replace Original Medicare coverage. Managed care plans provide basic Medicare coverage in addition to all other benefits needed to fill the gaps in Medicare, while individuals remain enrolled in Medicare and maintain all rights and protections. The two most popular are Health Maintenance Organizations (HMOs), which are the least expensive and most restrictive, and Preferred Provider Organizations (PPOs).

Medicare Part D: A comprehensive prescription drug program that subsidizes the costs of prescription drugs for individuals enrolled in Medicare Parts A and B. Medicare Part D went into effect January 1, 2006, and is part of the Medicare Prescription Drug, Improvement, and Modernization Act (MMA) of 2003. Unlike other Medicare services, individual states partially finance this benefit.

Medicare Special Needs Plans: Special Needs Plans (SNPs) are available in some parts of the country. SNPs were created to help coordinate services needed by people who have certain chronic diseases and conditions. SNPs offer all the coverage of Medicare Parts A (hospitalization), B (medical), and D (prescription drugs), plus additional benefits and lower insurance co-payments.

Medigap Policy: A Medicare supplemental insurance policy that is normally purchased through private insurance companies. Medigap typically covers the gaps in Medicare coverage.

MRSA (Methicillin-resistant staphylococcus aureus): A drug-resistant bug spread by contact with infected people and/or contaminated objects. It can cause infections in various parts of the body, which may be serious, and some can be life threatening. MRSA is rapidly spreading worldwide, with millions already infected. Persons with weak immune systems and living in nursing homes, hospitals, or other health care centers are most vulnerable. MRSA kills more people in the US each year than HIV and AIDS.

MUNIs (municipal bonds): A bond issued by a local or state government agency. Issuers might include school districts, public airports, cities, counties, seaports, redevelopment agencies, or other governmental groups. Interest income is typically exempt from state and federal income tax. However, certain municipal bonds may not be tax exempt.

Nasotracheal Intubation: A method of mechanical ventilation that entails passing a tube through the nose rather than the mouth, then through the larynx, vocal cords, and into the trachea.

Natural Death Act: See *Healthcare Decisions Act*

New Deal Program: The title given to a series of promises and programs initiated by President Franklin D. Roosevelt between 1933 and 1938. The goals of these programs were to provide relief, recovery, and reform to the citizens and the economy of the U.S. during the Great Depression. The First New Deal (1933) focused on short-term recovery programs for all groups, while the Second New Deal (1935–36) focused more on redistribution of power away from big businesses and toward consumers, farmers, and coal workers, incorporating relief to the needy and pensions for the elderly. The Securities and Exchange Commission (SEC) was created as a result of the New Deal.

NG (Nasogastric Tube): A method of artificial hydration and nutrition. In this procedure, a tube is inserted into the patient's nose, down through the esophagus, and into the stomach, so she/he can receive fluids and nutrition. Fluids can either be poured in or pumped in mechanically.

NPs (Nurse Practitioners): See CNPs

OASI (Federal Old Age and Survivors Insurance Trust Fund): One of the two primary trust funds created by the U. S. government for Social Security on January 1, 1940, and from which retirement benefits are paid to eligible retirees, their dependents, and survivors. This is a separate account in the U. S. Treasury.

Oral will: A will that is only communicated verbally. It is also referred to as a *Nuncupative will.* Very few states recognize oral wills.

Ordinary annuity (annuity-immediate): See Annuity

Orotracheal Intubation: The most common method of mechanical ventilation. This procedure is performed using a laryngoscope.

OSS (Optional State Supplemental): States programs designed to supplement the income of individuals who reside in an adult congregate living facility or who live in a foster home or other specialized living arrangement that accepts state clients. Some states provide what may be referred to as SS (State Supplements). State supplements are customarily intended to be used for room and board and certain other services provided by authorized facilities.

OTC (Over-the-Counter): This acronym refers to medications that may be purchased without a doctor's prescription.

PAD (Peripheral Artery Disease): A painful and dangerous disease caused by blockage when the arteries are clogged with plaque. Clogged arteries slow the supply of blood to the legs and feet.

Palliative care: Any form of medical care that focuses on reducing the symptoms of a disease, preventing and relieving suffering, and improving the quality of life for patients diagnosed with complex and serious illnesses. Unlike hospice care, patients are not necessarily in the end-stage of their illnesses. Palliative care may be offered in conjunction with curative and other types of medical treatment, although the goal of palliative care is not to provide a cure.

PERS (Personal Emergency Response System): A medical response service with emergency specialists on call twenty-four hours a day, 365 days a year. PERSs reduce concerns about personal safety and help to ensure early intervention, which may allow seniors to remain independent in their own homes. Research suggests the need for hospitalization is reduced by 26% and death by 80% when individuals get help quickly after a fall.

POA (Power of Attorney): A legal document that allows a competent person to assign power to another competent person to act as her/his agent regarding medical, legal, or business matters. The individual giving authority is the principal, or grantor, while the person given the authority to act is the agent.

POS (Point of Service): A Managed Care plan that provides basic Medicare coverage in addition to all other benefits needed to fill the gaps in Medicare. Additional coverage beyond basic Medicare, monthly premiums, amount of co-pays, and decisions as to whether a claim will be paid are all controlled by the managed care plan, not by Medicare. Under a POS plan, participants would be permitted to see physicians and other health care providers, as well as to receive certain services, outside the network. Members can also see specialists without being required to go through their primary care physician.

Pour-Over Will: A will that allows individuals to leave some or all of their assets in a trust established prior to their death. It also tells the courts that assets that were not transferred in to the trust prior to the person's death were intended to be included in the trust.

PPO (Preferred Provider Organization): A Managed Care plan that provides basic Medicare coverage in addition to all other benefits needed to fill the gaps in Medicare. Additional coverage beyond basic Medicare, monthly premiums, amount of co-pays, and decisions as to whether a claim will be paid are all controlled by the PPOs, not by Medicare. The basic premise of PPOs is that members agree to receive care only from a specified list of doctors, hospitals, and healthcare providers in order to get reduced healthcare costs. Specified healthcare providers are referred to as a network.

PT/TD: Acronym for pre-tax/tax-deferred status of investments. Contributions to such investments are funded with monies for which taxes had not been paid. Thus, contributions are tax-deductible. Contributions, as well as earnings, are tax-deferred each year and taxed at the time of distribution at ordinary income rates.

PVS (Persistent Vegetative State): A condition of severe brain damage to the extent that the patient appears to be in a state of wakefulness but without awareness. PVS is not legally recognized as death. This has led to several court cases involving people in a PVS, including Terri Schiavo. Ethical concerns are related but not limited to opinions about quality of life, personal autonomy, wishes of family members, appropriate use of resources, and professional responsibilities.

QMBs (Qualified Medicare Beneficiaries): State assistance programs that provide assistance for individuals who are unable to pay the deductibles, premiums, and co-payments required for Medicare Parts A and B.

Qualified Funds: Funds that qualify for tax-exempt or tax-deferred status.

Red Flag Checklist (Haymon, 1996): A checklist used to evaluate an individual's cognitive, physical, general, and social level of functioning, as well as her/his ability to handle money matters. It includes a critical checklist that screens for potential endangerment to self or others and an alcohol specific checklist, which uncovers alcohol-related problems. This was first published in *My Turn: Caring for Aging Parents & Other Elderly Loved Ones* (Haymon, 1996) and is included in *Baby Boomers-Sandwiched Between Retirement and Caregiving* (Haymon, 2009).

Respite Care: Short-term, temporary relief to persons who are caring for family members in their homes. Without this home care, most of these individuals would require permanent placement in long-term health care facilities. Respite care offers a much-needed break from exhausting challenges often endured by family caregivers.

Reverse Mortgages: A loan used to convert the equity in a person's home into a reversed cash flow, where the lender makes payments from the equity accumulated in the home to the homeowner. This steady income stream provides some seniors with financial security and allows them to remain in their own homes when they would otherwise not be able to because they couldn't afford the upkeep and utility bills, etc. Normally, the home has to be completely paid for or at least have substantial equity in it. Homeowners are allowed to live in their homes until they die or need to move to a care facility.

Revocable Living Trust: A type of trust where the terms may be changed or revoked by the grantor at any time after the trust is initiated. A revocable living trust is normally used as a supplement to a will. It often names a specific person to manage the grantor's affairs should she/he become incapacitated and usually specifies it is to become irrevocable at the death of the grantor. Ideally, a revocable living trust would be enhanced by a pour-over will, which specifies that all assets not already transferred to the living trust would be transferred to the trust at the grantor's death.

Roth 401k: A relatively new retirement plan that combines the most advantageous tax features of the traditional 401k and the Roth IRA. This option is also appropriate for individuals who are self-employed as sole proprietors (not incorporated). This was signed this into law August 15, 2006, making it retroactive to January 1, 2006.

Roth IRA: An after-tax/tax-free (AT/TF) retirement plan first offered in 1998, which offers the greatest tax advantages. Contributions are made after taxes have been paid on assets intended to fund the Roth. Growth within a Roth, as well as distributions, are tax-free, provided the funds have been held in the account for a minimum of five years and the investor is at least 59.5 years of age. In 2008, Roth contributions are prohibited if the individual earns a *modified adjusted gross income* over $110,000 ($160,000 if married and filing jointly). There are no income limitations for roll over funds from a Traditional IRA or 401k account to a Roth IRA account.

Sandwich generation: A term previously used to refer to baby boomers sandwiched between caring for their minor children and their aging parents. Now, this term is used to refer to baby boomers sandwiched between their own retirement and caring for elderly loved ones.

SCHIP (State Children's Health Insurance Program): Created in 1997 to provide health insurance coverage for children whose families did not qualify for Medicaid because their annual incomes were too high but who were too poor to pay for private health insurance. SCHIP provides federal funds to the states, allowing them to administer individualized programs. In 2007, the House and Senate authorized $60 billion (a $35 billion expansion) for the following five years. This will be funded primarily by an increase in cigarette taxes, from 39 cents to one dollar per pack.

SEC (Securities Exchange Commission): A U.S. government agency created by Section 4 of the Securities Exchange Act (1934) as part of President Franklin Delano Roosevelt's New Deal Programs. The SEC enforces the Securities Act of 1933, the Trust Indenture Act of 1939, the Investment Company Act of 1940, the Investment Advisers Act of 1940, and the Sarbanes-Oxley Act of 2002, in addition to other statues. The SEC was created to protect investors, maintain efficient and fair markets, enforce the federal securities laws, and regulate the securities industry/stock market. President Roosevelt appointed Joseph P. Kennedy (father of President John F. Kennedy) as the first chairman of the SEC.

Self-Directed IRAs: Retirement accounts that require a qualified custodian or trustee to hold account assets on behalf of the account owner. Qualified holders must make investments and investment decisions on behalf of the retirement plan according to IRS regulations. Individuals interested in a self-directed IRA should consult a financial advisor.

Self-funded Retirement Plans: Retirement plans established and funded by individuals for themselves rather than by their employers.

SEP (Simplified Employee Pension Plan IRA): A retirement account intended for self-employed individuals and small business owners who do not have a pension fund in the company's name. SEPs are pre-tax/tax-deferred (PT/TD) accounts and are funded with monies for which taxes have not yet been paid. Thus, contributions are tax deductible. Contributions, as well as earnings, are tax-deferred each year and taxed at the time of distribution at ordinary income rates.

Simple IRAs: Often referred to as IRAs but are actually treated differently. A Simple IRA is an employee pension plan that allows the employee and the employer to make contributions that are tax-deductible. The portion contributed by the employee is deducted from her/his taxable income, and the portion contributed by the employer is deducted as an allowable business expense. This means the pension is funded with assets for which taxes have not yet been paid. Withdrawals will be taxed as ordinary income at the time of withdrawal.

Simple Wills: Wills most commonly used for simple estates and normally outlining the individual's preference as to distribution of her/his assets in a straightforward manner.

Skilled Nursing Care: Healthcare that requires a licensed medical provider.

SLGS (State and Local Government Series): See U.S. Treasury Securities.

SS: Acronym for Social Security.

SSI (Supplemental Security Income): State programs designed to help individuals who have few assets and low income. These programs are designed to ensure persons who are 65 or older, disabled, or blind have a minimum level of income. This is primarily for people who live below the poverty level.

State Supplements (SS): Programs designed to supplement the income of individuals who reside in an adult congregate living facility, live in a foster home, or other specialized living arrangement that accepts state clients. State supplements are customarily intended to be used for room and board and certain other services provided by authorized facilities.

Supplemental Insurance: Healthcare insurance intended to cover the gaps in Medicare. Some supplemental policies also cover deductibles and co-payments.

Surrogate Caregiver: See Healthcare Surrogates

Testamentary Trust Will: A trust that occurs upon the death of an individual (the testator), typically under her/his will. Since the testator is deceased when this trust arises, she/he typically does not have any influence over the discretion of the trustee. However, the testator may leave a letter specifying her/his wishes. Testamentary trusts tend to be motivated more by the needs of the beneficiaries (particularly minor beneficiaries) than they are by tax considerations.

Testamentary Trusts: Trusts that allow for assets to be transferred into the trust only after the grantor dies. For example, a single parent might include a testamentary trust in her/his will assigning her/his assets to a trustee who has been appointed the responsibility of managing these assets for the benefit of minor children. Since a testamentary trust is not automatically created upon the death of the individual but normally specified as a provision of the will, the assets allotted to a testamentary trust are required to go through probate prior to commencement of the trust.

TIPS (Treasury Inflation Protected Securities): See Treasury Securities.

Tracheal Intubation: A method of mechanical ventilation where a flexible plastic tube is placed into a person's trachea to provide a means of ventilation and to protect her/his airway. Typically, this type of tube is only left in place for short periods of time (one to four weeks).

Traditional IRA: An individual retirement account that is funded with pre-tax/tax-deferred (PT/TD) funds. Contributions are funded with monies for which taxes have not yet been paid and are therefore tax-deductible. Contributions, as well as earnings, are tax-deferred each year and taxed at the time of distribution at ordinary income rates.

Treasury Bills: See U.S. Treasury Securities.

Treasury Bonds: See U.S. Treasury Securities.

Treasury Notes: See U.S. Treasury Securities.

Treasuries: See U.S. Treasury Securities.

Trustee: An institution or individual designated to manage assets within a trust in accordance with the instructions of the trust.

Trusts: Documents intended to help individuals manage their estates while they are still living, as well as ensure their intentions are in place in the event they should die. A trust allows individuals to manage assets by transferring and distributing specific assets and obligations to different people. Trusts also allow individuals to specify particular circumstances for receipt of benefits, as well as to spread distribution of benefits over a period of time instead of as single gifts. Trusts allow individuals to accomplish goals after their deaths. Therefore, many individuals prefer to have trusts instead of wills. However, a pour-over will should be included in the trust as part of the estate plan.

U.S. Treasury Securities: Debt financing instruments of the U.S. federal government. Marketable U.S. government bonds include |FCO|Hyperlinktreasury notes, treasury bonds|FCC|, treasury bills, and Treasury Inflation Protected Securities (TIPS) issued by the Department of the Treasury through the Bureau of the Public Debt. These bonds are considered liquid and are traded on the secondary market. Non-marketable treasury securities include

Government Account Series—debt issued to government-managed trust funds, savings bonds, and SLGS (State and Local Government Series) that are not to be traded on the secondary market.

VA (Department of Veterans Affairs): A U.S. government agency responsible for administering programs of military-veterans benefits, their families, and/or survivors. VA benefits include but are not limited to pensions, nursing home care, hospitalization, and outpatient medical treatment, as well as disability benefits and services for the blind. VA benefits also customarily pay for prosthetic appliances and a clothing allowance for those who have prosthetic devices. Alcohol and drug treatment is also provided. Death benefits such as burial flags, burial in a national cemetery, and a grave marker, as well as reimbursement for burial expenses, may also be provided. Life insurance is often provided for survivors of disabled veterans.

Variable annuity: A secure, flexible, financial investment created in the U.S. in 1952 and offered through insurance companies to accommodate *qualified,* as well as *non-qualified,* funds. Variable annuities guarantee income for life and provide income for a spouse or other designated individual after the death of the investor. There is typically the benefit of life insurance. Sub-accounts within the annuity allow for investments in equities inside the annuity. There is a tax penalty if qualified funds are distributed before 59.5 years of age. Gains vary according to separate accounts within the annuity. All annuities grow tax-deferred during the accumulation phase.

Will: See Last Will and Testament

Yuppies: A label assigned to baby boomers in the 1980s.

SAMPLE LETTER
REGARDING SOCIAL SECURITY

Re: Social Security

Dear :

I am one of the seventy-eight million baby boomers who will soon be eligible for Social Security. Ten thousand of us will turn 62 every day for the next two decades! Most of us are concerned about the state of our present pay-as-you-go Social Security system. I'm sure that you are aware of these statistics, as well as many of our concerns.

The Social Security Administration offered this press release on April 23, 2007: "The projected point at which tax revenues will fall below program costs comes in 2017. The projected point at which the Trust Funds will be exhausted comes in 2041." So in less than nine years, there will be more going out of the Social Security fund than will be coming in, and in about thirty years, the fund will be depleted if immediate steps are not taken. This translates into great concern as to whether there will be sufficient funds to pay Social Security benefits to the tens of thousands of boomers who will be retiring every week.

Other reports paint an even bleaker picture of the state of affairs for the entire Social Security Program. For example, in the "*Summary of the* 2007 *Annual Reports*" of the Federal Social Security Administration, it was revealed that,

"Medicare's Hospital Insurance (HI) Trust Fund is already expected to pay out more in hospital benefits this year than it receives in taxes and other dedicated revenues. The growing annual deficits in both programs are projected to exhaust the HI reserves in 2019 and Social Security reserves in 2041."

This reiterated the notion that the entire Social Security

reserve would be exhausted by 2041—the same projection that was offered in 2006 and earlier in 2007.

The conclusive paragraph to this report was signed by the trustees of the Social Security Administration and reads:

"The financial difficulties facing Social Security and Medicare pose enormous, but not insurmountable, challenges. The sooner these challenges are addressed, the more varied and less disruptive their solutions can be. We urge the public to engage in informed discussion and policymakers to think creatively about the changing needs and preferences of working and retired Americans. Such a national conversation and timely political action are essential to ensure that Social Security and Medicare continue to play a critical role in the lives of all Americans."

Perhaps I'm missing something here, but in light of the information given in this report, it seems we need more than a "national conversation." I propose we open these decisions to political process, as opposed to allowing the trustees to make these very serious decisions. I believe every US citizen should be allowed to vote on possible resolutions. After all, our Constitution begins with "We the people..." not "We the Congress..." or "We the trustees..."

I, along with every person I have talked with about this grave subject, have little confidence in our government's ability to "fix" this problem. Members of Congress have been trying to "fix it" for the past forty years, and every decision they've made has not only created more problems but has created problems that are even more serious.

I've recently learned that a lot of folks didn't know they only have to pay Social Security Tax (6.2%) on the first $102,000 they earn in 2008, regardless of how much they make. The reason they don't know this is because mainstream America doesn't earn $102,000 a year! Just for the record, in 2007, the average worker made less than $40,000 a year, while the average income for those 65 and older was less than $25,000.

What is much more disturbing is that the top Major League Baseball players were paid an average of $20 million a year, the top National Football League players averaged $20 million, and the top National Basketball Association players averaged $20 million. The top ten endorsement athletes averaged $28 million, with Tiger Woods leading the field, earning $100 million in 2007. Top actors average $20 million per film, with percentages of gross receipts adding another $50 million to $160 million. Plus, Wall Street's bonuses were a record $38 *billion* in 2007. All of them paid only 6.2% Social Security Tax (12.4% if self-employed, which is probably the case with Tiger Woods) on just $97,500—the income cap for 2007.

While there is certainly room for debate over the notion of eliminating the Social Security wage limit, many believe, as I do, that this would be much fairer. If the annual income cap were to be eliminated, everyone would pay 6.2%/12.4% (or whatever the going rate is) on total annual earnings. Thus, instead of Tiger Woods paying $12,090 (12.4% since he is self-employed) in Social Security Tax, in 2007, he would have paid $12.4 million.

The total for all the MLB players would have contributed about $300 million in additional Social Security taxes, perhaps another $250 million for the top fifty actors, $200 million for the NFL, $200 million for the NBA, and another $1.24 million for every $20 million contract/salary. There are thousands of those. Plus, Wall Street bonuses would contribute another $2.35 *billion*. The math is simple. Billions of dollars could easily be collected in Social Security revenues each year by simply eliminating the income cap.

Although I am definitely not in the same league as the NFL players or Tiger Woods, I am blessed to be included in the group that would be required to pay more in Social Security Taxes on total earnings should the cap be removed, and I am more than willing to pay my fair share. On the other side of this coin, it is only fair that payouts be computed using a flat percentage of the amount a person has paid in *without* a maximum benefit cap. Those who have paid substantially more in Social Security taxes should draw more in benefits when they reach retirement age. Yes, those who have paid in huge amounts would receive huge monthly benefit checks, but that's fair because Social Security retirement benefits are based on the amount of Social Security taxes paid in by the individual.

To impose a "wealth factor" or remove the maximum income cap without removing the maximum benefit cap would reduce the Social Security system to that of another welfare program. It would also "punish" individuals for working hard, which is the opposite of the principles on which our country was founded.

I am aware that some folks think that removing the maximum income and benefit caps would just postpone the problem, and when these young athletes and actors reach retirement age, the problems of Social Security would once again have to be dealt with. This would not be the case, provided these additional funds are *invested* and not *spent*. Surely the "powers that be" must have learned something over the past seventy years.

I am also aware that some argue that removing the income cap would open the floodgates for tax evasion with individuals "hiding" taxable income. There is less likelihood of this if the maximum benefit cap is also removed and individuals know they will be entitled to greater benefits when they retire. There will always be dishonest people and those who don't want to pay their fair share. However, the Social Security tax is not easily evaded because it is a flat percentage that must be paid before other deductions are allowed.

As I stated earlier, we must do more than simply engage in a "national conversation." This problem is best resolved sooner than later.

In addition to introducing possible solutions to the Social Security crisis, I respectfully urge you to propose that this matter be opened to political process allowing all citizens to vote on ways this grave matter might be resolved. Together we can affect change, and we must. We have our children's and grandchildren's futures to protect.

Sincerely,

The nearly eighty million baby boomers will find themselves, at some point in time, on either the retirement side, the caregiver side, or sandwiched in the middle of these passages in life. We hope this book will save others time, energy, and resources, as well as unnecessary stress and heartache. If you have found the information in *Baby Boomers—Sandwiched Between Retirement and Caregiving* to be helpful, please tell other boomers, financial planners, caregivers, and professionals who work with the elderly and/or their caregivers about it.

We would love to read your reviews and invite you to post your comments on our Web site: www. babyboomerssandwich. com. If you have a blog or Web site, consider sharing your thoughts about this book, and if you feel so inclined, please recommend it and refer others to our Web site.

Perhaps you would like to write a book review for your local paper or community magazine. We would be happy to send a press release.

If you distribute a newsletter, we would appreciate you including your review and our Web site address. You might also ask your favorite podcast, radio, and television stations to have Dr. Haymon as a guest and ask local bookstores to invite her to come for a book signing.

If you own a business and would like to sell this book, please contact us for discounted prices. If you are a financial planner or work in the caregiving profession and would like to give copies of this book to your clients, discounted rates are available for bulk orders. Individuals may also place bulk orders at discounted rates.

Dr. Haymon offers seminars and speaks at conferences all over the United States. Continuing education credits for a wide range of professionals may also be provided. Please contact her at www.babyboomerssandwich.com or 1–888–2 old-age (1–888–265–3243) for more information or to schedule her to speak to your organization or community.

listen|imagine|view|experience

AUDIO BOOK DOWNLOAD INCLUDED WITH THIS BOOK!

In your hands you hold a complete digital entertainment package. Besides purchasing the paper version of this book, this book includes a free download of the audio version of this book. Simply use the code listed below when visiting our website. Once downloaded to your computer, you can listen to the book through your computer's speakers, burn it to an audio CD or save the file to your portable music device (such as Apple's popular iPod) and listen on the go!

How to get your free audio book digital download:

1. Visit www.tatepublishing.com and click on the e|LIVE logo on the home page.
2. Enter the following coupon code:
   561e-6faa-3b4b-0eea-d751-0836-2df8-6a5b
3. Download the audio book from your e|LIVE digital locker and begin enjoying your new digital entertainment package today!